I0800474

IMAGES
of America

THE FORGOTTEN CAPE
1940–1960

On the cover: "Just beyond the Center of Harwich Port lies the magnificent Wychmere Harbor, one of the Cape's loveliest harbors." Its signature beach roses and vistas of wooden boats are observed in this photograph taken just off of Route 28. A brochure from the Harwich Board of Trade in 1960 invited visitors to Wychmere: "the Yachtsmen's paradise-filled with gleaming white hulls of luxury cruisers, sleek Sailboats, the fishing fleet and a multitude of small craft. Spend the summer or the rest of your life in this charming township where the pines meet the sea." (Courtesy of the Nickerson Room, Wilkens Library, Cape Cod Community College.)

IMAGES
of America

THE FORGOTTEN CAPE
1940–1960

Mary Sicchio

ARCADIA
PUBLISHING

ISBN 978-0-7385-5009-1

Published by Arcadia Publishing
Charleston, South Carolina

Printed in the United States of America

Library of Congress Catalog Card Number: 2006940924

For all general information contact Arcadia Publishing at:
Telephone 843-853-2070
Fax 843-853-0044
E-mail sales@arcadiapublishing.com
For customer service and orders:
Toll-Free 1-888-313-2665

Visit us on the Internet at www.arcadiapublishing.com

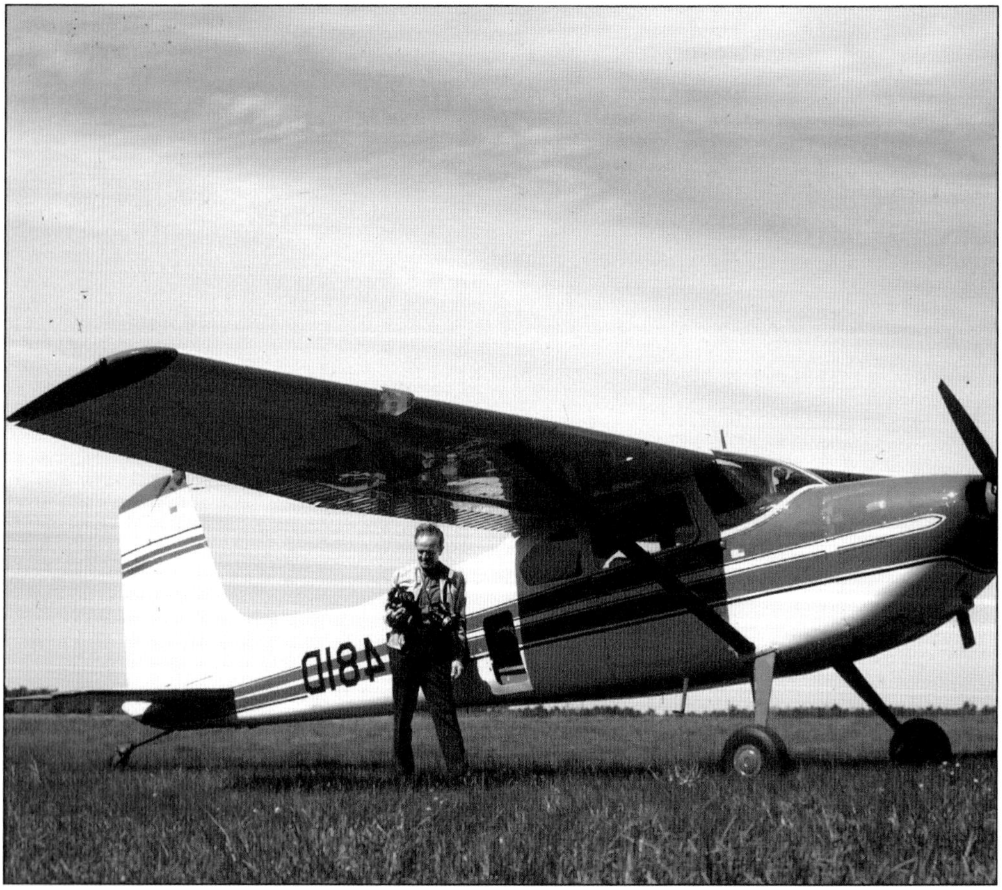

This book is dedicated to Richard Cooper Kelsey (1915–1988), Cape Cod's image maker, and to his extraordinary body of work.

Contents

ACKNOWLEDGMENTS

I would like to acknowledge the wonderful, quirky collections of the Nickerson Room, Wilkens Library, Cape Cod Community College. The Richard Kelsey Photograph Collection, given to the college in 1978 by Sarah K. Kelsey, widow of Richard Kelsey, is part of its collections as well as the Cape Cod Chamber of Commerce Collection of brochures, tourist maps, and publications (1920–1980).

I need to thank the wonderful volunteers who indexed, processed, and valued these collections: Eileen Kraus, Frieda Roberts, Grace Hudson, Irene Hutchinson, and Jean Gardner Also I need to thank Joseph Wong, Cape Cod Community College student, who helped scan photographs for this publication; Jim Coogan for his great help in identifying photographs and who makes everything Cape Cod authentic; and lastly, Charlotte Price, who always knew the magic and power of manuscripts.

INTRODUCTION

Just as the Cape Cod Chamber of Commerce in the 1940s through 1960s was promoting Cape Cod as "an alluring vacationland where the blue begins, and the frets of life cease," a young exuberant man with a camera, Richard Cooper Kelsey, arrived in Chatham, Massachusetts.

Kelsey began compiling a photographic record of small-town life, of Cape Cod tourist landmarks, and the real people of Cape Cod with precision and clarity.

Kelsey, once called the "dean" of Cape Cod photographers, began his career after a World War II Coast Guard stint. He learned to fly just before the war at Chatham Airport and received his license in 1941. He came out of the war with a solid background in aerial and public relations photography and worked for a time in advertising for the old *Boston Transcript*. He did every kind of photography, specializing at one time in children's portraits and weddings. His photographs have appeared in all Cape Cod newspapers, and real estate advertisements, publicity brochures, and guidebooks.

He was a gregarious, popular spirit, and many recalled the tragic headlines on December 24, 1987, which read "Photographer Richard C. Kelsey, 72, dies in crash". There are still many collectors of Kelsey photographs and some who still collect Kelsey stories, but it is widely acknowledged that many of his photographs are works of art that cover an amazing spectrum of Cape Cod life. Since his photographs ran from 1940 to 1987, they recorded the changing face of Cape Cod.

The photographs in this book are culled from the over-7,000-item Richard Cooper Kelsey Collection (1941–1986) in the Nickerson Room, Wilkens Library, Cape Cod Community College.

Richard Kelsey (1915–1987) portrayed a Cape Cod of much beauty and charm, an earlier, more youthful time, a time just within reach of memory. His photographs capture Cape Cod at some of its finest moments, when nature, man, and community were less regulated, rural, and uncluttered.

The first chapter features Cape Cod landmarks from the views of the Cape Cod Canal to the Provincetown Monument. Included are views from vintage automobiles, square dancing at the Eastham Windmill, Easter sunrise at Chatham Light in 1957, and Seebees on Wequasett Lake. Many of these scenes are still visible today, but many are gone, obstructed, and changed, and the cast of Cape Cod characters is ever evolving.

The 1940s–1960s was a time when Cape Cod folks (see chapter 2) were accepted with all their quirkiness as much as the Cape Cod landscape. It was time when local surf-casting sportsmen were rewarded as much by the adventure of fishing off Nauset Inlet as by the abundant bass catch. Women wore dresses to square dances, children wore earmuffs, and gentlemen wore soft hats to beach picnics. A chapter on Cape Cod folks would not be complete without a portrait of the Cape Cod mythmaker Joseph C. Lincoln, the glamorous Gertrude Lawrence, and the stars of the Dennis Playhouse, as well as some of the local old salts.

Also equally engaging are the tourist brochures of the Cape Cod Chamber of Commerce and boards of trade that defined Cape Cod with their language of seduction, longing, and beauty. With permission, I have tried to match the words from tourist brochures, guidebooks, and handbooks with the photographs to match the words that correspond to the precise time and feelings of the photographs. As stated in the Cape Cod Handbook of 1953, the Cape Cod Chamber of Commerce's constant goal "is to preserve the natural charm and attractiveness of Cape Cod."

Not all the images in this book are quaint, however; the reality of storms, shipwrecks, and rescues are dramatized by Kelsey's images of Hurricane Carol at Allen Boatyard in Harwich and the rescue of the ship *Pendleton* by the Chatham Coast Guard in 1952.

Included are some of Kelsey's most signature and famous aerial shots taken in the 1970–1980 period. Several photographs of the nor'easter of 1978 that caused the break in Monomoy Island and much destruction on North Beach in Chatham are used. These photographs illustrated newspaper headlines but also were used by geologists and scientists studying erosion on Cape Cod.

Kelsey's photographs illustrate a Cape Cod many generations once knew and that future generations can only imagine. The Cape Cod of the mid-20th century is perhaps not really forgotten, and the photographs of Kelsey make it alive and vivid once again.

One

THE LAND AND ITS LANDMARKS

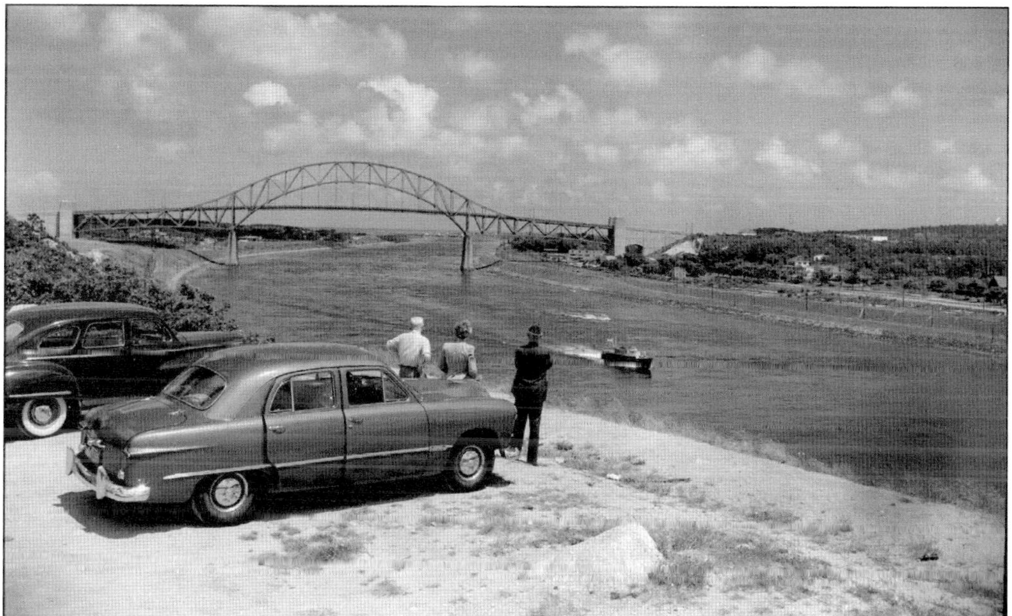

These 1951 visitors to Cape Cod stop at a popular overlook along the Cape Cod Canal in their vintage Ford automobile. They are viewing the canal and the Sagamore Bridge, which were widened and refurbished in the 1940s by the Army Corps of Engineers and are widely considered one of the engineering marvels of the modern world. A 1944 publication *Cape Cod Holiday* described the view this way: "through the waters of the canal one can watch the ships and flags of the nations of the world majestically gliding over its deep blue waters to and from New York and Boston."

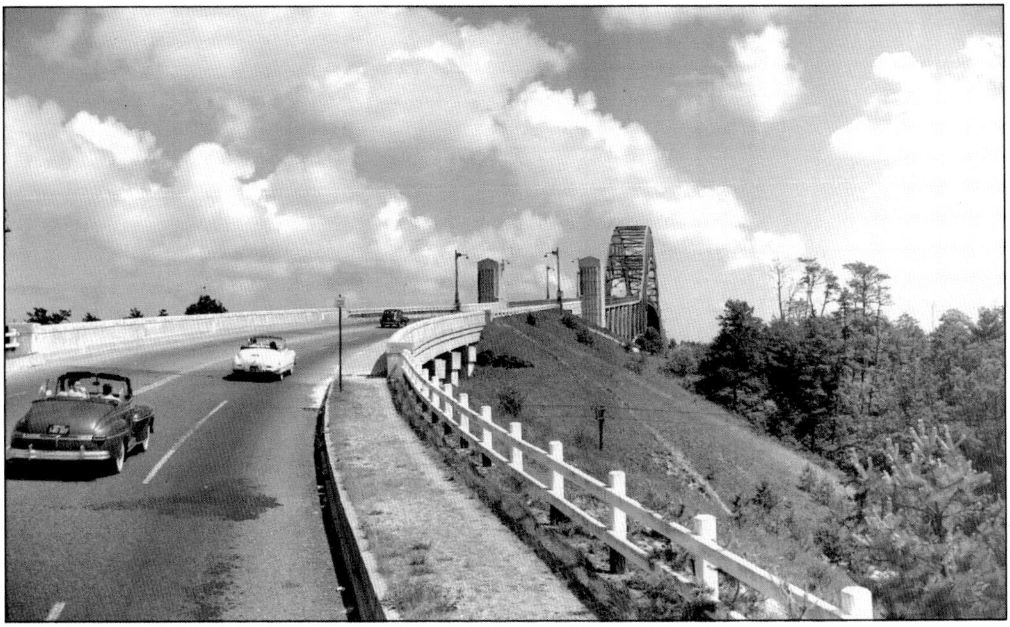

The dramatic approach to the Bourne Bridge recalls the excitement of entering Cape Cod and all the anticipation of a Cape Cod summer. These vintage convertibles recall many youthful summers.

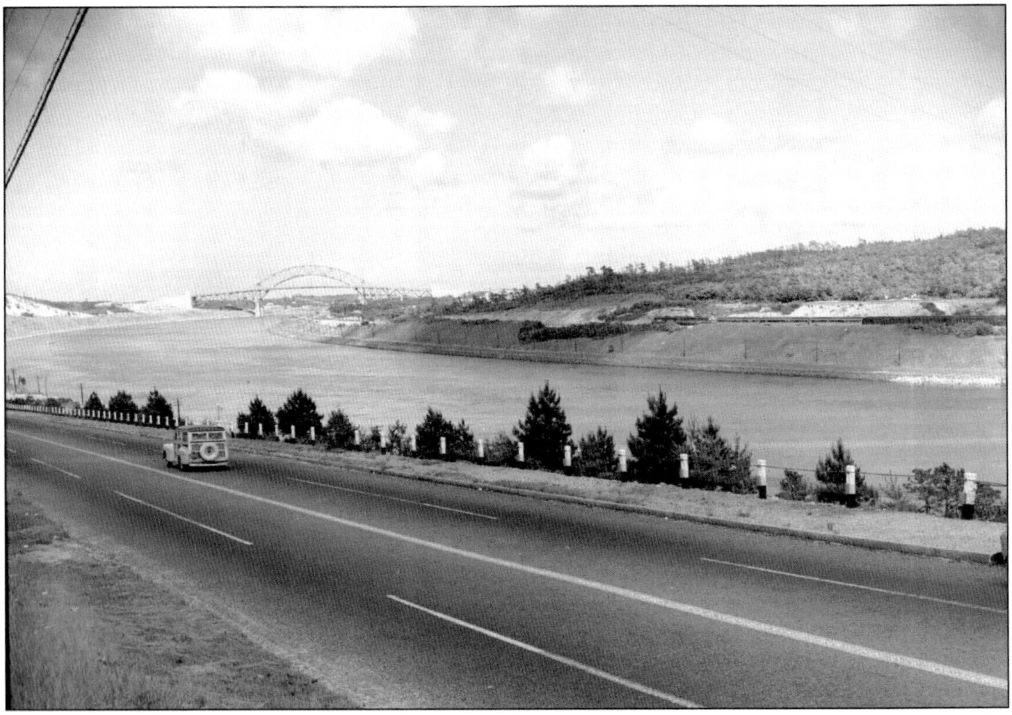

This lone 1942 Ford Woodie travels by the Cape Cod Canal with the Sagamore Bridge in the background. A brochure from the Cape Cod Chamber of Commerce described this scene as "one of the strikingly beautiful bridges which span the Cape Cod Canal at the gateway to The Cape's vacationland."

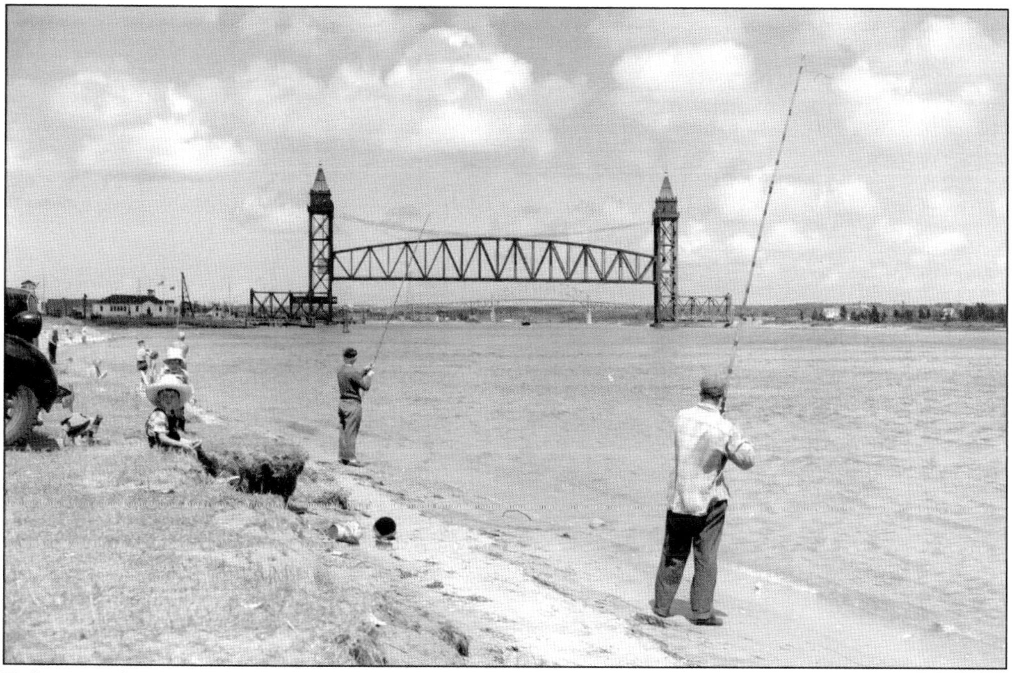

Fishing and picnicking along the Cape Cod Canal at Taylor's Point within view of the vertical lift railroad bridge was and still is a popular recreational activity along the canal banks.

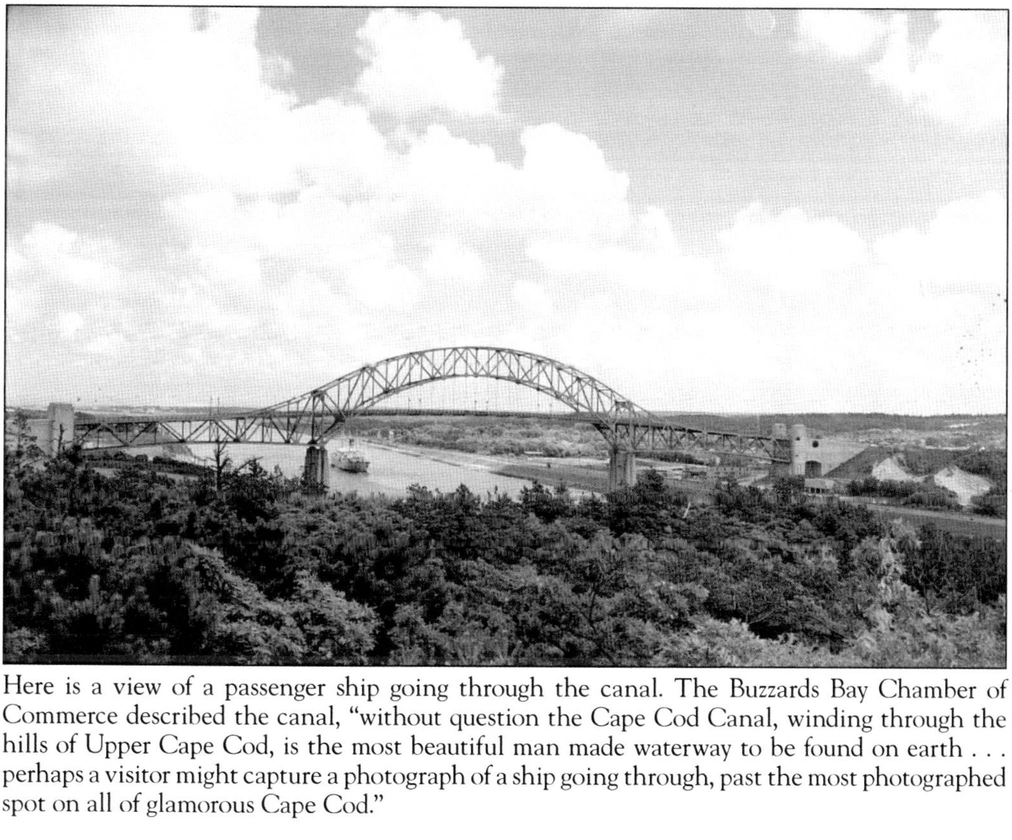

Here is a view of a passenger ship going through the canal. The Buzzards Bay Chamber of Commerce described the canal, "without question the Cape Cod Canal, winding through the hills of Upper Cape Cod, is the most beautiful man made waterway to be found on earth . . . perhaps a visitor might capture a photograph of a ship going through, past the most photographed spot on all of glamorous Cape Cod."

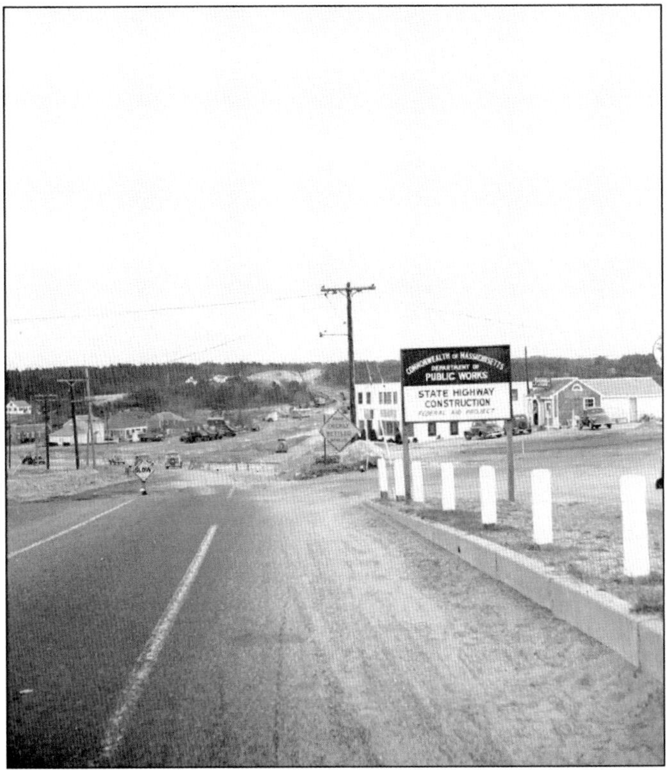

This photograph shows the paving of the new Mid-Cape Highway connecting the Cape Cod Canal to Route 132 in West Barnstable. This new route was opened in 1950.

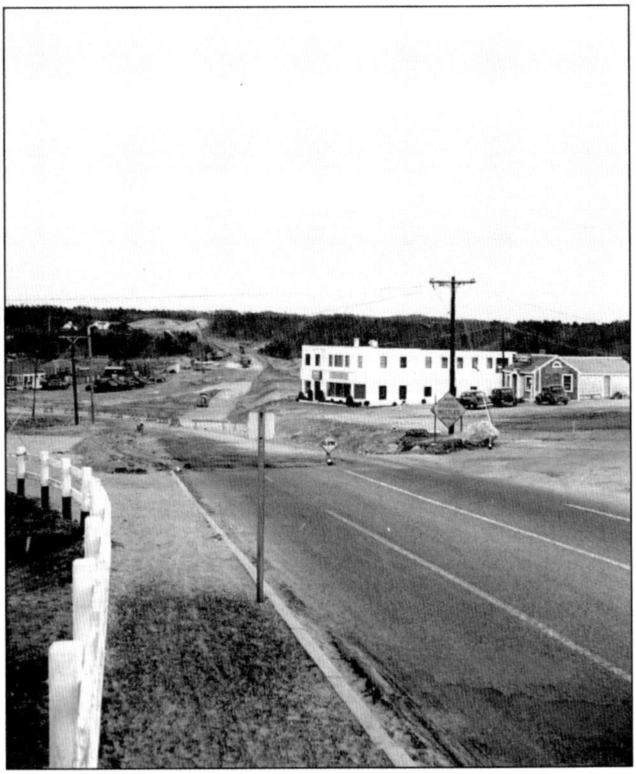

Also shown is the bottling plant for Coca-Cola Company of Cape Cod. Its huge glass windows and art deco design were a landmark along the banks of the canal. The Coca-Cola Company of Cape Cod, under the direction of Murray G. Kayajan, was an important employer on Cape Cod.

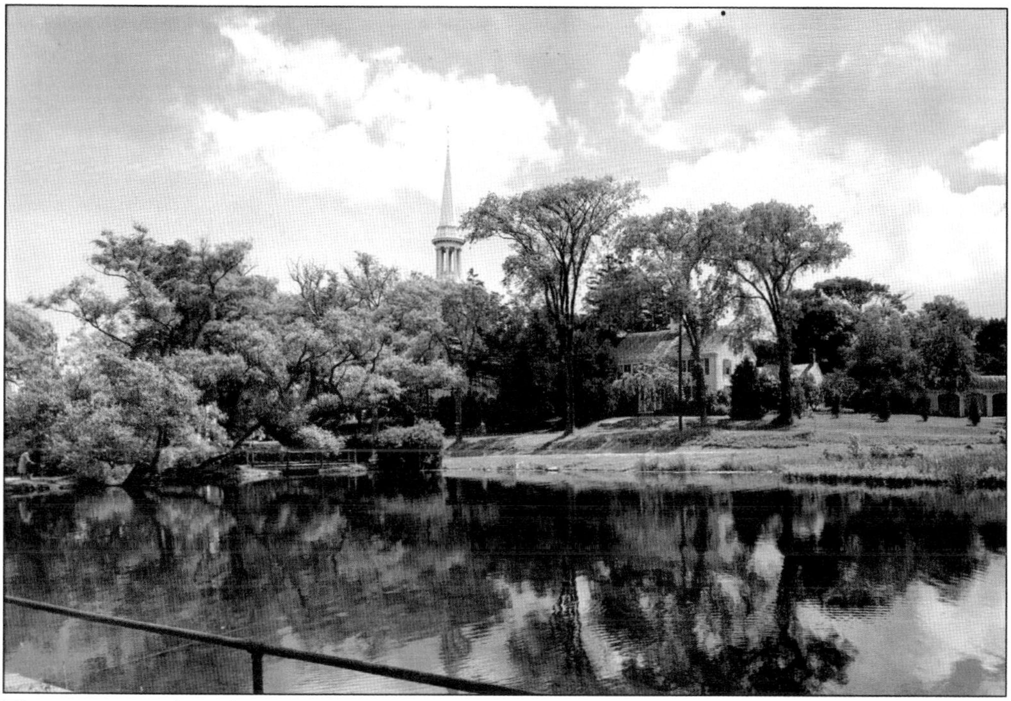

This is a view of Sandwich, the home of the famous Sandwich glass, showing the old gristmill, the mill pond, and the lovely church spire designed by Christopher Wren. This photograph illustrated a Sandwich Chamber of Commerce brochure advertising "Sandwich on beautiful Cape Cod—Perfect Choice for Fun and Relaxation."

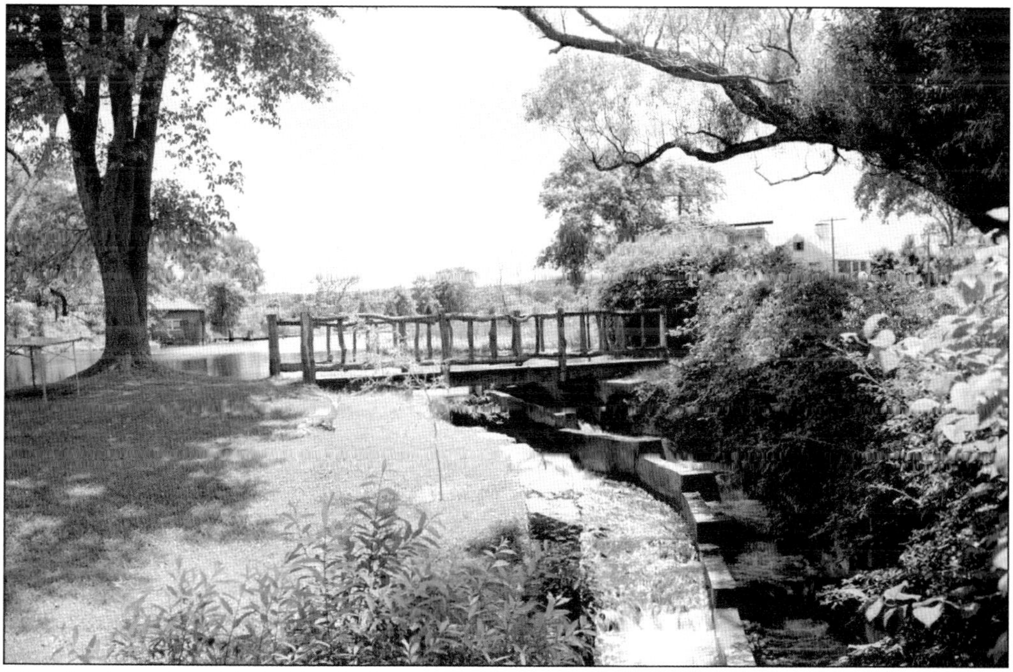

Mill Creek, with a fish ladder for herring, welcomes all to Sandwich, the oldest town on the cape, the doorway that prides itself on hospitality.

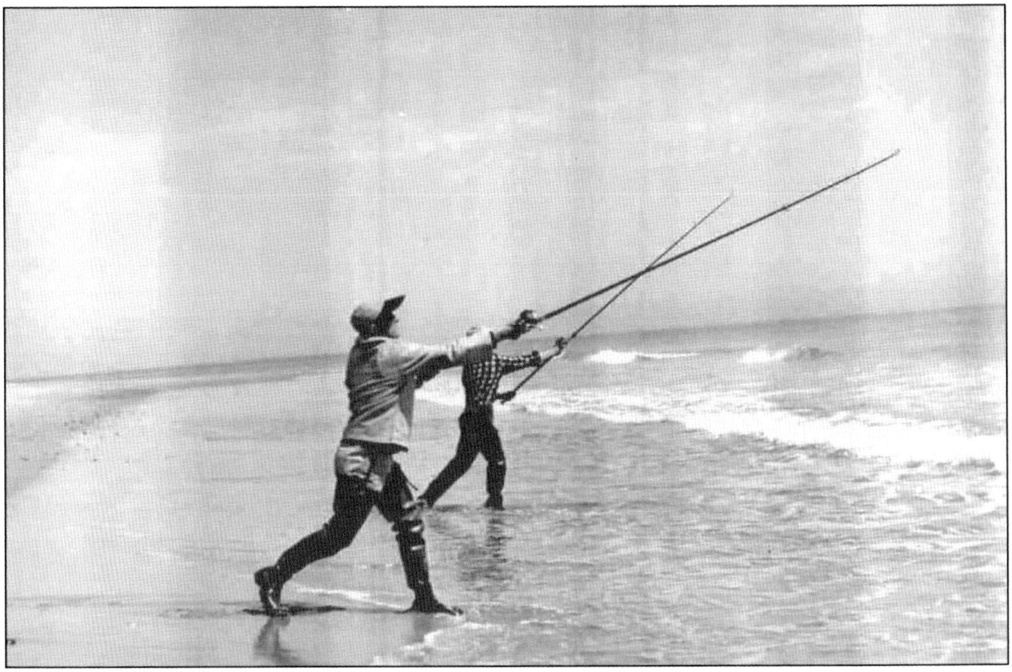

This photograph of sportsmen showing their excellent casting form was used in the *Sportsmen's Guide to Cape Cod* from the Cape Cod Chamber of Commerce to illustrate that the Sandwich area is one of the best places for catching stripers and blues: "Cape Cod is literally surrounded by the famous striper. A 50 pounder is no rarity and miles of wave battered beaches are tailor-made for the surfcaster."

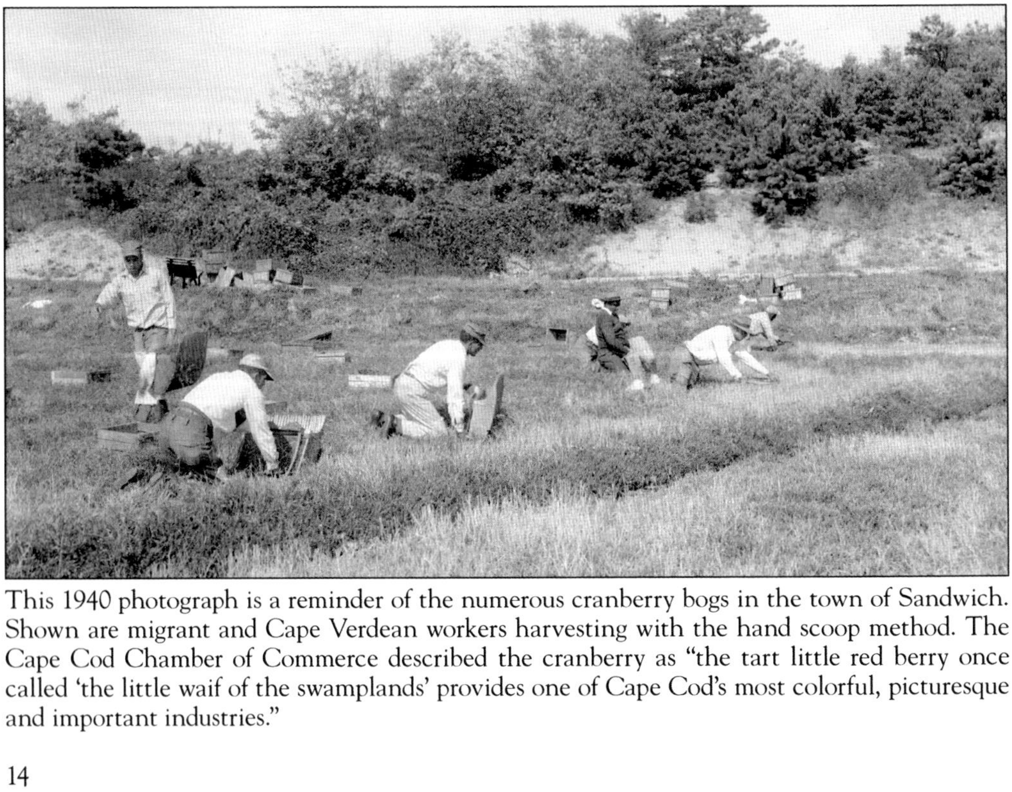

This 1940 photograph is a reminder of the numerous cranberry bogs in the town of Sandwich. Shown are migrant and Cape Verdean workers harvesting with the hand scoop method. The Cape Cod Chamber of Commerce described the cranberry as "the tart little red berry once called 'the little waif of the swamplands' provides one of Cape Cod's most colorful, picturesque and important industries."

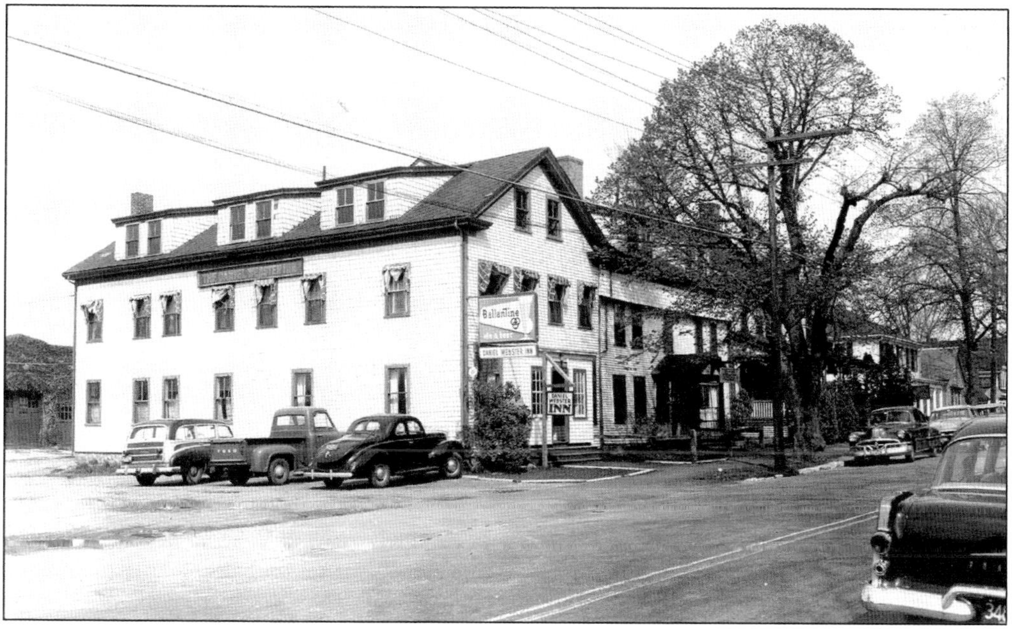

This century-old taproom shows that it did welcome all sorts of automobile tourists with a 1955 Pontiac, a Ford pickup truck, a station wagon, and a Chevrolet parked nearby.

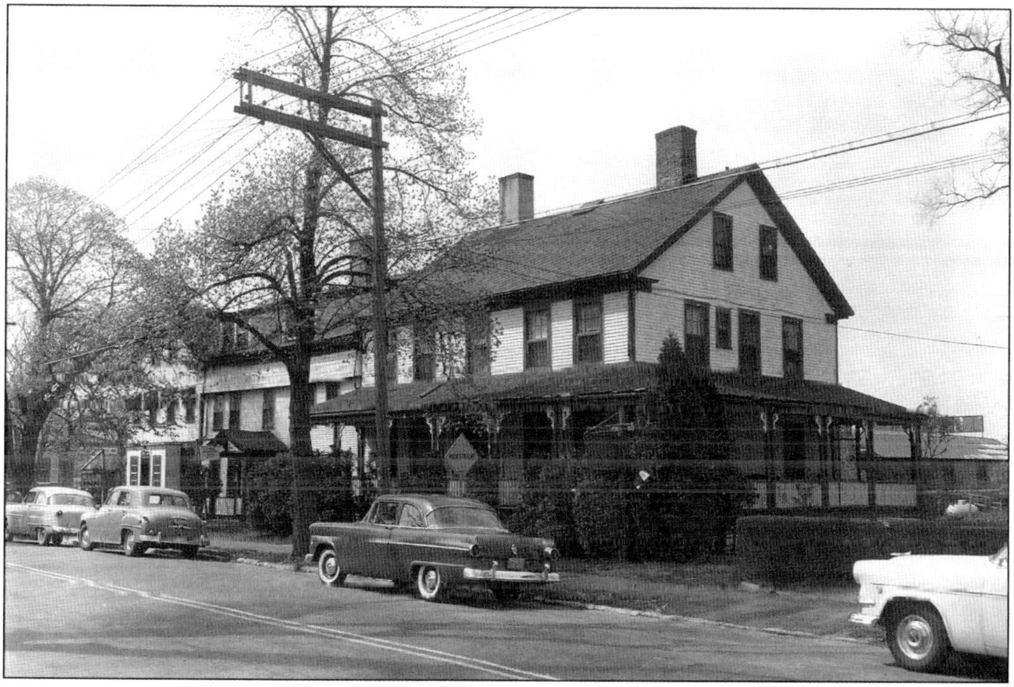

Billed as "the oldest Inn on Cape Cod" in the 1956 Cape Cod telephone book, the original Daniel Webster Inn building on this site on Main Street in Sandwich was built in 1694. It was named after its most-famous visitor in 1915. This photograph shows the inn before the major fire on April 17, 1971. James McCue wrote about the inn in *Cape Cod Holiday*: "From a quaint old Tavern to a modern Inn, guests have included: Daniel Webster, Grover Cleveland, Joe Jefferson, Governor Gould, catering to the auto tourists."

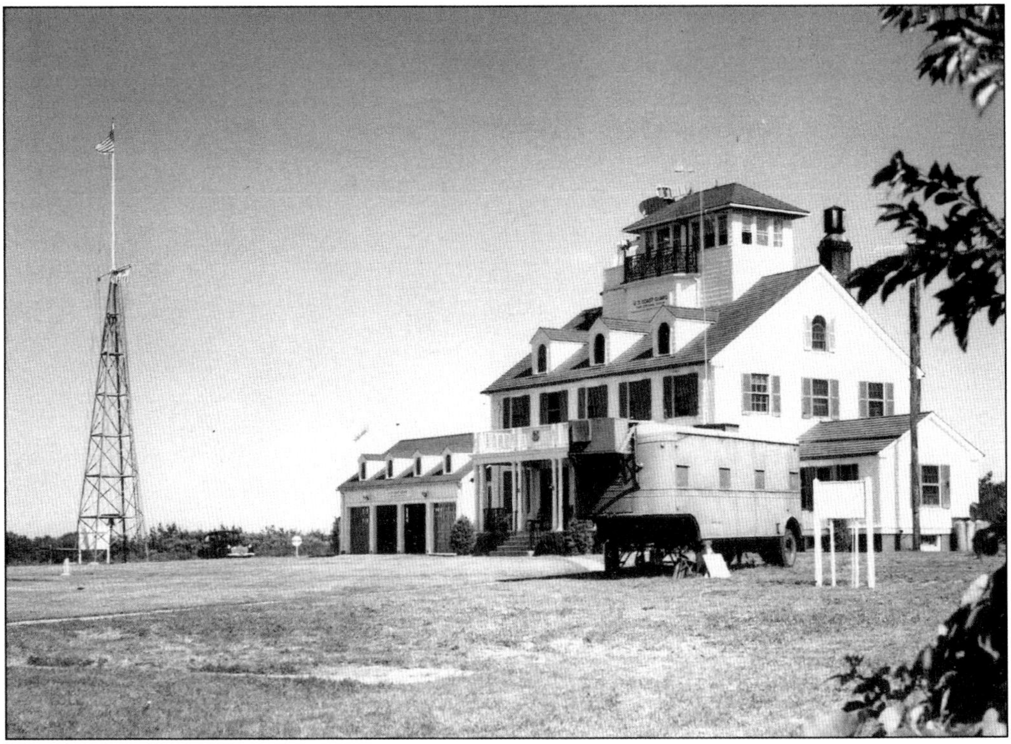

Shown here is the Coast Guard station at the entrance to the Cape Cod Canal in Sandwich with a flagpole for displaying distress signals. The 1948 Sandwich Board of Trade publication read, "The Yacht Basin at the Sandwich end of the canal is a must to be visited and to enjoy that good old salty flavor found there. Also at the basin you will see the Sandwich Coast Guard Station with its men ever on the alert with its sleek boats and trim equipment."

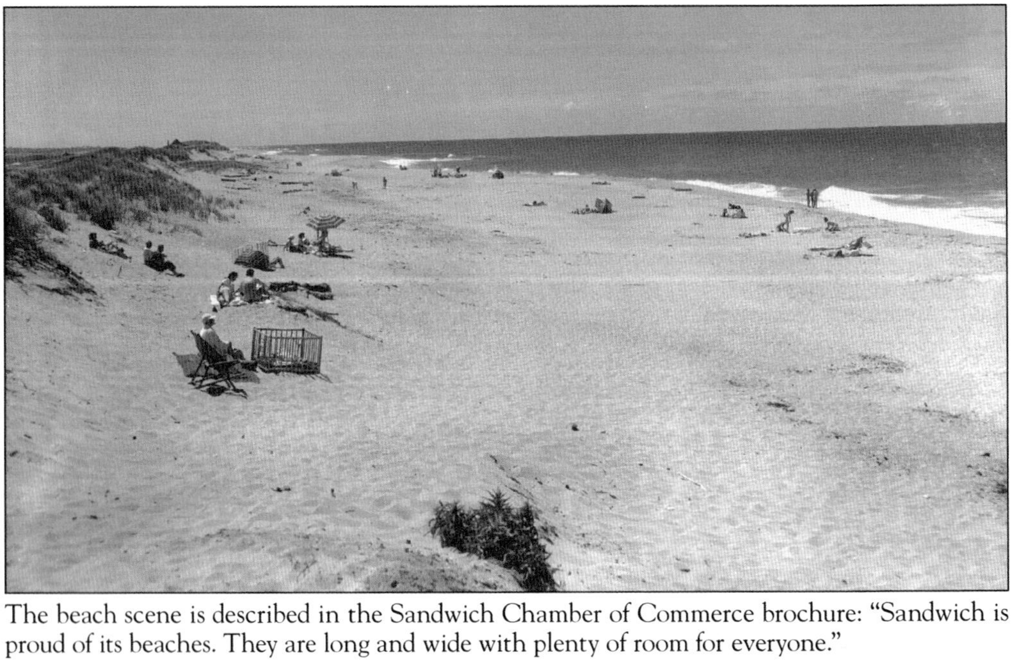

The beach scene is described in the Sandwich Chamber of Commerce brochure: "Sandwich is proud of its beaches. They are long and wide with plenty of room for everyone."

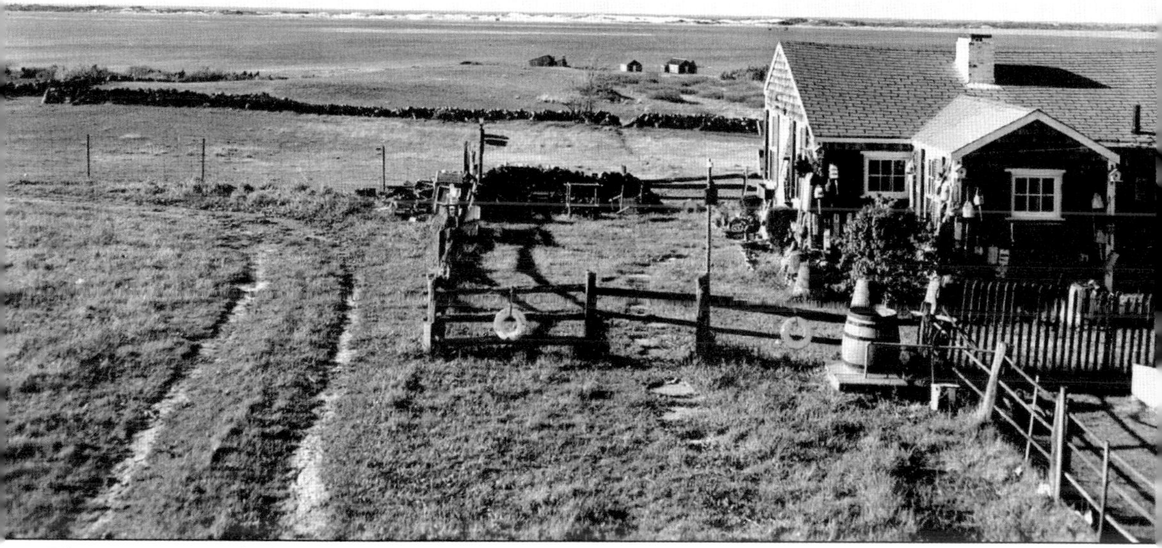

This cottage overlooking Sandy Neck, according to Sandy Neck rangers, was once a piggery overlooking Harris Meadows. Buildings in the background include the Stewart cottage, Dorothy Kelly's boathouse, the Leonard's boathouse, and cabins of Sandy Neck summer residents. This pristine photograph of the seven miles of sand dunes that comprise Sandy Neck shows an early spectacular view of Cape Cod.

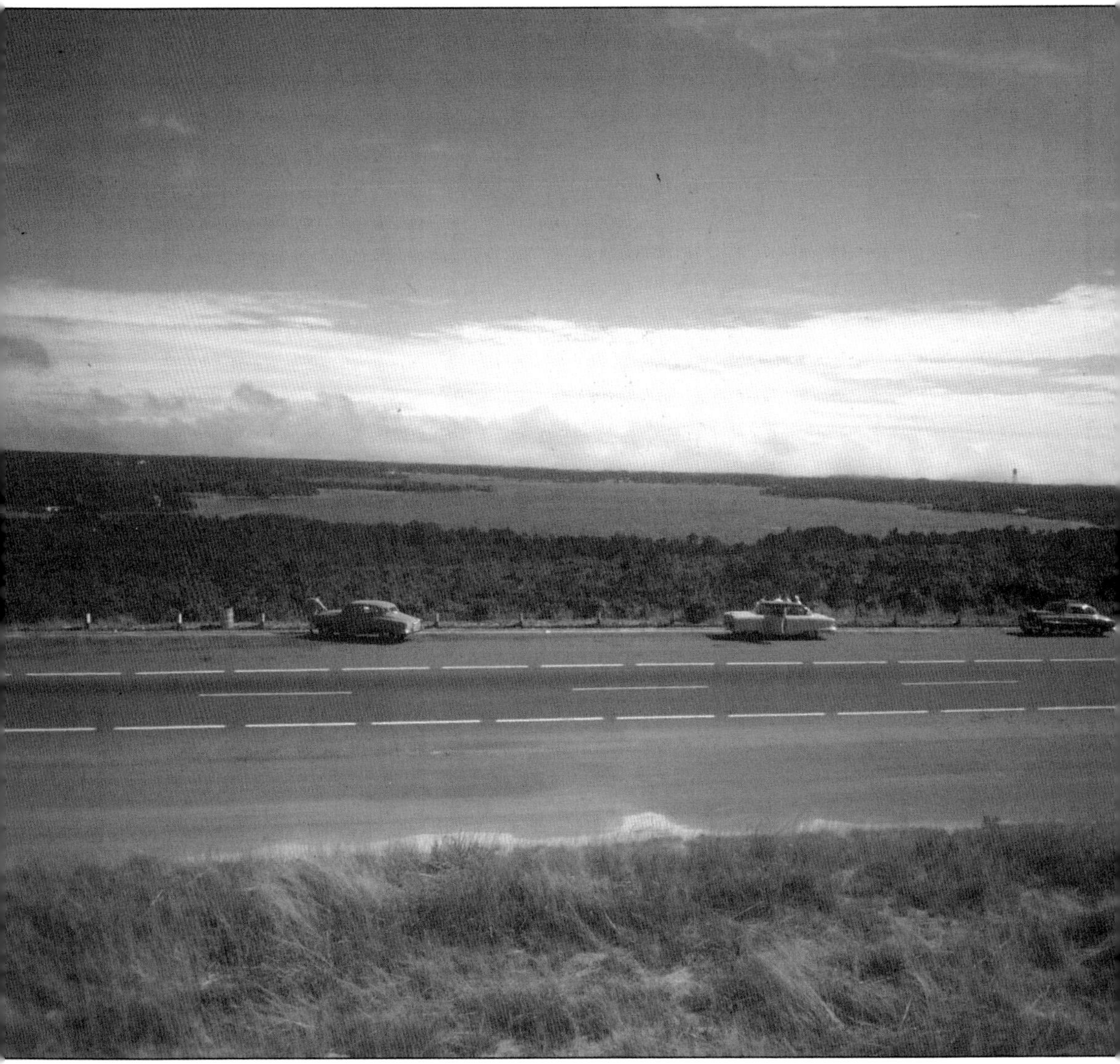

This picturesque view from Mid-Cape Highway overlooks Wequaquet Lake. Visitors in a Nash, Studebaker, and Chevrolet Coupe enjoy this now obscured overlook by the largest lake in the town of Barnstable with a glimpse of Hyannis and Centerville. This spot was considered one of the best scenic viewing spots according to the 1950 Cape Cod Chamber of Commerce listing: "For best views of land and ocean we suggest Shoot Flying Hill on the north side of Wequaquet Lake, reached from Highway 132 or Centerville-West Barnstable road." It has also been called more recently the "gold coast," with nine miles of shoreline.

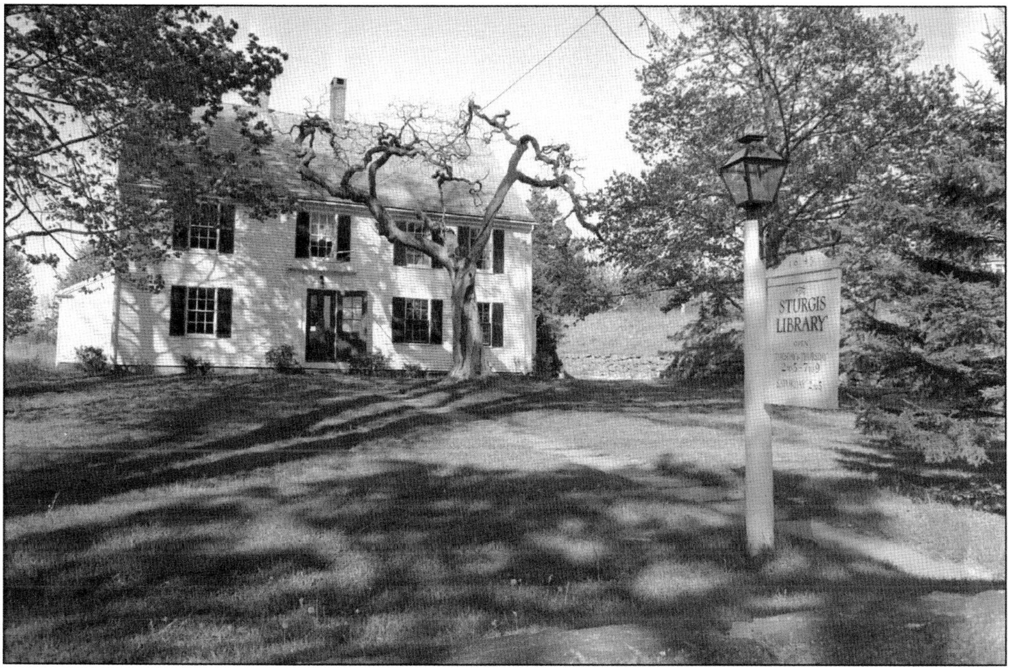

Sturgis Library along Route 6A in Barnstable Village is shown in 1951. It is often called the jewel of the historic district. The Lothrop Homestead of 1644 comprises the earliest half-saltbox portion of this building, and the old mulberry tree has long graced its front yard. Its major claim is that it is the oldest building to house a public library in the United States.

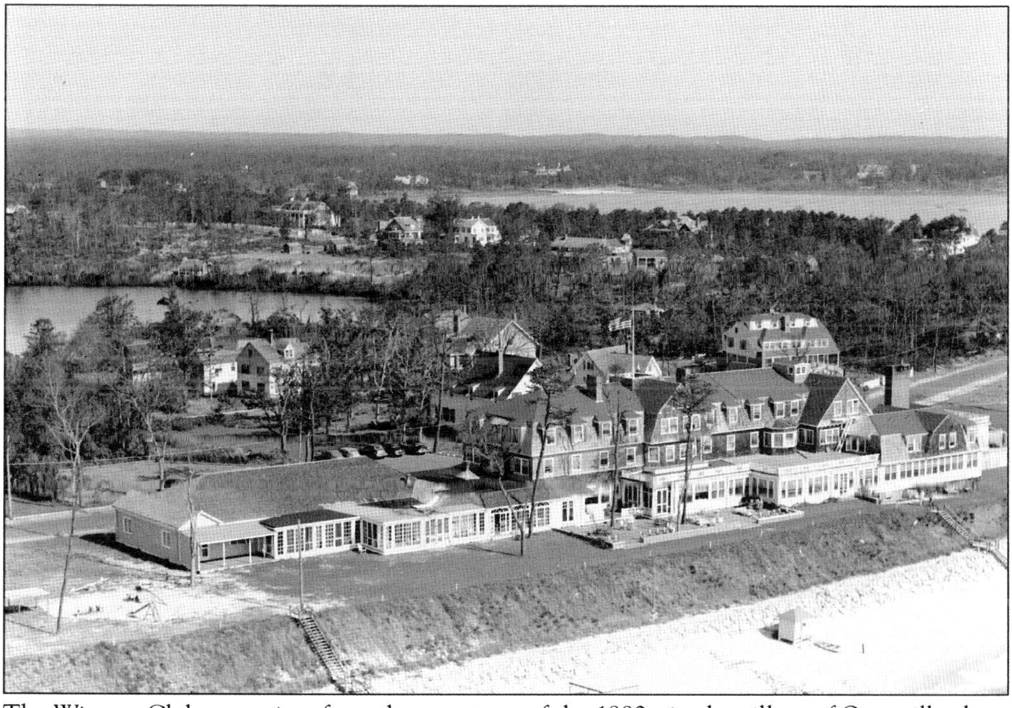

The Wianno Club, a survivor from the resort age of the 1880s, in the village of Osterville along Sea View Avenue displays its overpowering size, irregular roofline, and tower elements.

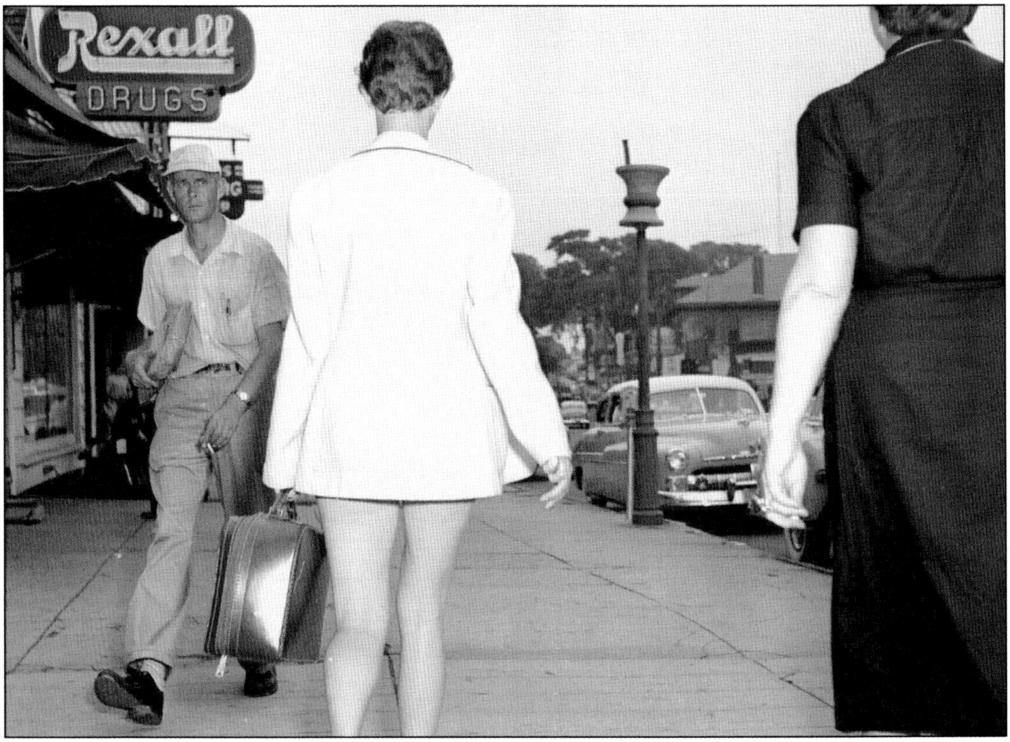

Titled *Here Comes Summer!*, this photograph shows the busy streets of Hyannis and the new fashion of short shorts outside the Voss Rexall Pharmacy, 298 Main Street. Its slogan was "the place to know, the place to go." Ora Hinkley reported in 1931, "as to points of interest, Hyannis is full of life and interest. It is a human place and loves people. If you do, come along and see them."

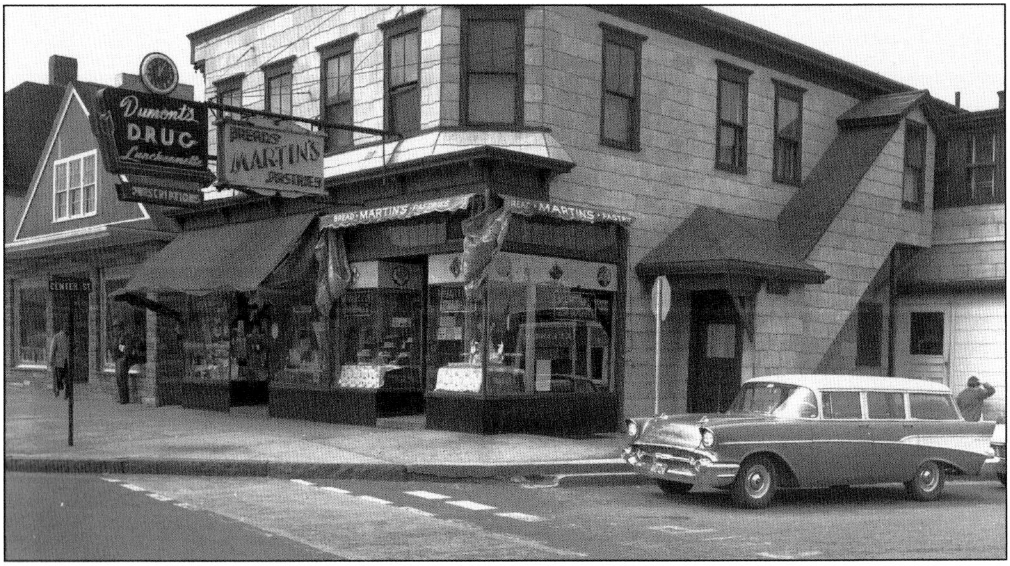

This is Hyannis Center in 1958, called "the Metropolis of Cape Cod," showing Martins Bakery and Dumonts Drug and Luncheonette. Alfred A. Dumont, also known as "your friendly druggist," was the proprietor. Martins Bakery had stores in Hyannis, Osterville, and West Dennis and billed itself in the 1953 Cape Cod telephone book as "for 28 years the Cape's Best Bakers."

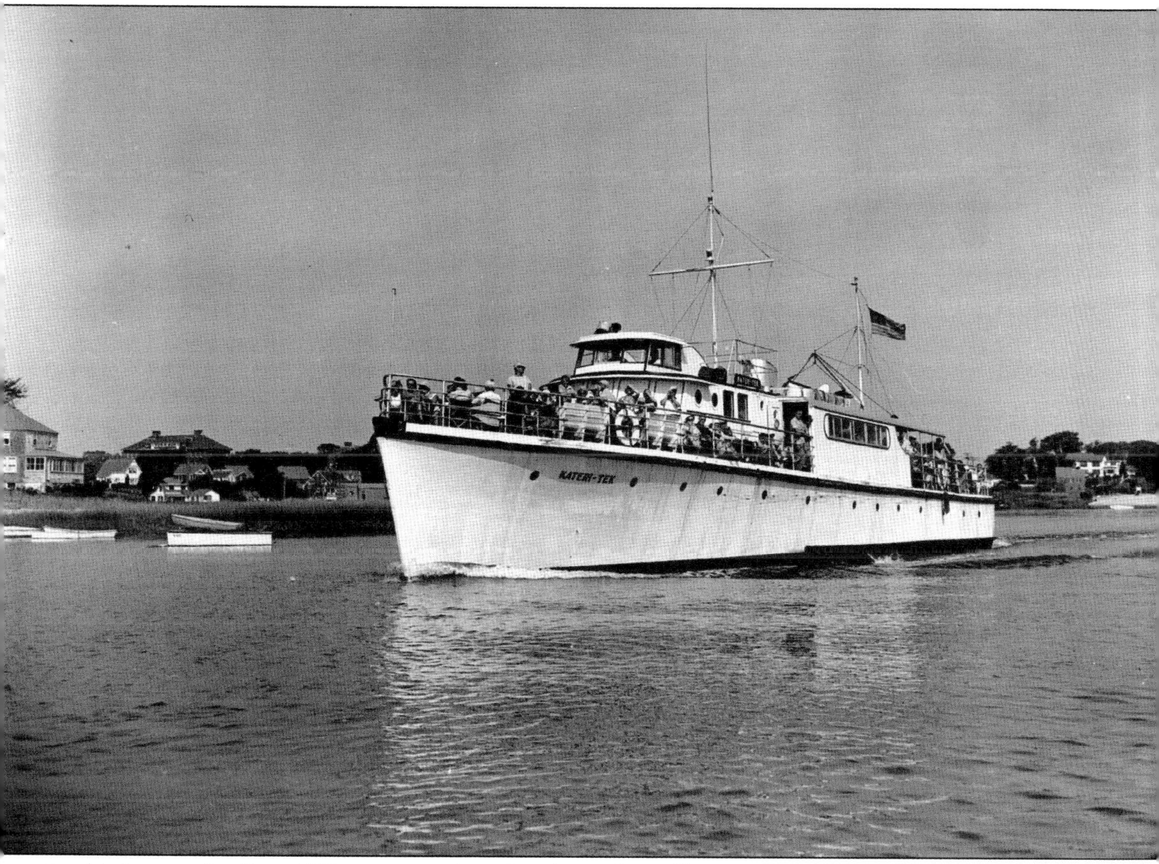

In this image, the *Kateri-Tek* excursion boat heads out from Pleasant Street, Hyannis to Martha's Vineyard on a beautiful summer's day in 1952. Its sister passenger ship, *Catherine-Tek,* also made daily trips to Nantucket for a $5 fare, round trip. It was listed under salt water cruises in *Cape Cod Vacationer*: "Daily cruises to the romantic islands of Martha's Vineyard and Nantucket—spacious boats—snack bars—time ashore for sightseeing."

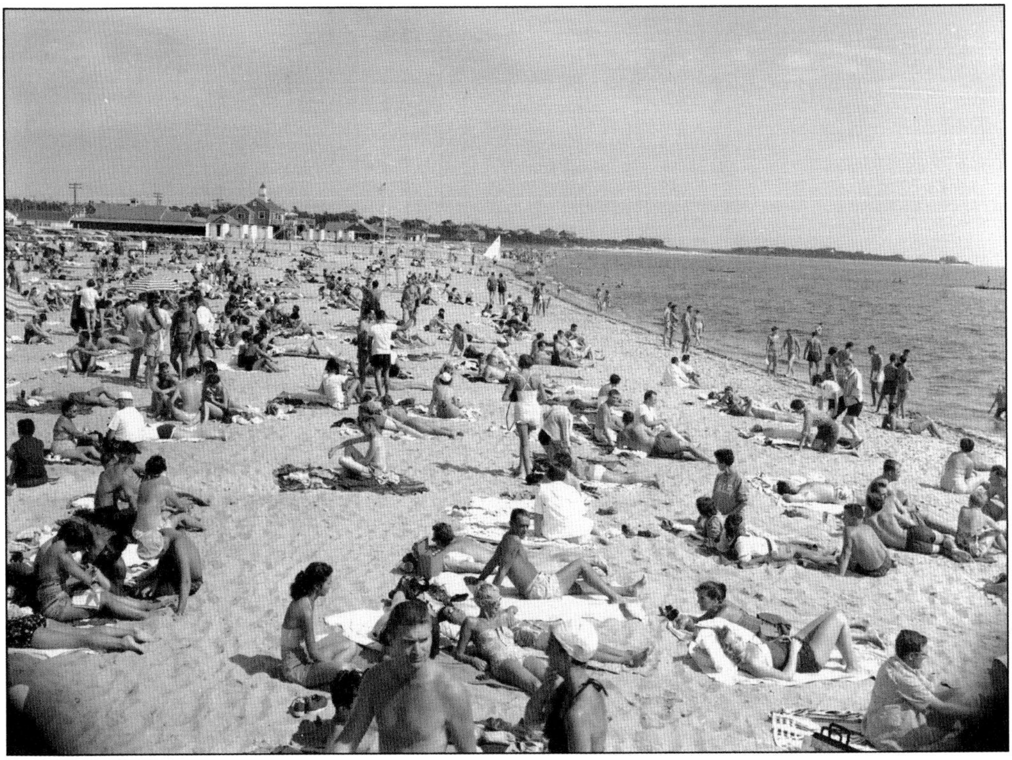

Craigville Beach put Centerville on the map as the "home of the world famous Craigville Beach" according to the Centerville Board of Trade. This busy beach shown with bathhouses in the background was originally founded by a Christian Camp Meeting Association in 1872.

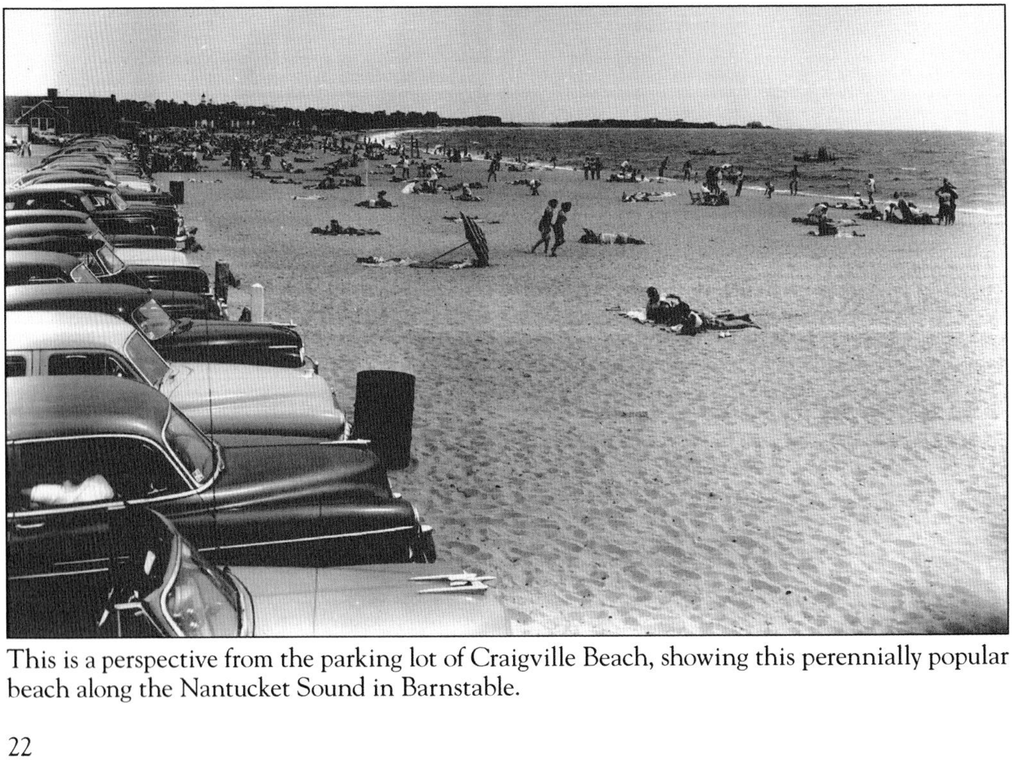

This is a perspective from the parking lot of Craigville Beach, showing this perennially popular beach along the Nantucket Sound in Barnstable.

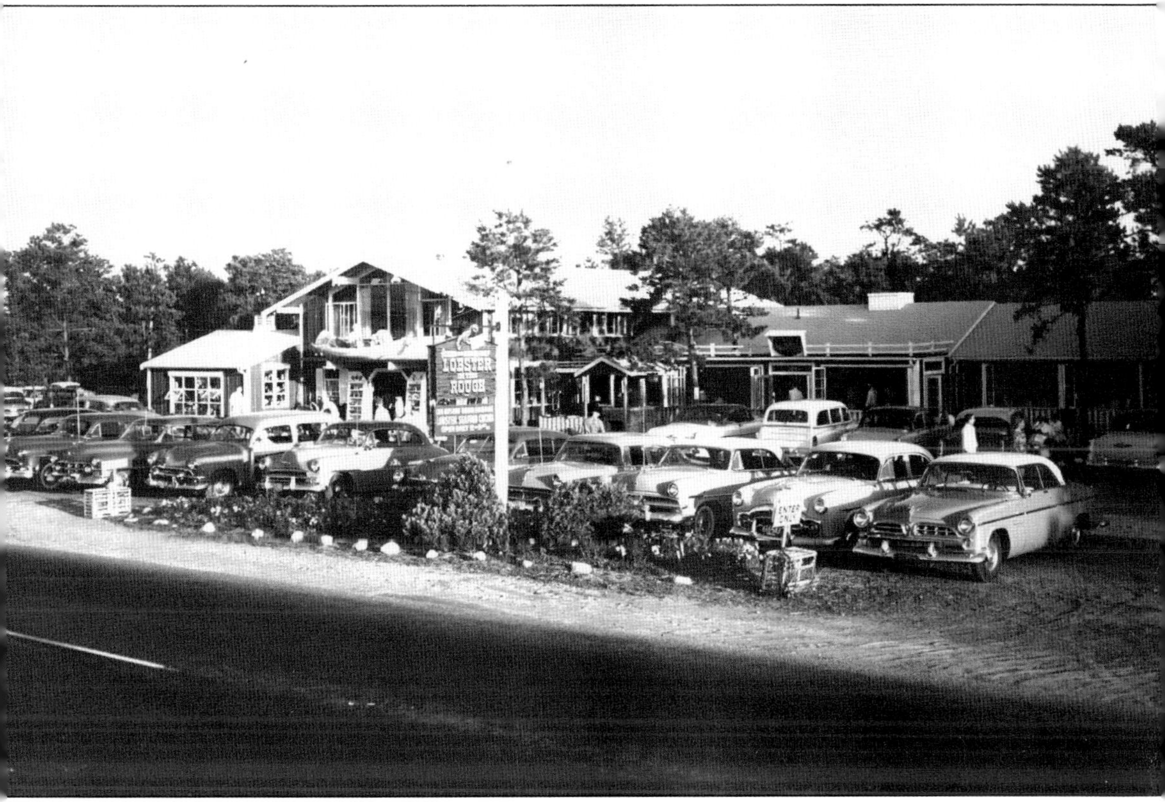

Lobster in the Rough on Route 28 West Yarmouth was a restaurant and gift shop founded by Ken and "Midge" Daley in 1952. The Daleys wanted to establish a family eatery for those who loved lobster but could not afford the high prices. Their motto was "Cape Cod's most unusual eating place." DeSotos, Fords, Mercurys, Cadillacs, and Pontiacs are all shown pulled up to this popular eatery.

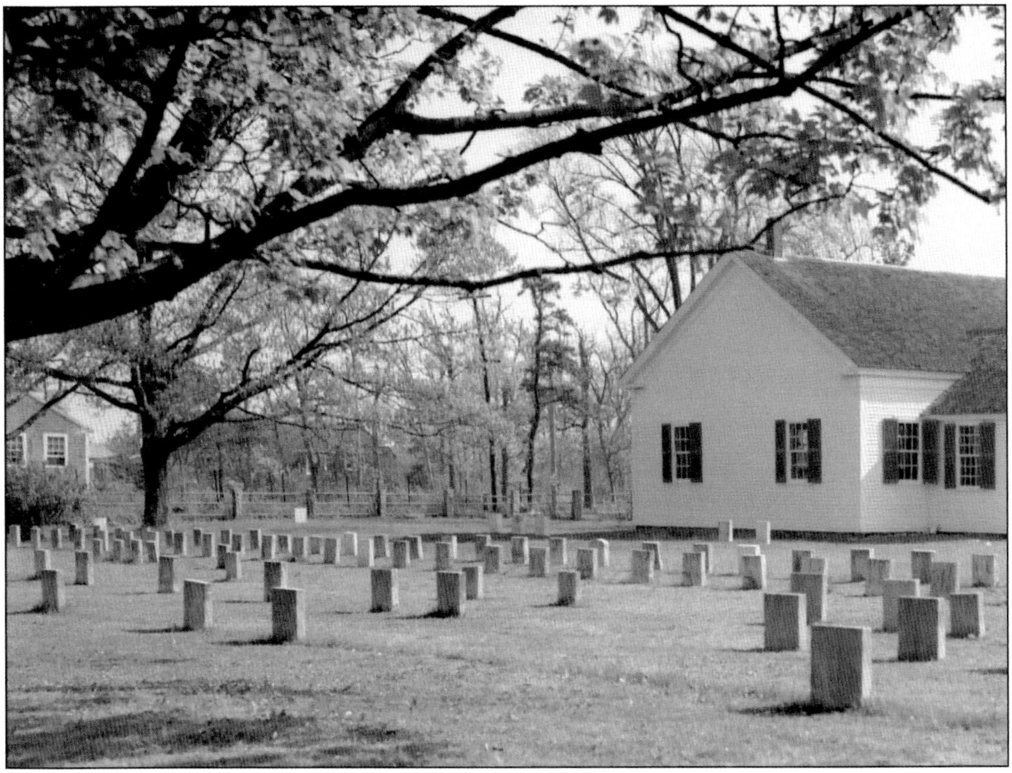

The Bass River Quaker Church and Cemetery is located in South Yarmouth and built in 1809. This photograph was taken in 1951, just prior to the reactivation of this Quaker church in 1954. The graveyard has post–Revolutionary War Quaker graves with their simple, uniform, and unadorned gravestones.

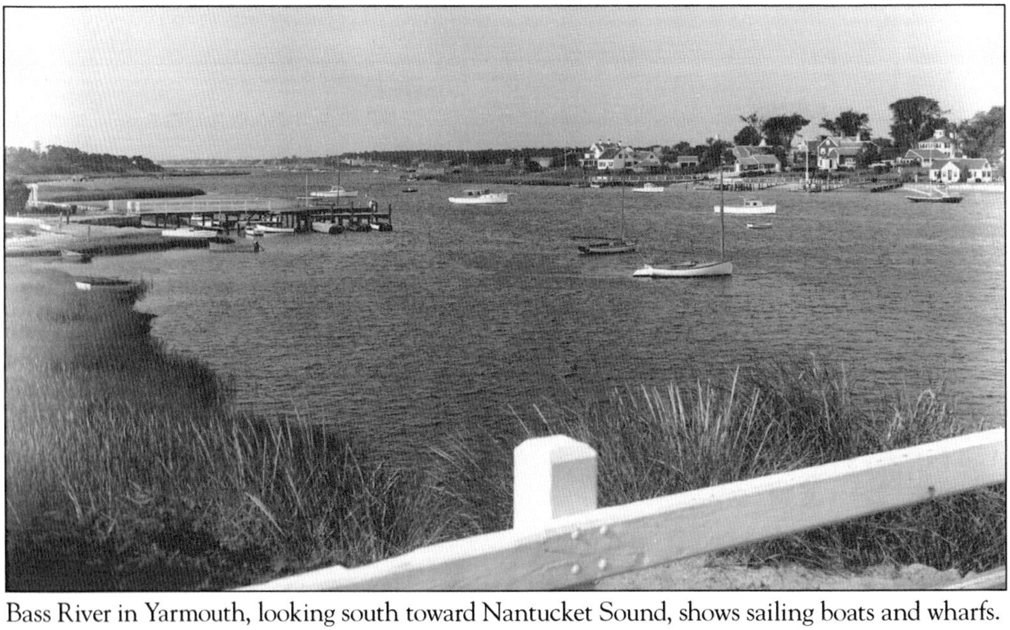

Bass River in Yarmouth, looking south toward Nantucket Sound, shows sailing boats and wharfs.

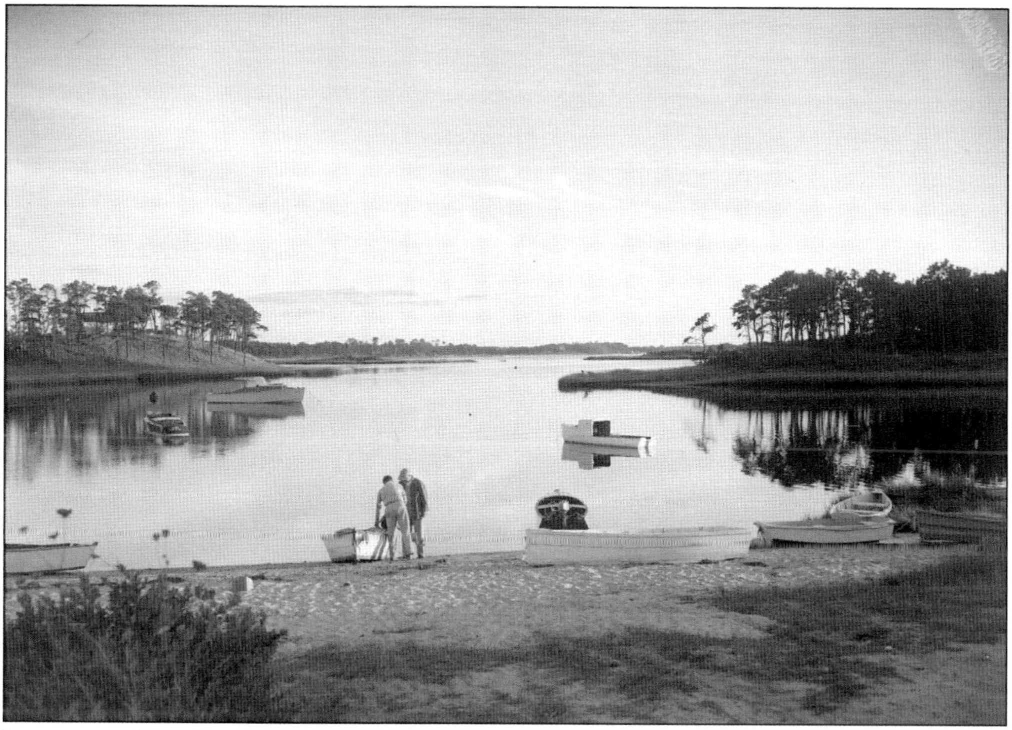

Two views of Bass River at High Bank Bridge in South Dennis are seen here, with Wilbur Park on the right. In the photograph above, an early morning launch barely disturbs this tranquil scene. The lack of moorings and peaceful nature of the photograph below testifies that this is an early-1950s photograph.

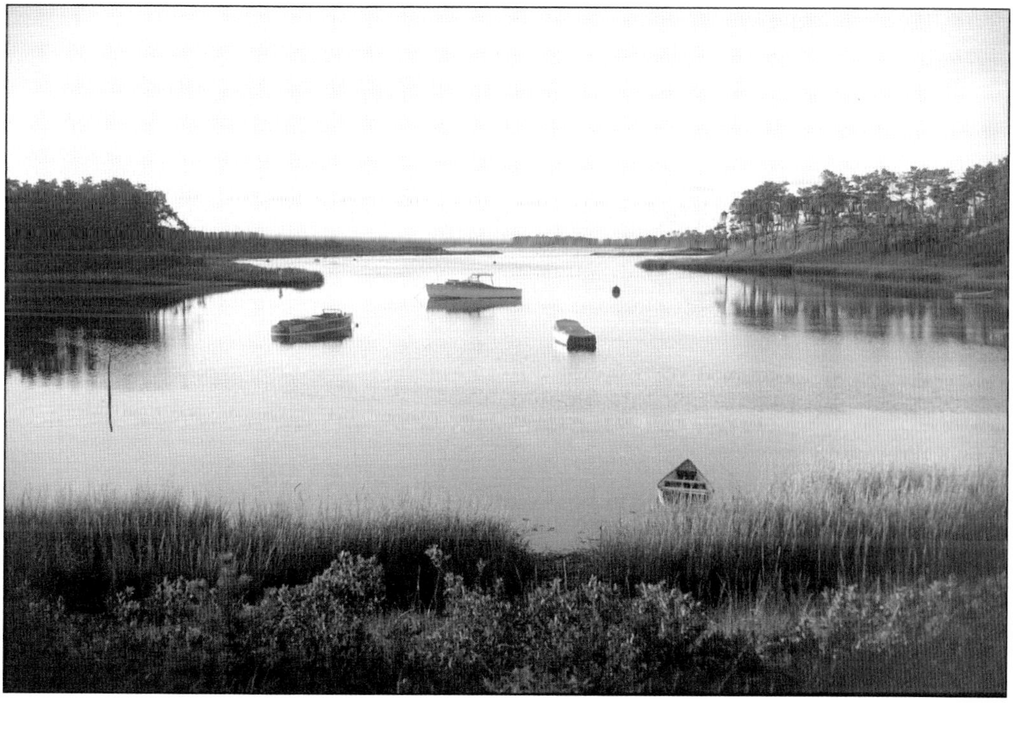

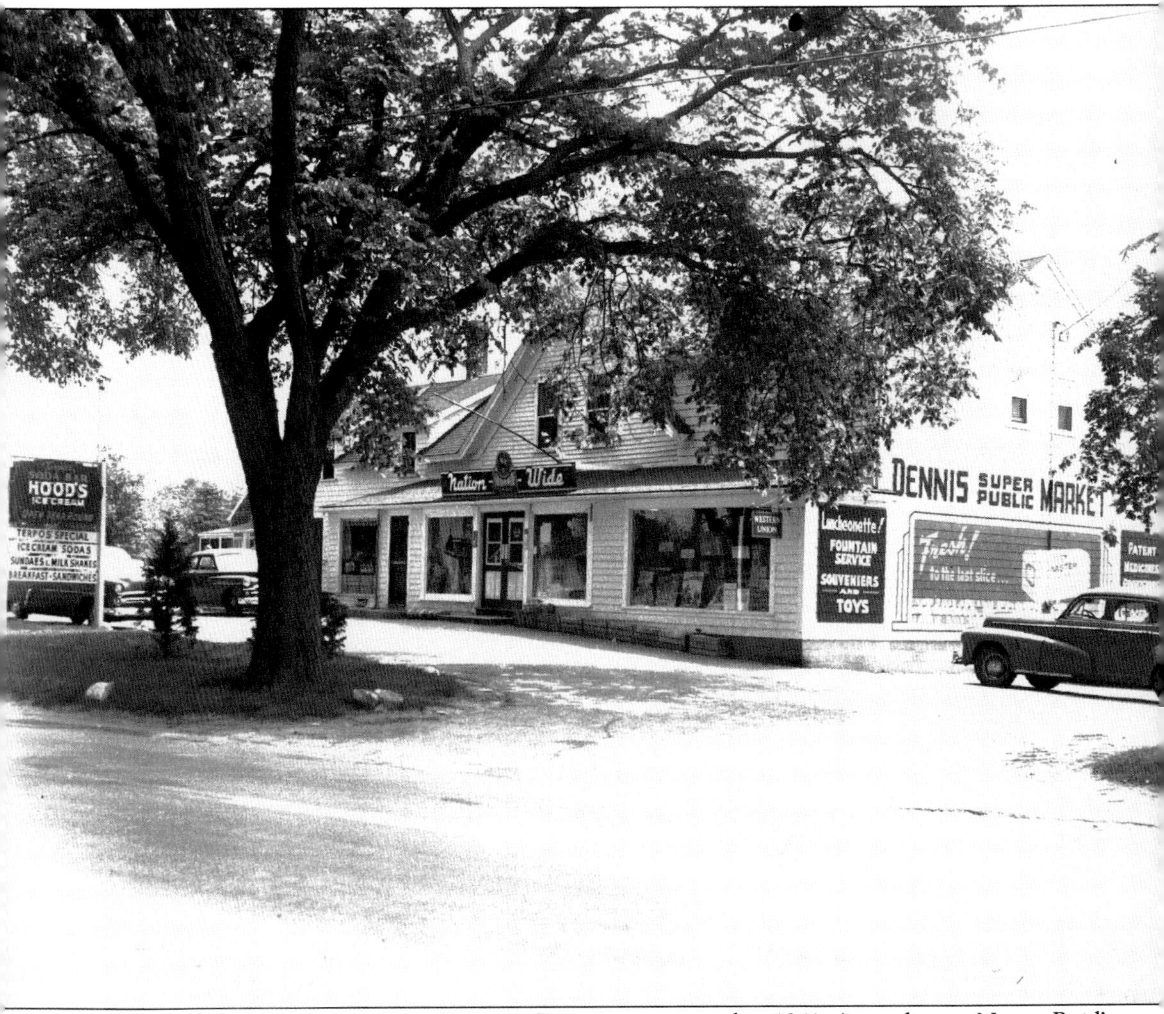

Dennis Public Market on Main Street in Dennis was opened in 1941. According to Nancy Reid's Dennis history, the market was named for Elias "Louis" Terpos, the longtime owner. Old-timers still refer to the market as "Louie's." On the signboard, one can see "Terpos Special" advertised and the lunchonette built at the suggestion of Gertrude Lawrence.

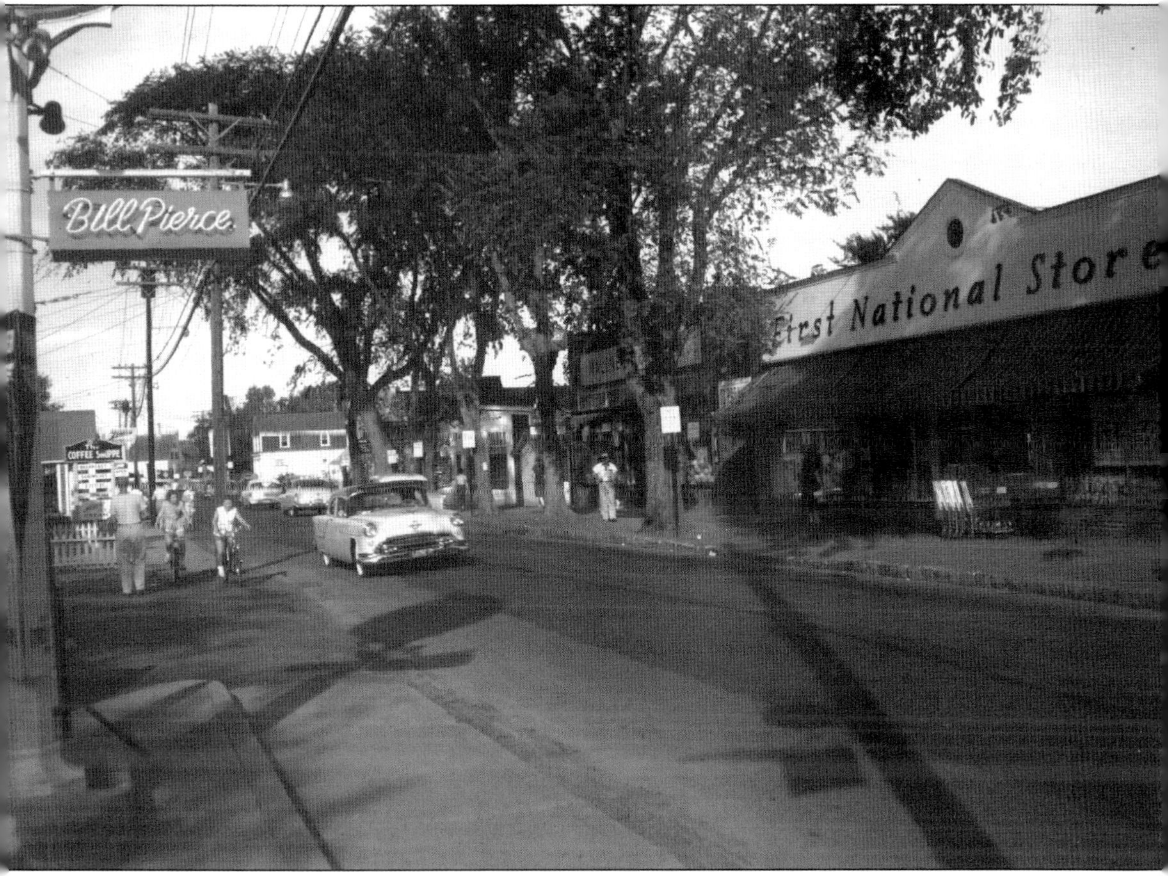

Main Street in Dennis Port was the shopping destination for most Dennis folks and others from Harwich, Brewster, and Yarmouth in the 1950s. Both sides of the street, lined with elms, were also lined with stores. The First National Store, at 120 Main Street, Bill Pierce's Tydol Flying A Service Station, the Coffee Shoppe, and Bob West's Zenith Store draw automobile traffic, bicyclists, and pedestrians to this busy street.

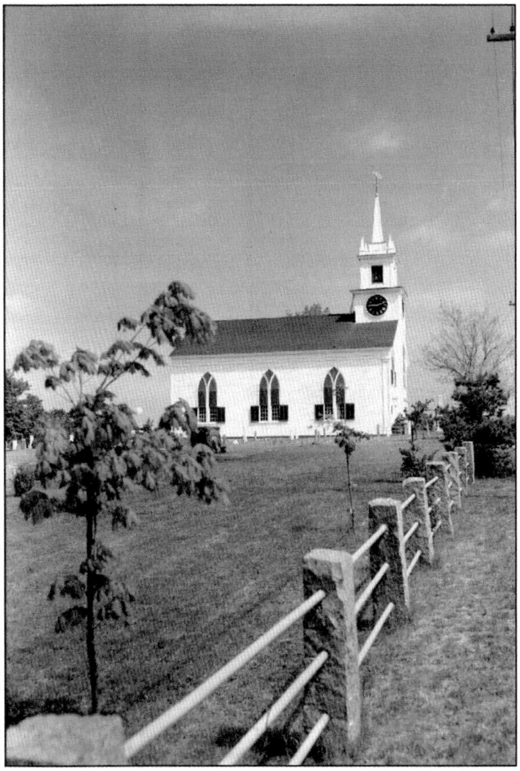

The Congregational church of South Dennis, the Sea Captains Church, stands on a bluff overlooking the Grand Cove of Bass River, with its quiet churchyard and cemetery beyond. Its signature clock tower and steeple with trinity-style spirettes on the upper tier have been carefully preserved since 1835.

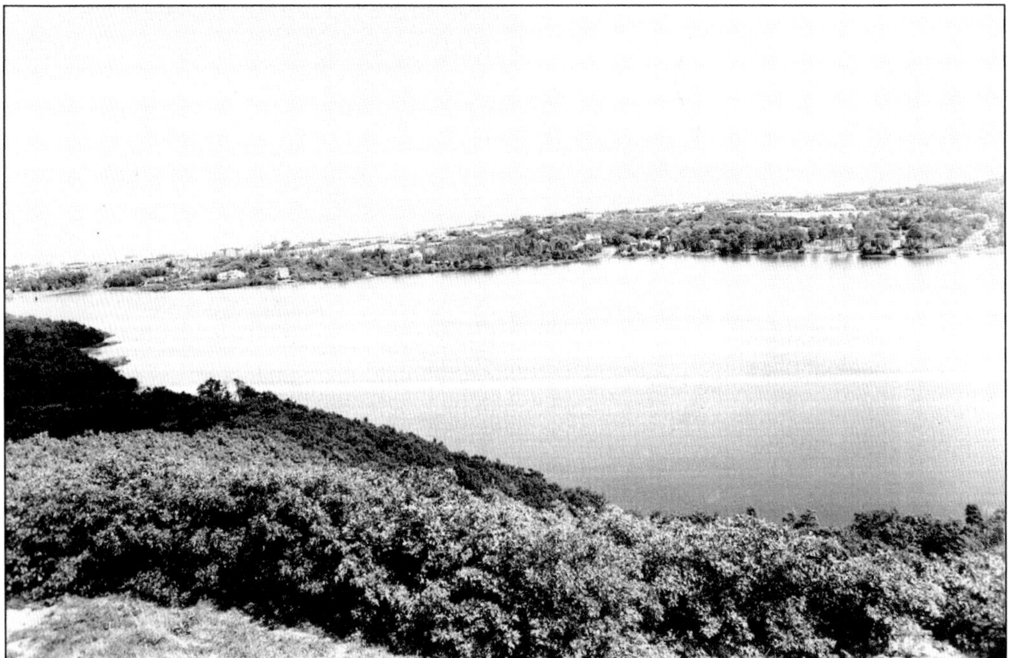

Scargo Lake is located on the north side of Dennis, just south of Route 6A, also with a herring run leading to Sesuit Creek. This area has many Native American legends attached to it, including its Wampanoag name, meaning "bass" for its shape.

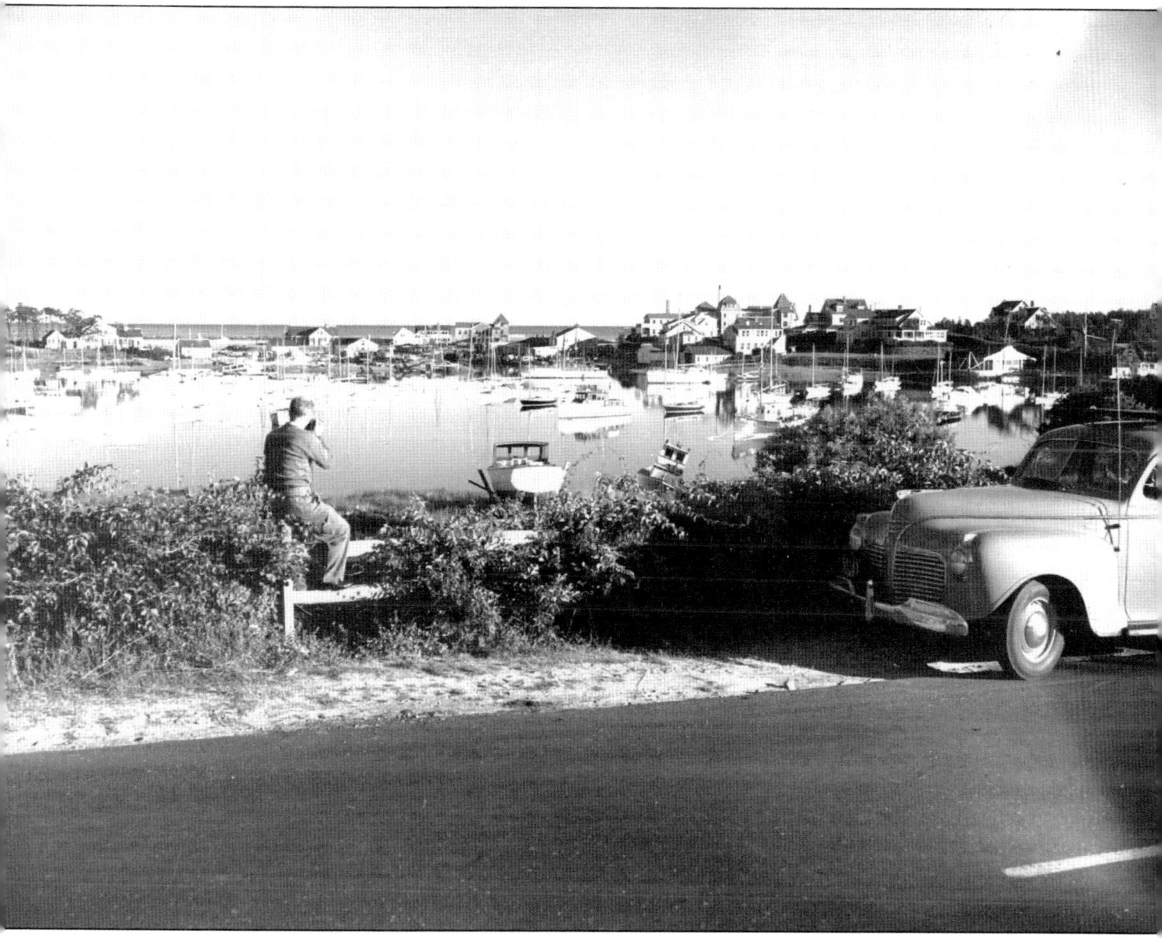

Richard Kelsey took many classic photographs of Wychmere Harbor located on the protected south shore. This hub of Cape Cod, as advertised by the Harwich Board of Trade, was "an uncommercialized and uncluttered inlet for those seeking quiet and privacy."

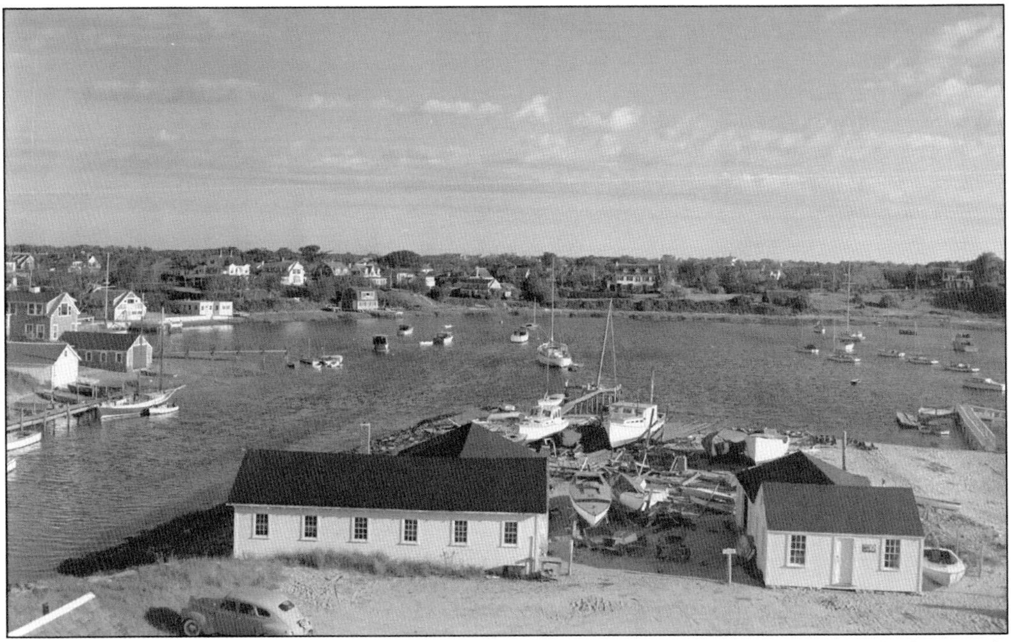

Boat craft of all kinds can be identified here at Wychmere Harbor looking north from the boatyard.

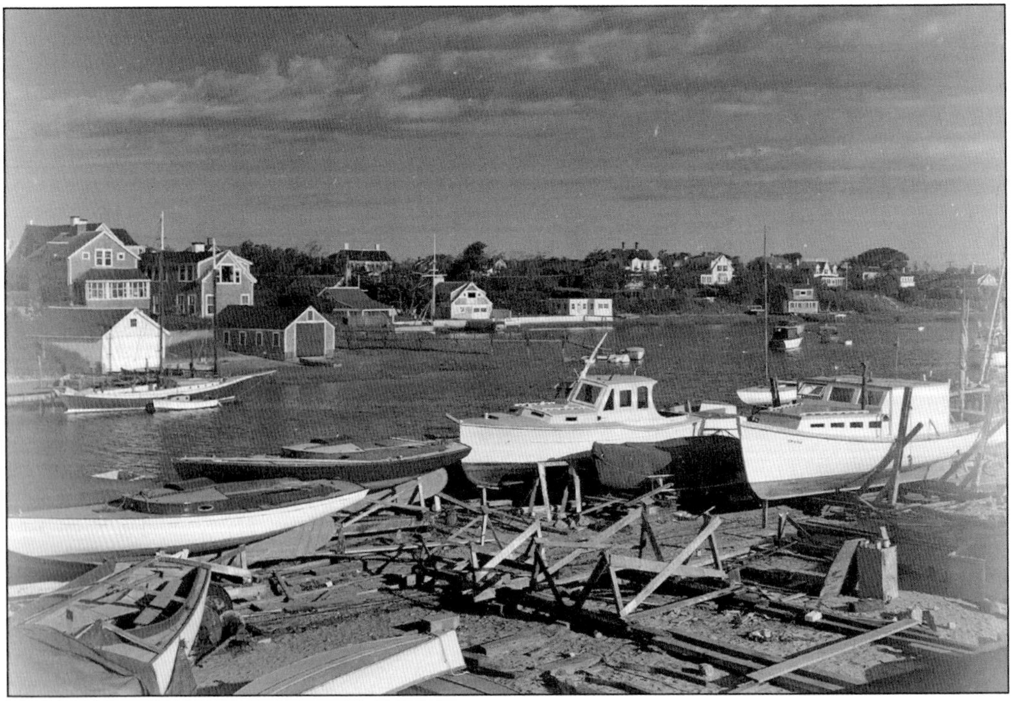

An undated advertisement brochure for the Wychmere Seashore Cottages stated, "All along the high Wychmere shore a superb sea-view is presented, with unbroken water-line nearly from east to west."

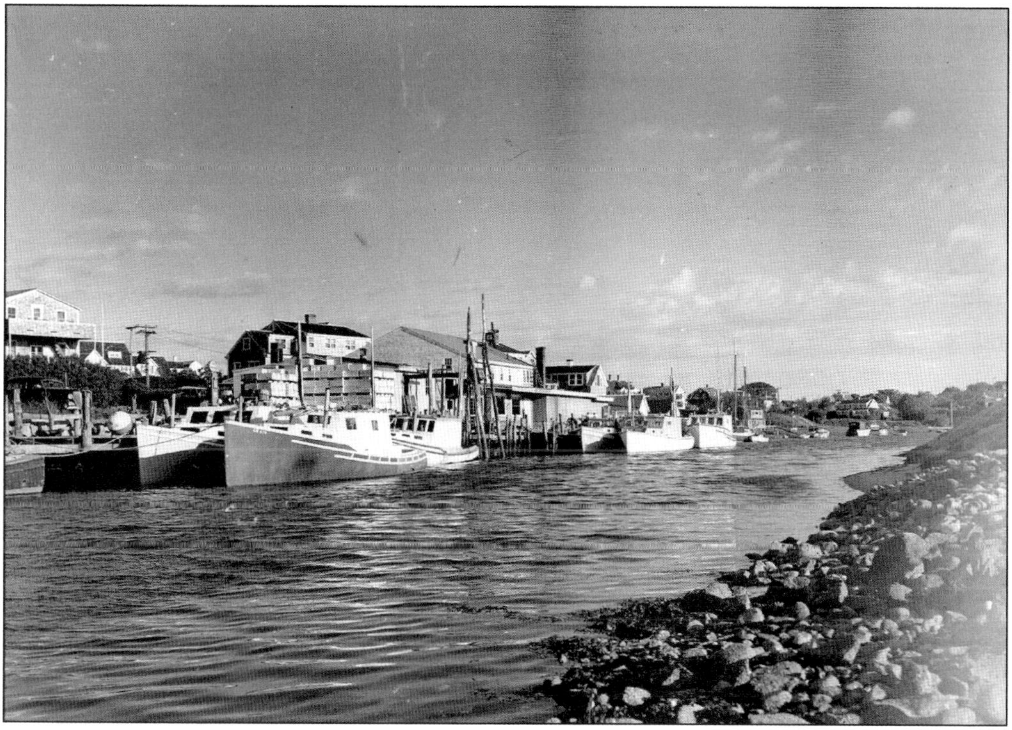

Here are two more views of Wychmere Harbor. "Here are your deep-sea charter boats for cruising and fishing in gentle Nantucket Sound," advertised the Harwich Board of Trade. In the photograph below, the distinctive rooftop of the Snow's Inn can be seen behind the yacht.

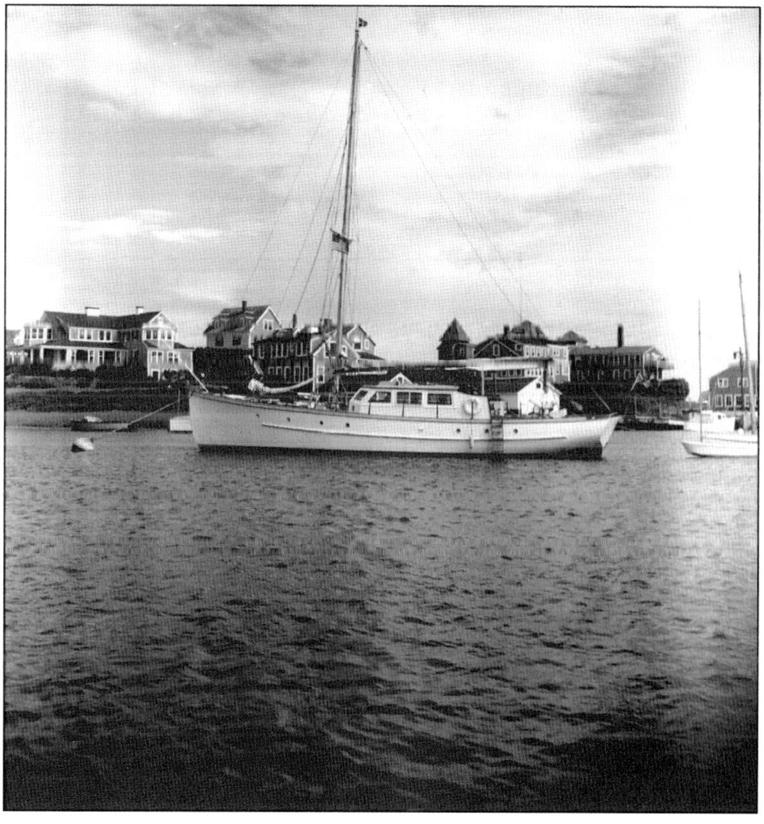

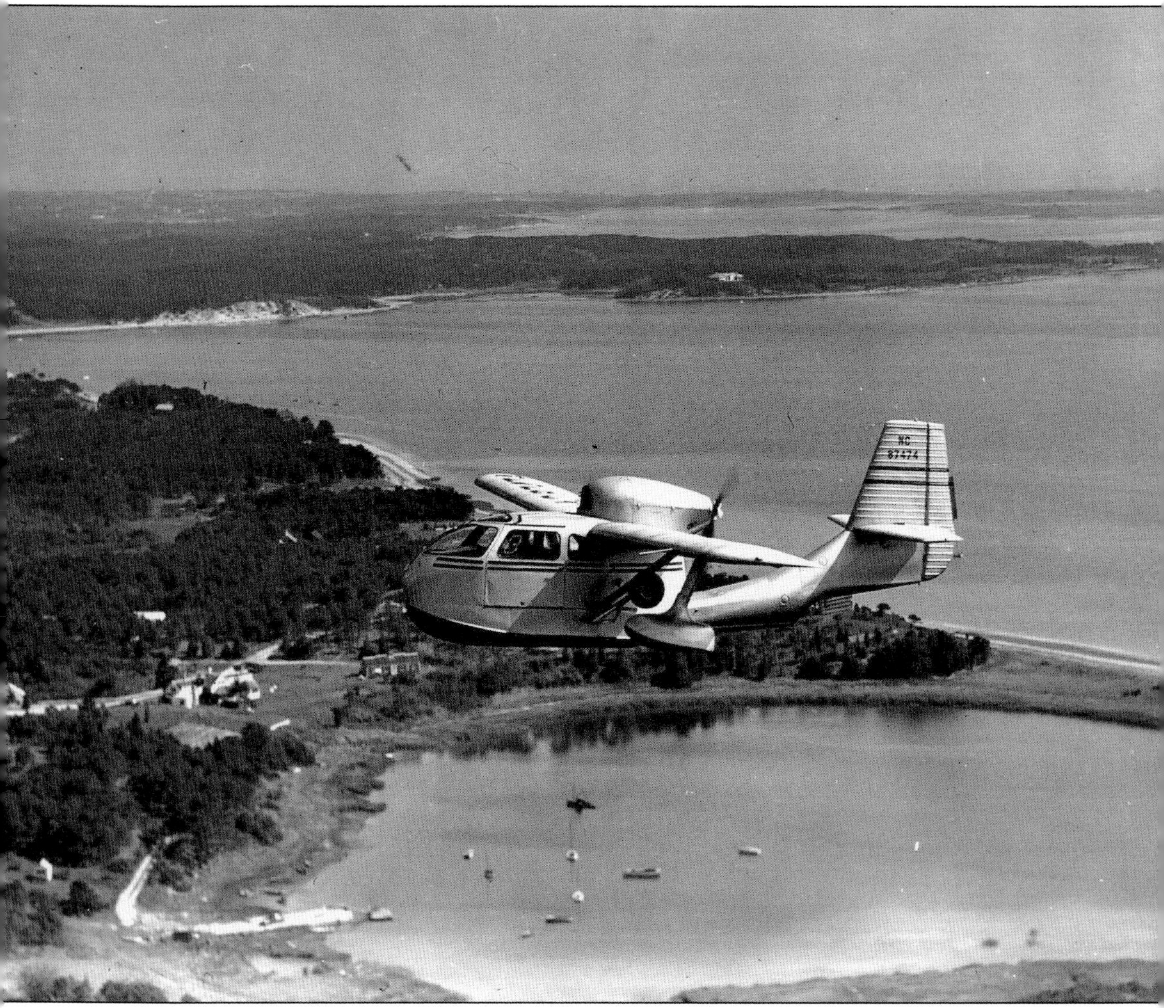

A Seebee flies over Wequassett in 1946. A 1951 Cape Cod Directory of Hotels and Inns listed, "Wequassett Inn and Cottages, on Pleasant Bay, East Harwich. A charming inn with individual cottages overlooking Pleasant Bay and offering you a complete vacation-a combination of the best seashore and country living."

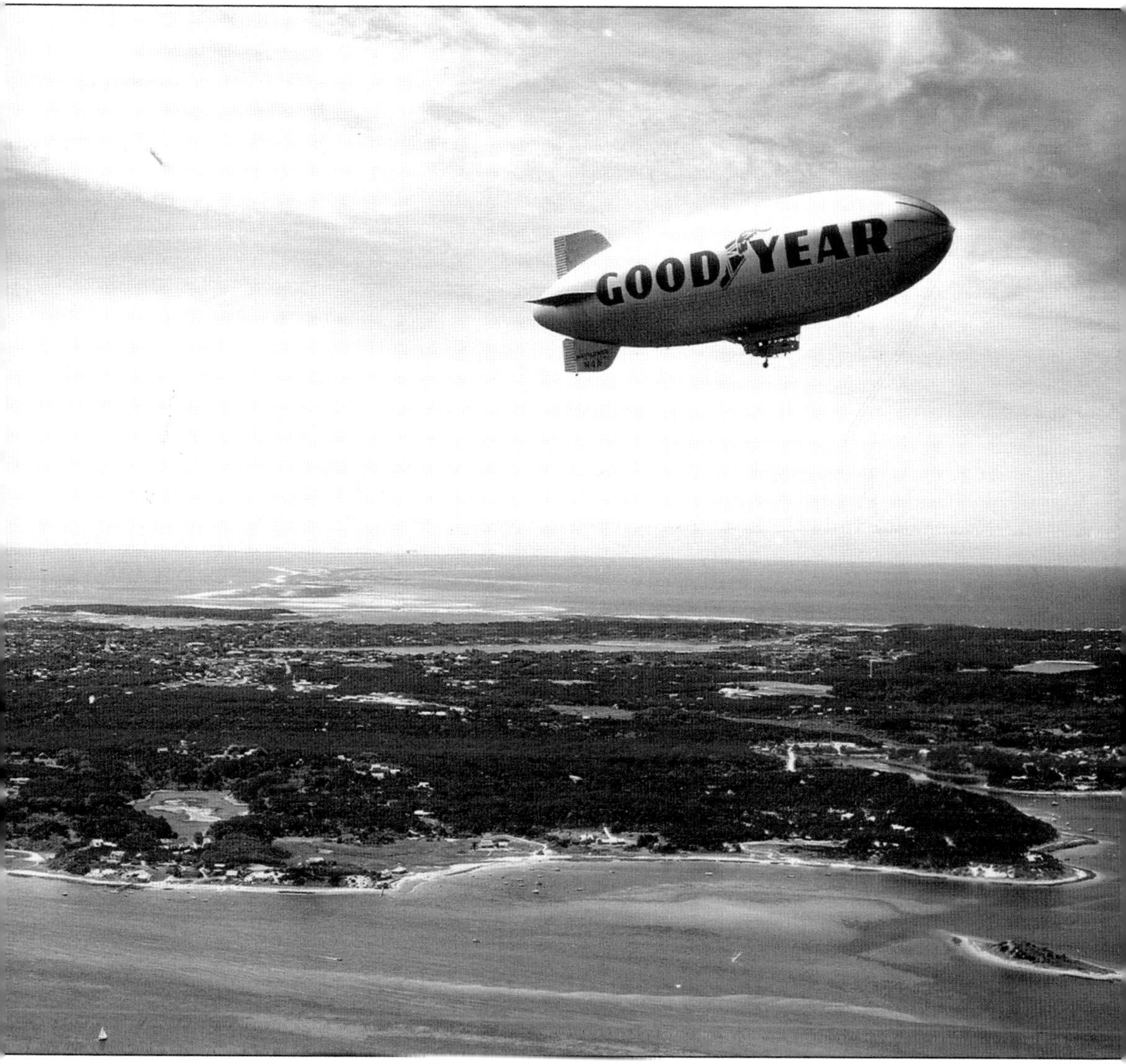

The Good Year blimp over Pleasant Bay is pictured here in 1966 with a clear image of Chatham below. The Good Year blimp made frequent trips over Cape Cod in the 1960s. Here it is poised over Pleasant Bay looking south to Monomoy. The view is over North Chatham, and in sight are Bassing Harbor, Fox Hill, and the top of Strong Island.

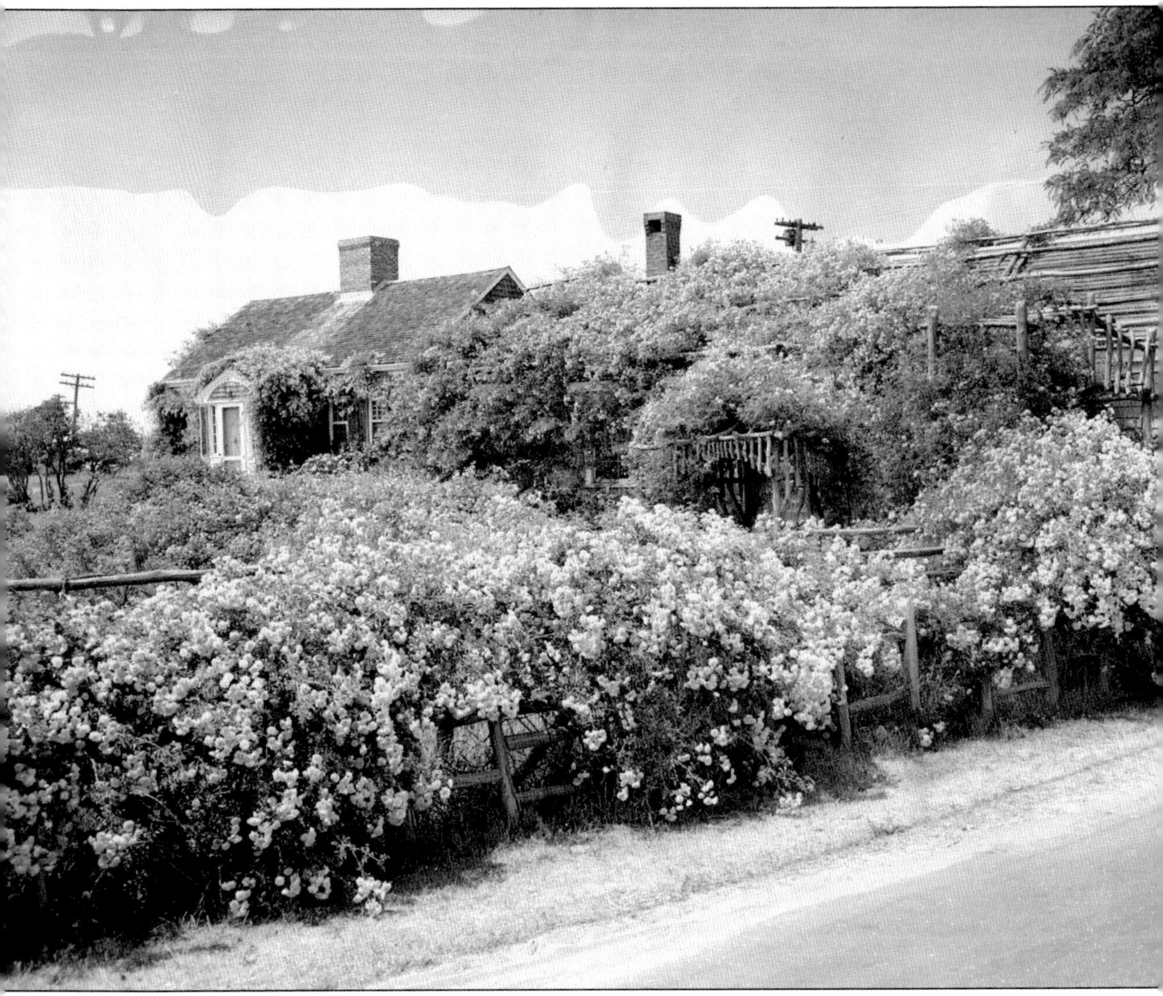

A rose-covered cottage with no address given was found among the stock photographs of Richard Kelsey. It is the picture of rural postcard perfection that was part of the Cape Cod image.

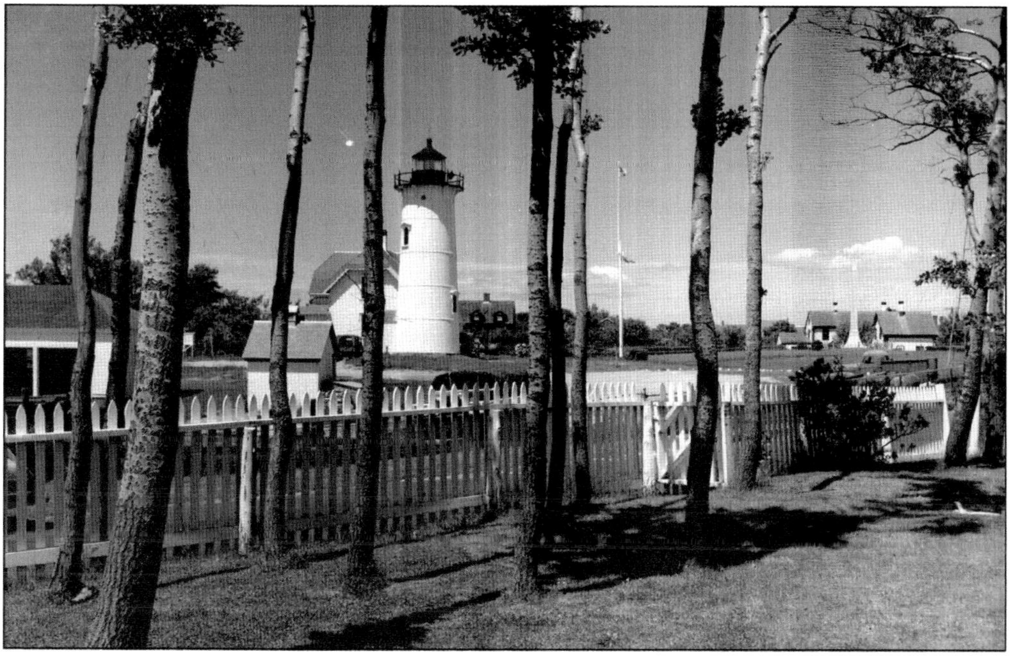

Shown from an unusual angle in the photograph above, Chatham Light is seen from the Beach Club with the Mack Memorial in the background and surrounded by a picket fence and tall oak trees. Below, an aerial shot of the Chatham Light from the 1940s shows the area on a sunny quiet afternoon. Chatham Light is one of the many beacons that have guided mariners for centuries.

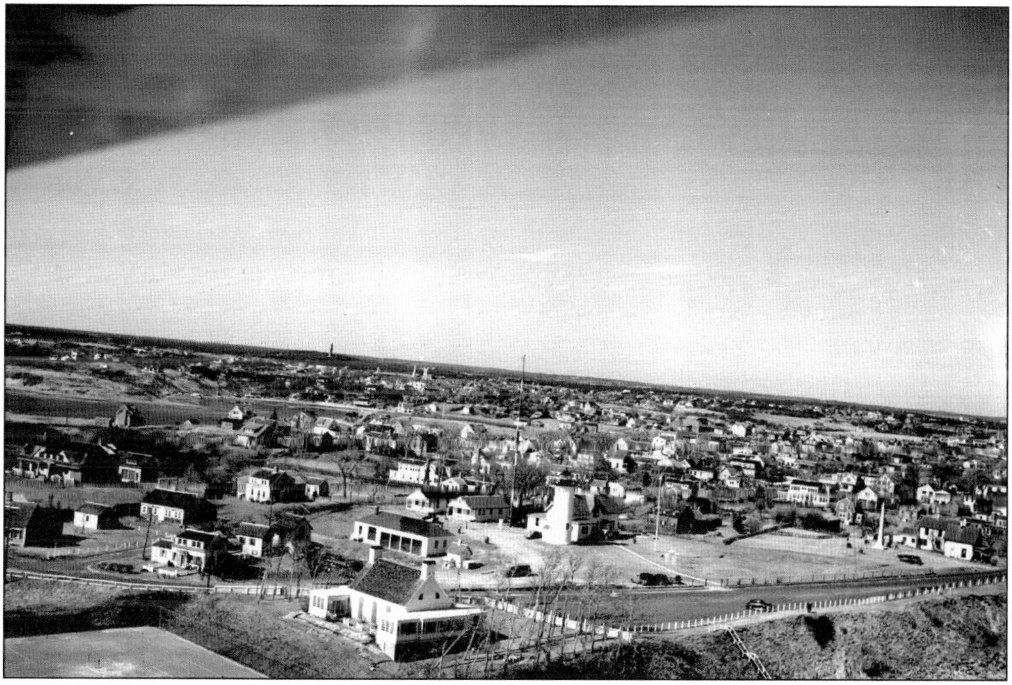

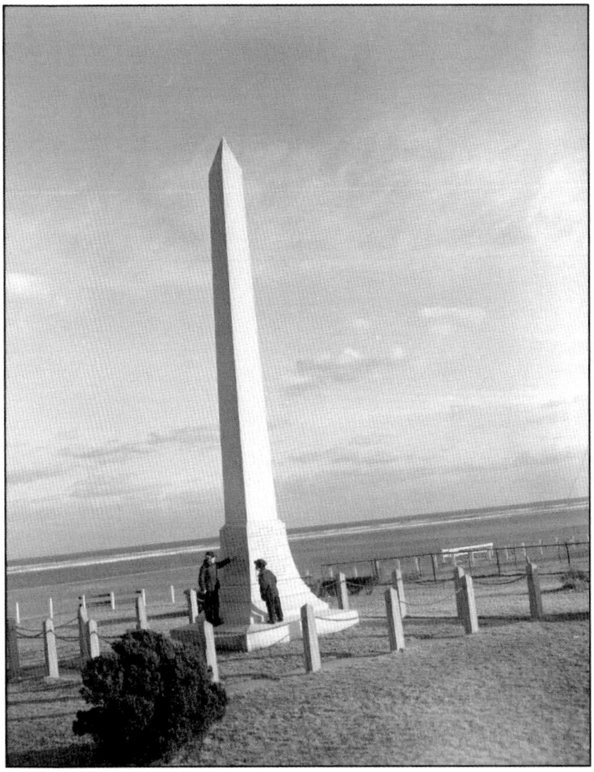

In the photograph above, two young boys play innocently by the imposing structure of the William Harry Mack Memorial of 1903. This memorial honors the victims and the heroes of the "Monomoy Disaster," where 12 men perished on the barge *Wadena*. The photograph below pictures a class trip by the Chatham Light, around the same earmuffs era, and shows an enthusiastic greeting to an unseen lighthouse tender.

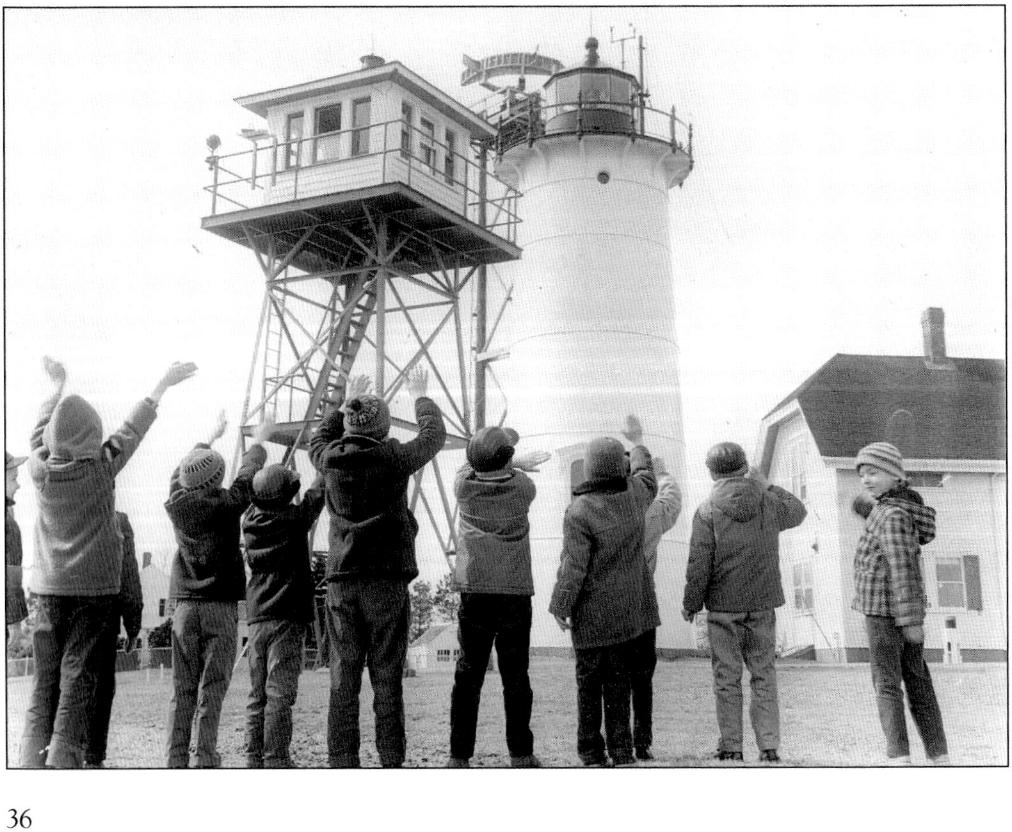

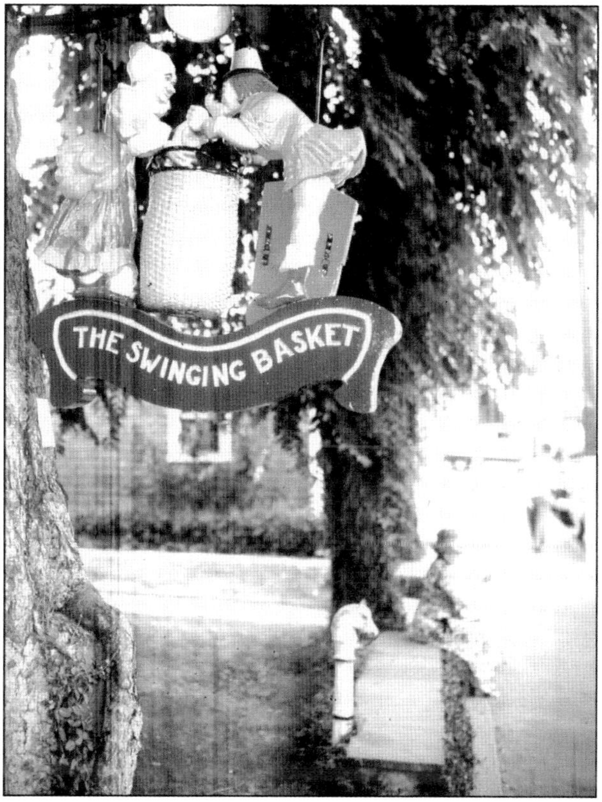

Commerce in downtown Chatham developed early. Seen in the above image is a close-up of signage for the Swinging Basket on Main Street in Chatham, Cape Cod's "most beautiful and complete gift shop," where one could relax in the gardens to the music of a Hammond organ according to a 1952 advertisement. In the photograph below, Main Street in Chatham is a still life snow scene in this late-1940s-to-early-1950s photograph, showing Monomoy Liquor Store owned by Barry Gibson at the far end and realtor Margaret Carr's storefront next to the Candy Manor.

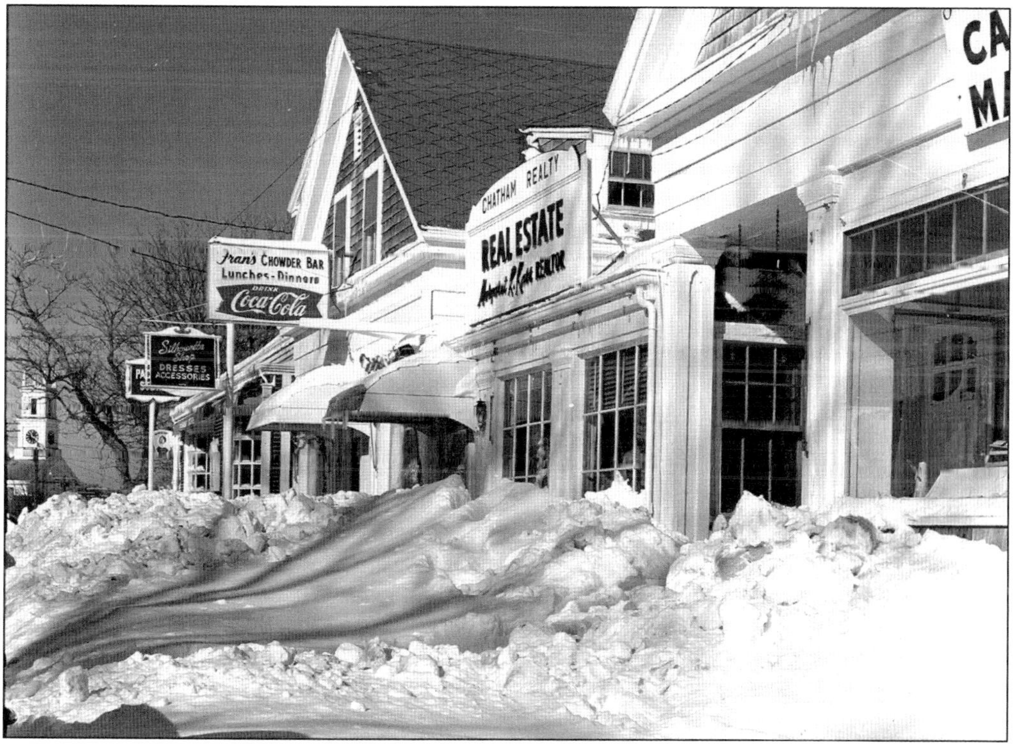

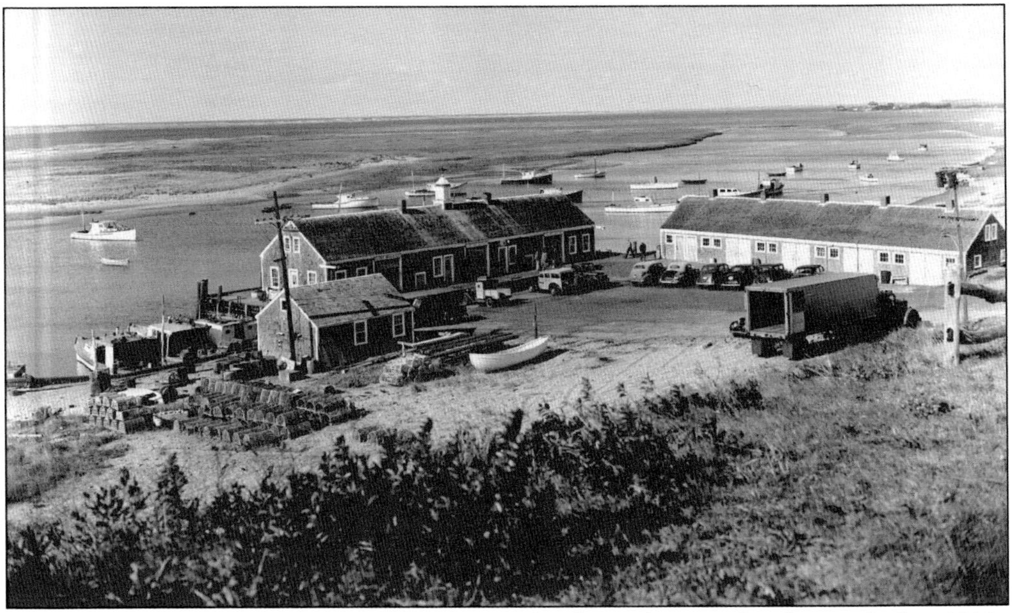

Two views of Chatham Fish Pier are shown here. The above photograph, taken in the late 1940s, shows the boating sheds to the right and Nickerson's Fish and Lobster Market to the left owned by Willard Nickerson Jr. An unusual double-ender lies abandoned out front.

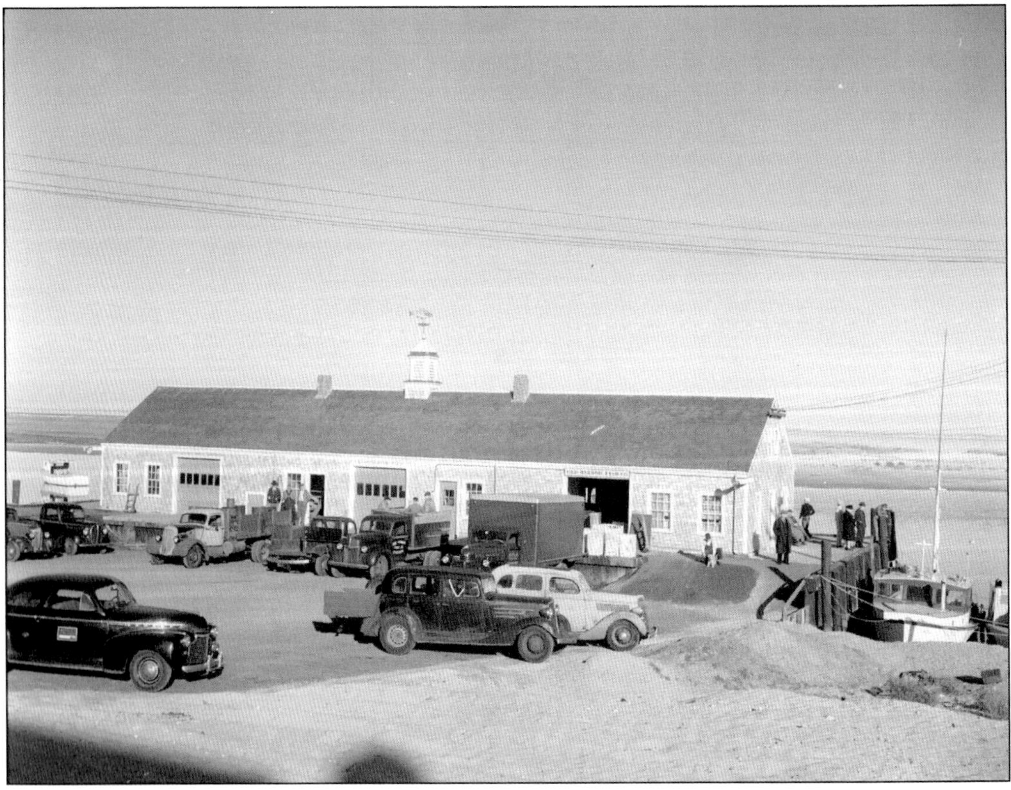

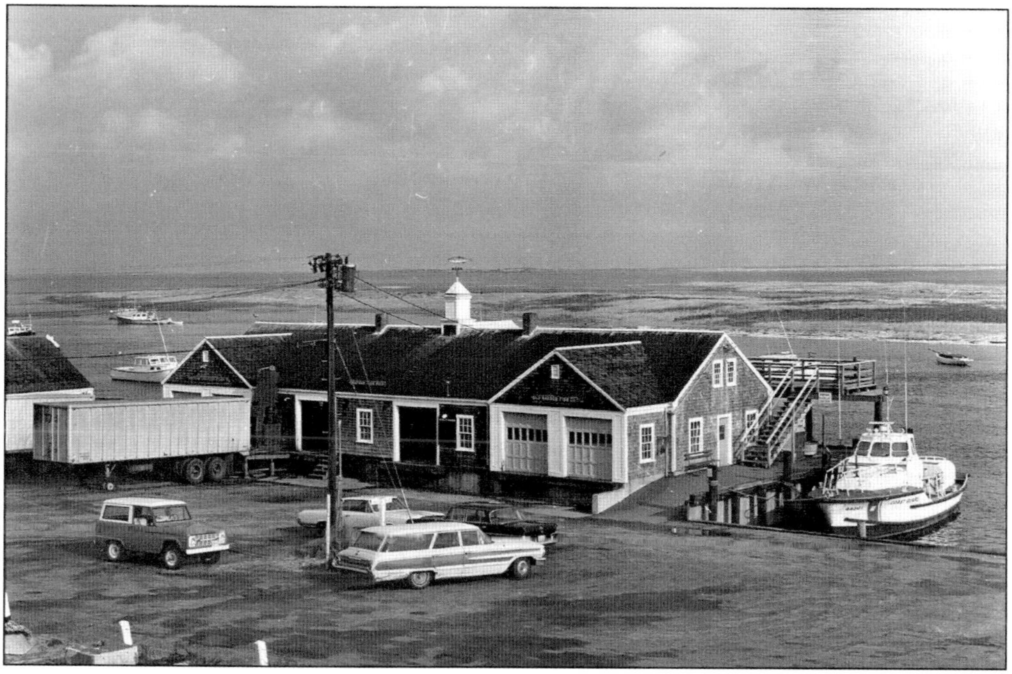

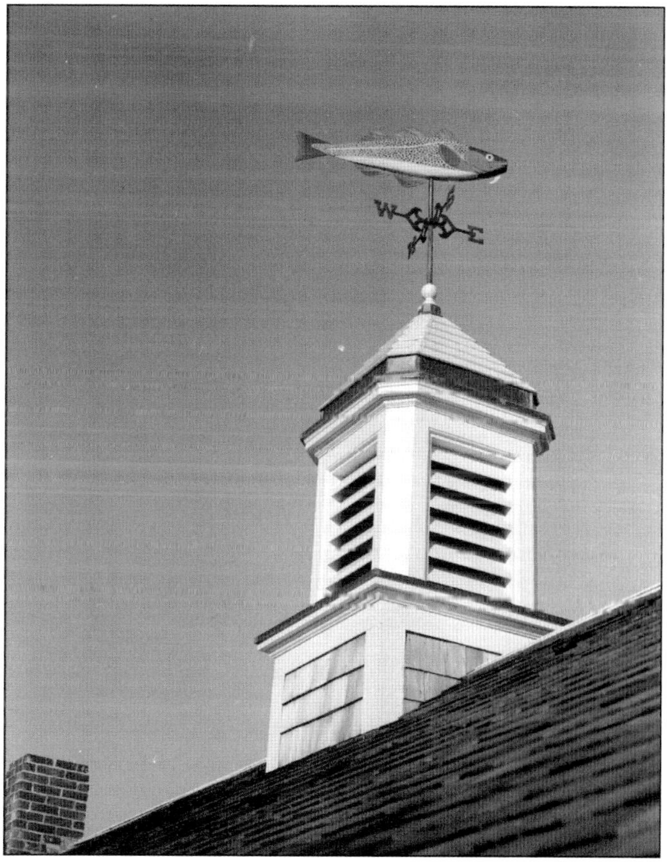

Pictured here are two later views of Chatham Fish Pier in the 1960s. In the image above, a 44-foot Coast Guard vessel is moored on the side, and the cars of local fishermen (Merritt Wright's Mercedes and Bud Ducky's car) are on the far left. Below is a close-up of the fish-topped cupola on the Chatham Fish Pier building.

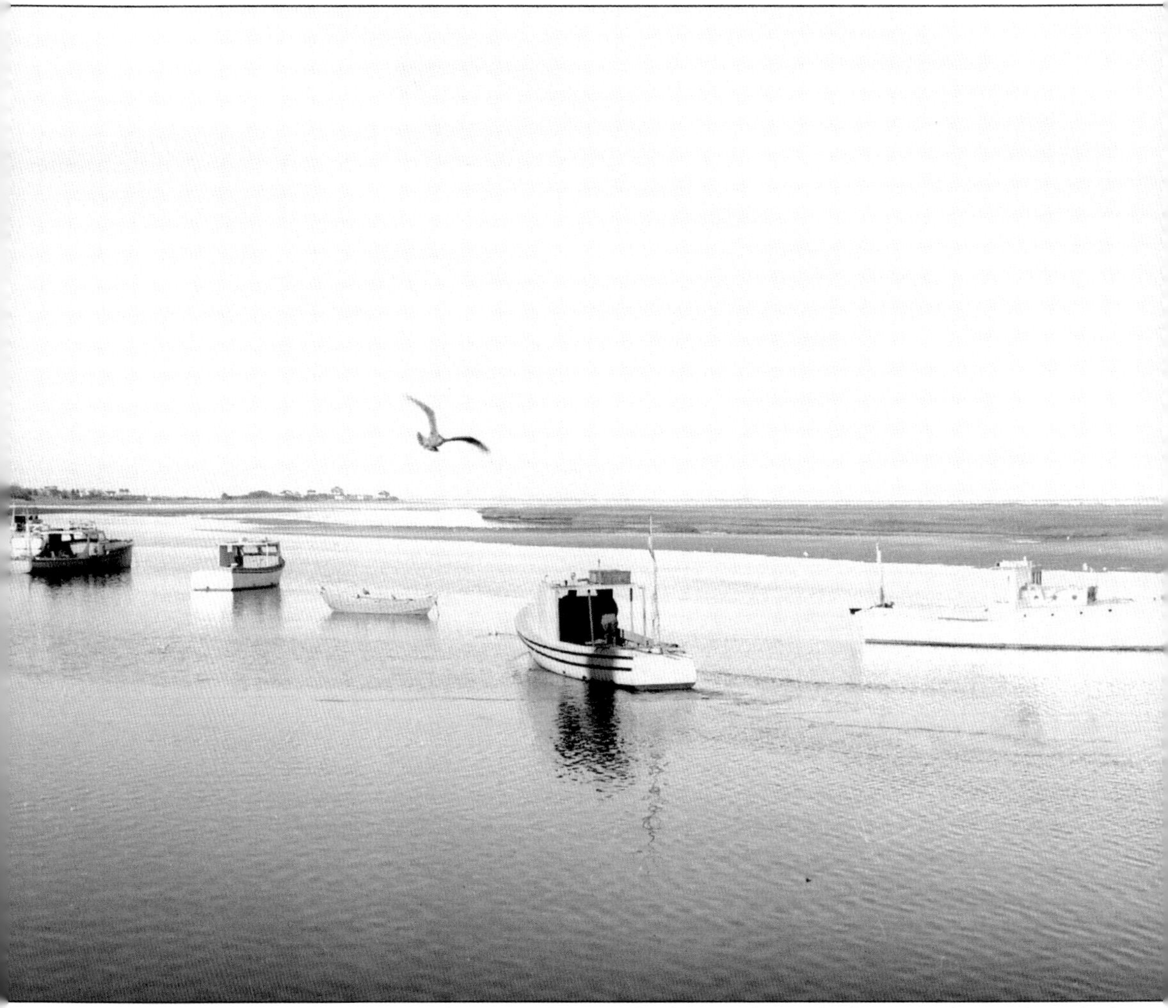

Here is a serene view of Aunt Lydia's Cove by the Chatham Fish Pier looking north. It is described in the 1890 Eldridge Map and Guide: "Surely Nature smiled upon Chatham, it will be sought by those who enjoy natures gifts here so lavishly bestowed."

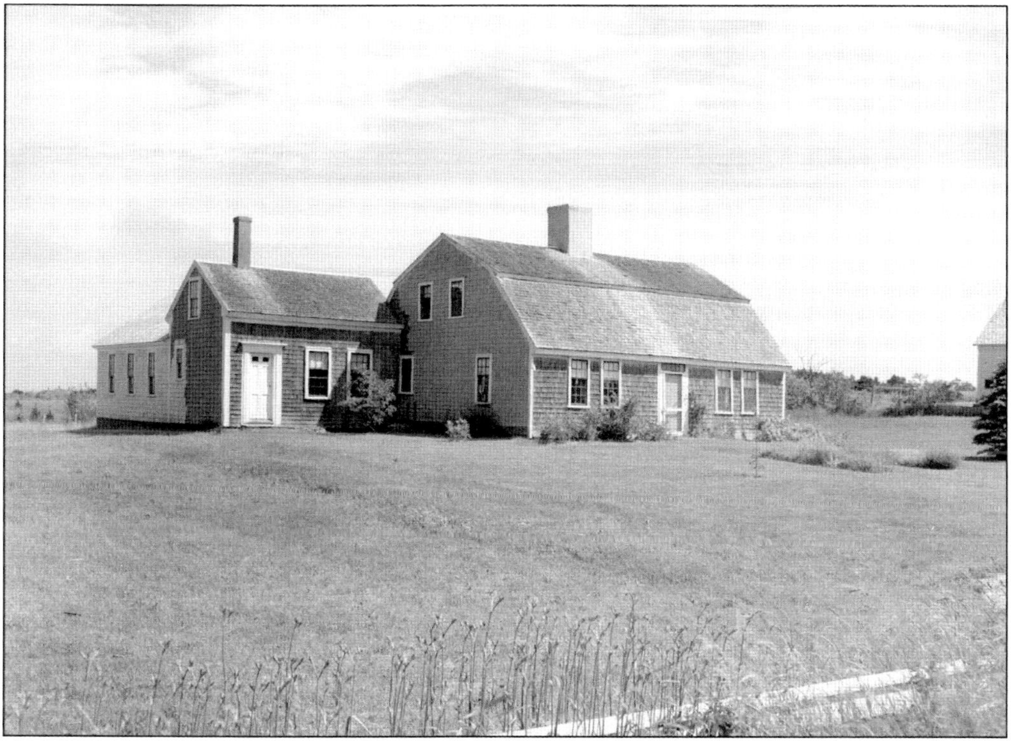

Two architectural treasures in Chatham include the 1752 Atwood House with its gambrel construction and headquarters to the Chatham Historical Society and also the Bowed Roof Guest House on Queen Anne's Road with hosts C. Joseph and Vera Mazulis in the 1970s.

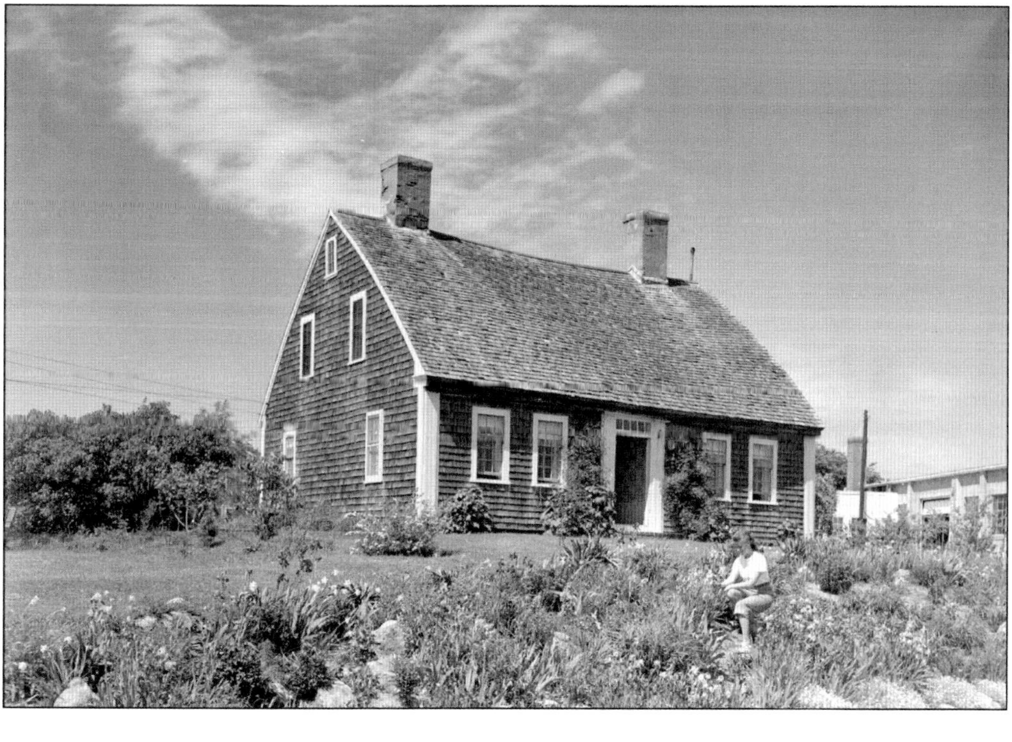

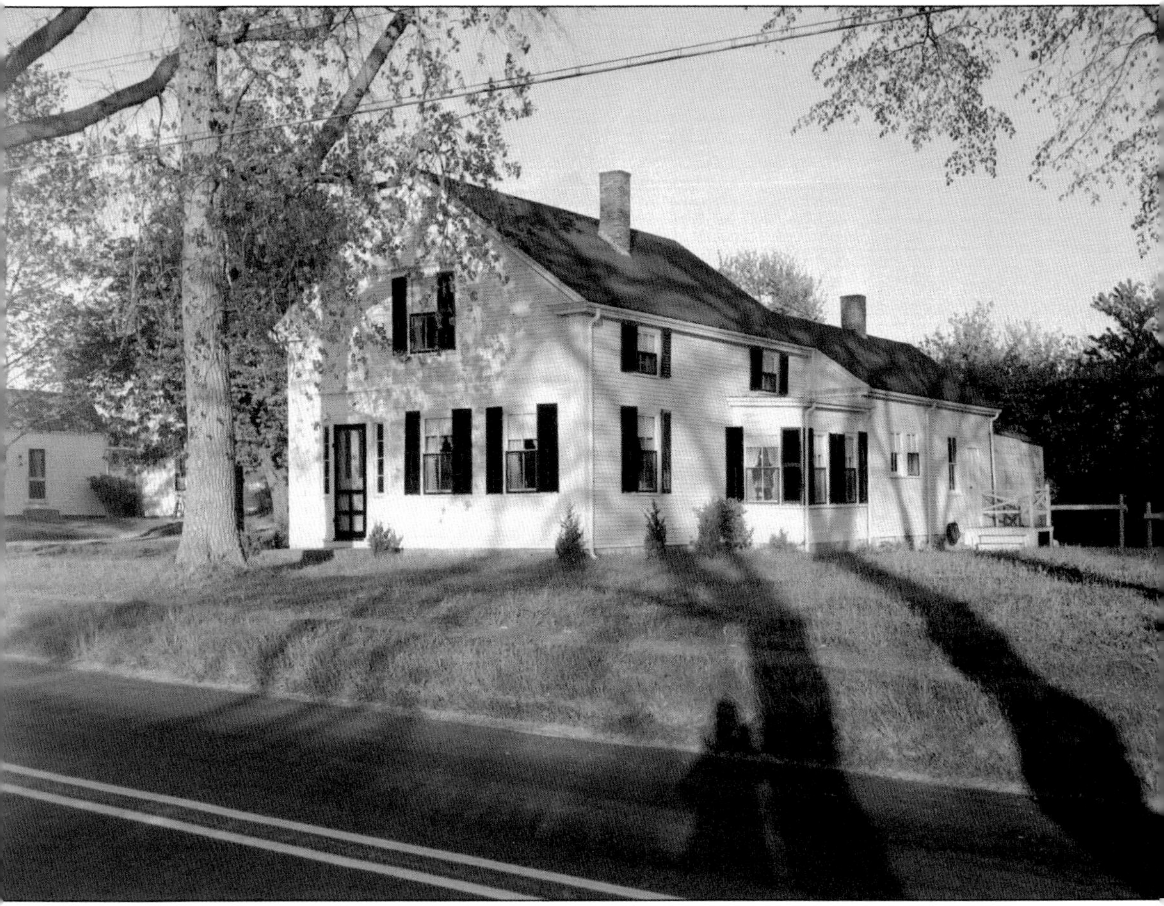

Here is Joseph Crosby Lincoln's birthplace and residence until he was 13 years old, pictured in 1951 on Route 6A in Brewster. This simple structure, built in 1840 in the Greek Revival style, was the early home of this storyteller of many quaint sea captain stories with a rural folksy flair that defined Cape Cod and caught the attention of tourists to the area.

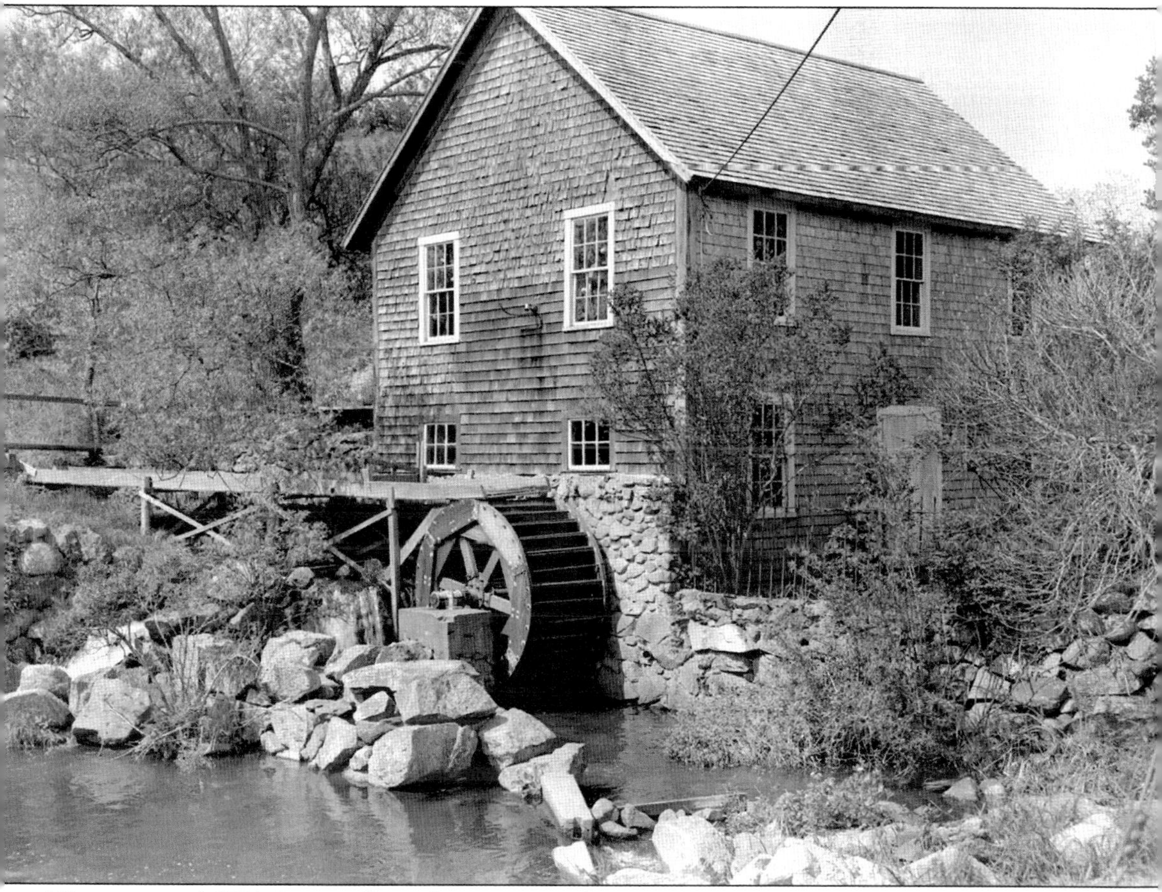

The renowned "Old Grist Mill" in the Stony Brook area off of Route 6A in West Brewster was among the stock photographs of Richard Kelsey. It was often used to illustrate brochures and articles promoting the beauty and quaintness of Cape Cod. A 1968 Brewster Board of Trade brochure that welcomed all to Brewster, "the Heart of Cape Cod," described the old mill as "one of the few remaining water wheel driven grist mills in the country . . . following the stream once known by its Indian name Saquatuckct, but now called Stony Brook."

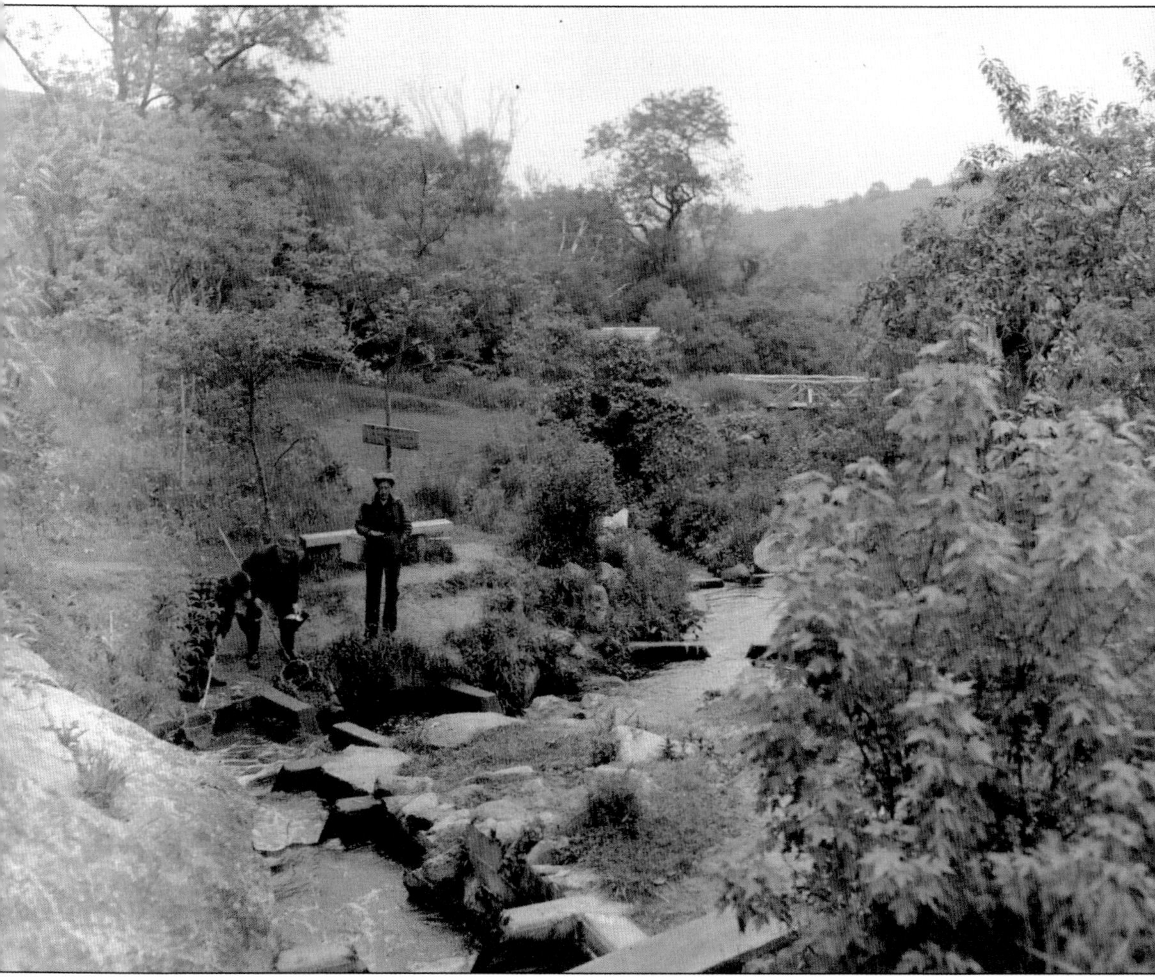

Three unidentified gentlemen are witnesses to the never to be forgotten sight of the incredible surge of the spring herring migration from the saltwater ocean to the freshwater ponds at the Brewster Herring run. The herring ladder was made famous by John Hay in his publication *The Run*.

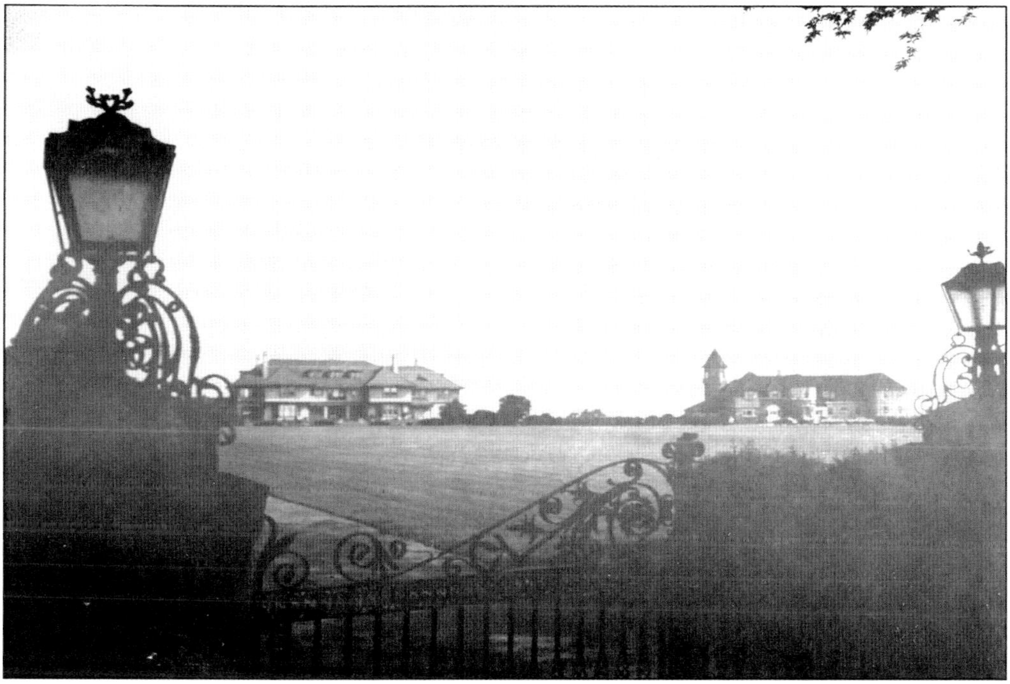

Shown here are two mansions gracing the towns of Brewster and Orleans. The Nickerson Estate, once the private residence of Roland Nickerson, is now a resort hotel; and Southward Inn, once offering food and shelter for the discriminating guest with its Georgiana dining rooms, operated in the 1920s through the 1960s.

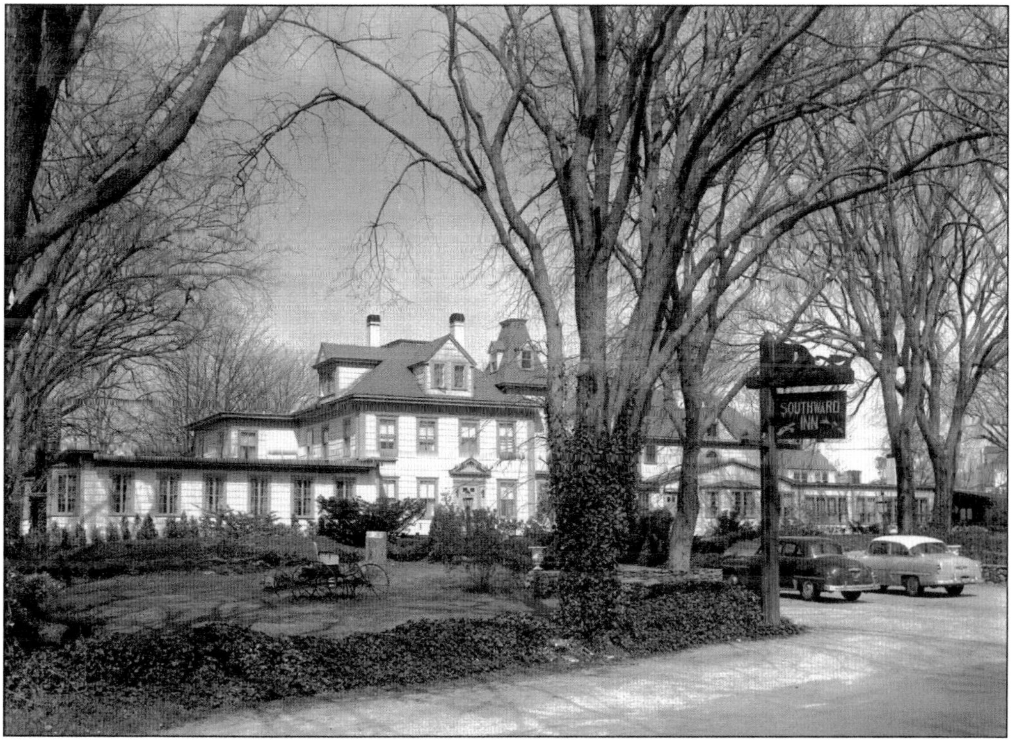

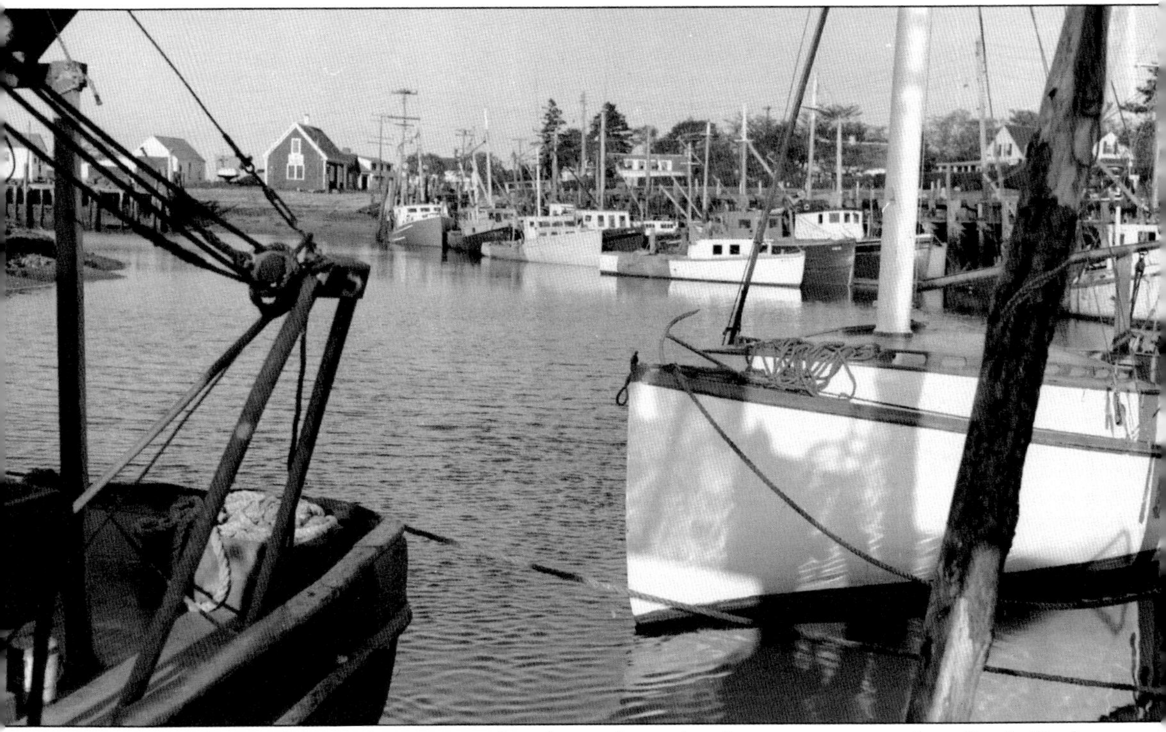

Charter boats, fishing draggers, and a fleet of wooden boats are moored at Rock Harbor, Orleans, on Cape Cod Bay. The Orleans Board of Trade once boasted that Rock Harbor was the "most thoroughly Cape Cod of all, with the active coming and going of the shell fishing fleet at Rock Harbor."

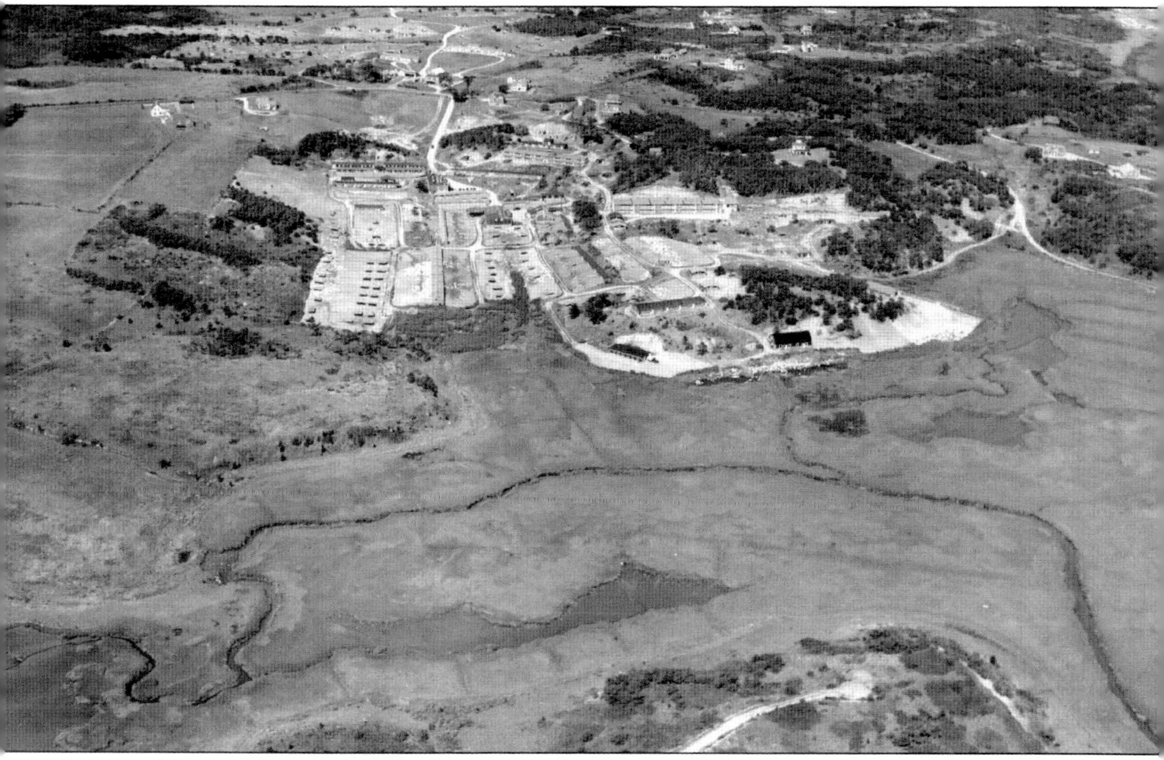

This aerial view of Mayo's duck farm in East Orleans was taken in 1947. Founded in 1895 and managed by Lucy L. Mayo for many years, it had a bakery and a restaurant, called the Quacker, on Beach Road in East Orleans. It closed in 1976, but it marketed thousands of ducks in its heyday.

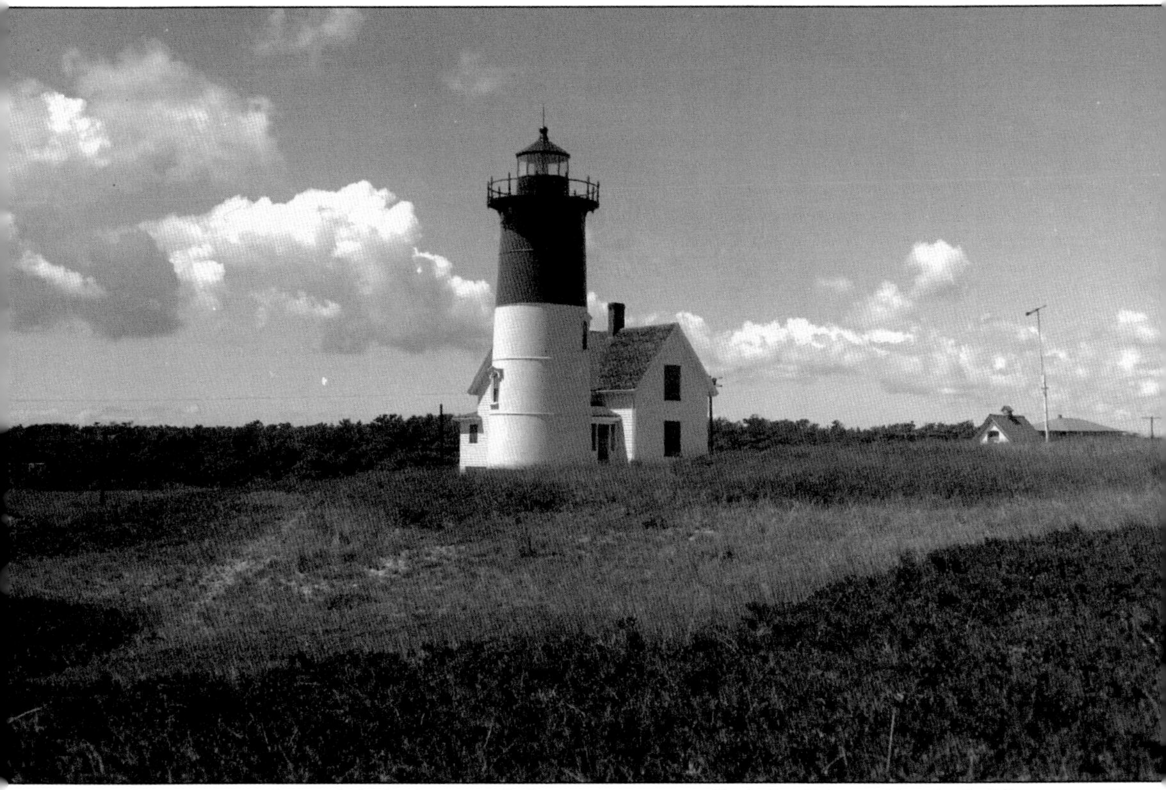

The Nauset Light with light keeper's lodge, sometimes called the "I Love You Light" because of its three-flash signals, stands with its distinctive red-and-white color scheme and gingerbread that decorated the light keeper's lodge. They are pictured here before storms and erosion caused them to be moved further back from the shoreline. But the light did not save all, as Eastham Vacationist's Handbook from 1951 states, "and grief did come to Eastham homes from shipwreck at sea very often during the last century. In Eastham in 1837 there lived 31 widows of seamen—which fact tells its own story."

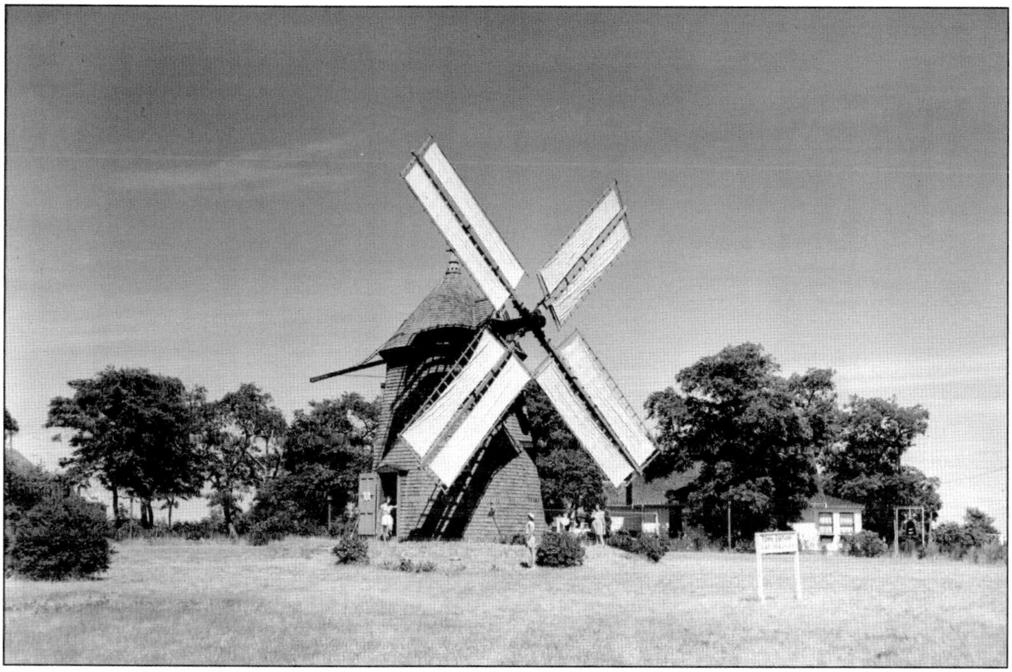

Two views of the old windmill at Eastham with and without sails are seen here. According to the 1890 Eldridge map and guide, "Eastham windmill with its sails set in a stiff breeze can still occasionally grind corn at Windmill Park, in Eastham center. A Town Miller is in attendance to explain the mill and its history throughout the warm weather."

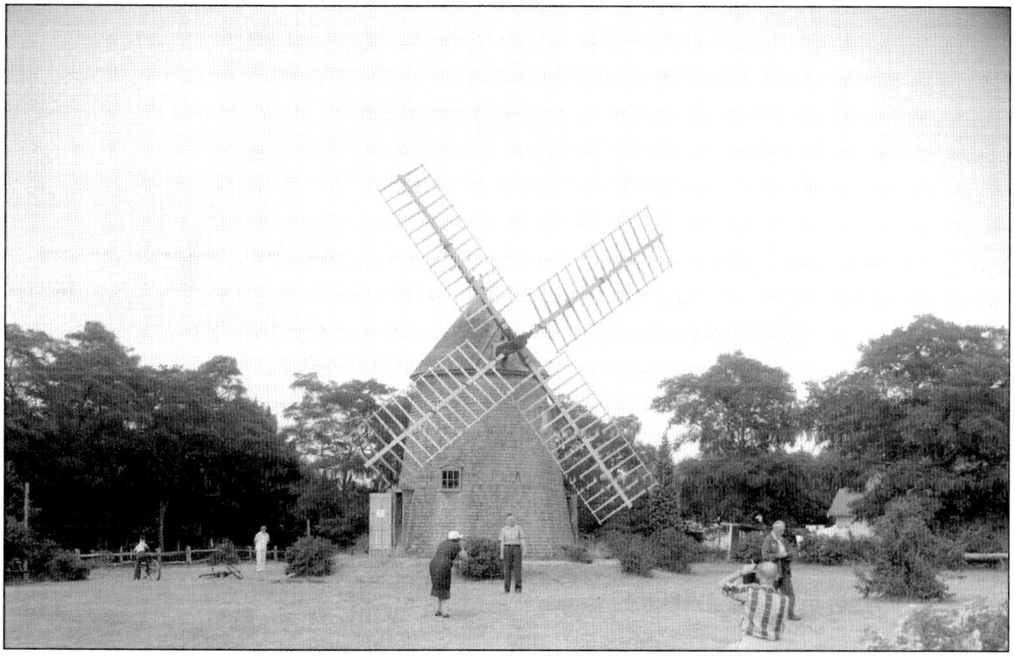

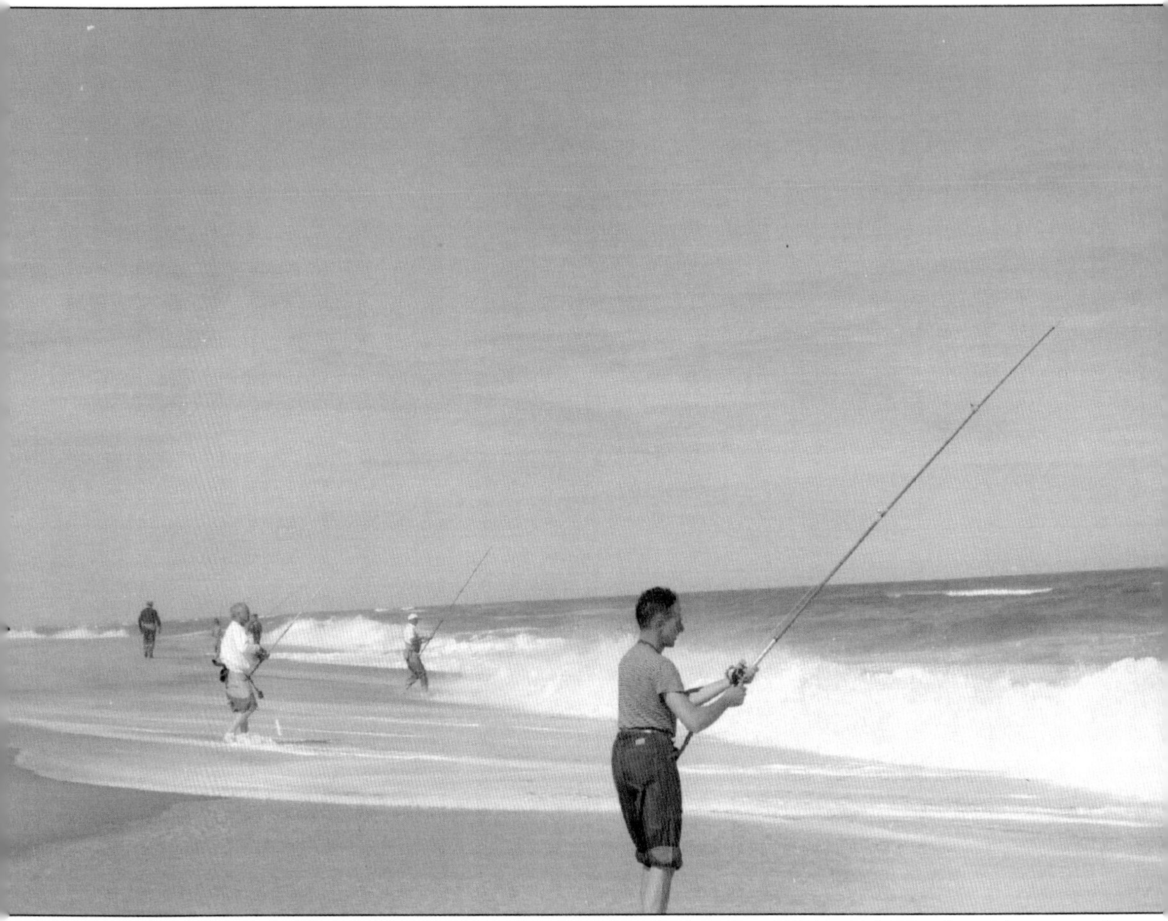

A sportsman is surf casting on Nauset Beach, Cape Cod, in 1948. The 1951 *Eastham Vacationist's Handbook* from the Eastham Chamber of Commerce states, "for fishing at its best, fish in Eastham . . . surfcasting all along the tides at Nauset Beach lures the experienced and the novice to try for the 'big one.' "

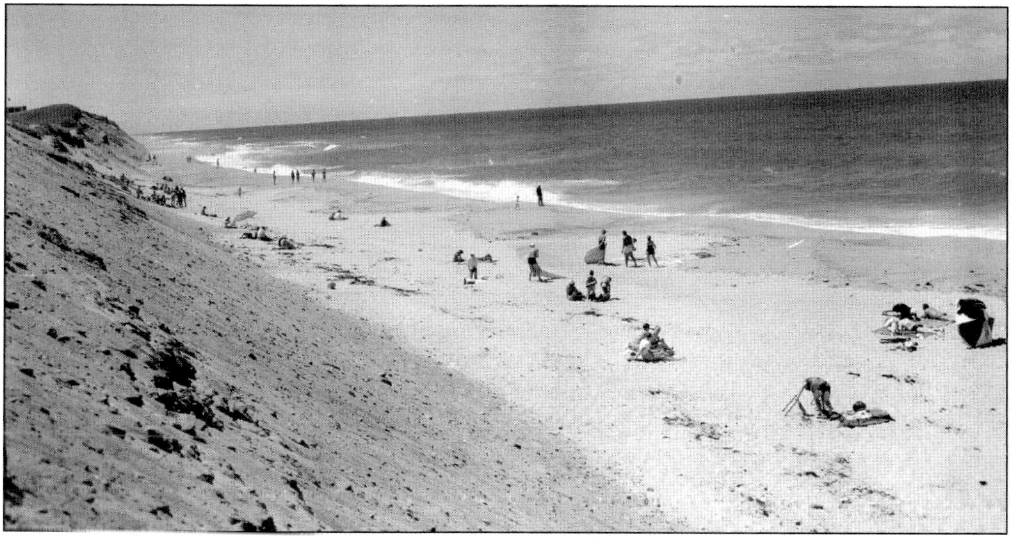

Views of Nauset Beach from the late 1940s are captured from the parking lot showing Jeepsters and convertibles at this Atlantic beach. The 1951 *Eastham Vacationist Handbook* described the beach, "one of Eastham's greatest attractions for visitors is the stretch of beach on the backshore called the Nauset or the Great Beach. Here fishing and bathing in the surf is unexcelled."

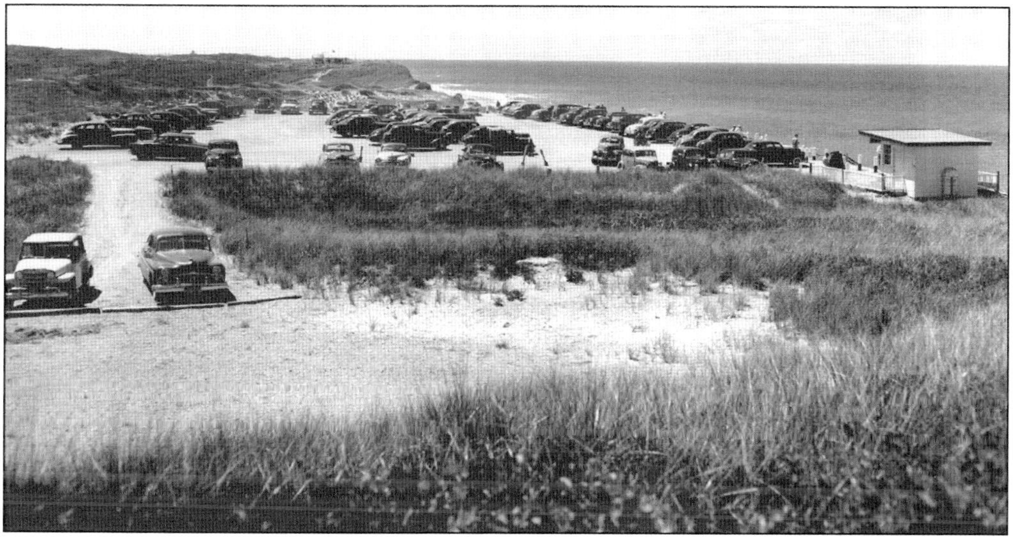

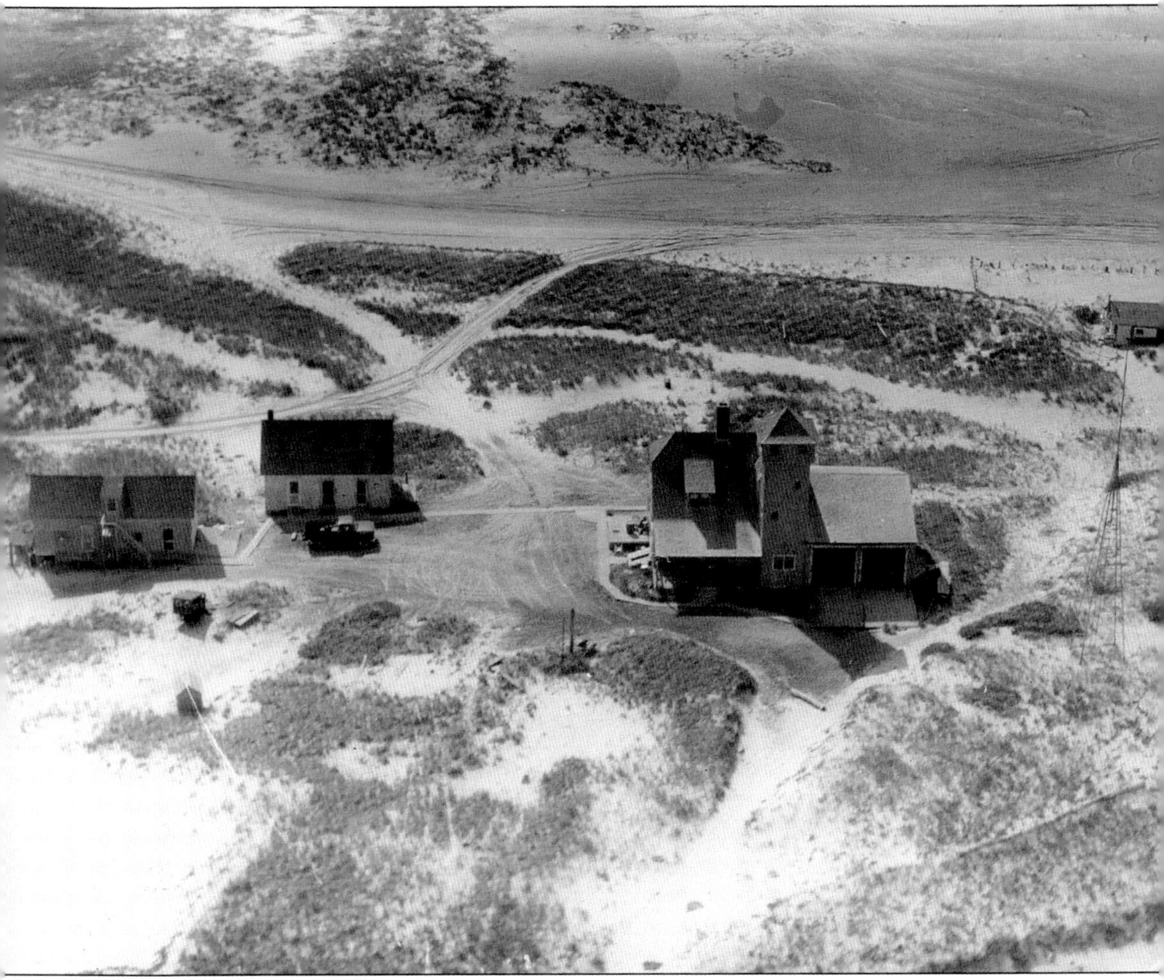

The Old Harbor Life Saving Station of Cape Cod in this late-1960s photograph shows the station in its original location at the entrance to Chatham Harbor. The boathouse, main building, stable, and several outbuildings are shown in this aerial photograph. The drama of the moving of this station by barge to Race Point in Provincetown on November 8, 1977, was captured in a series of photographs by Richard Kelsey. The move saved the station from the many violent winter storm surges on that coast and placed the station under the protection of the National Seashore.

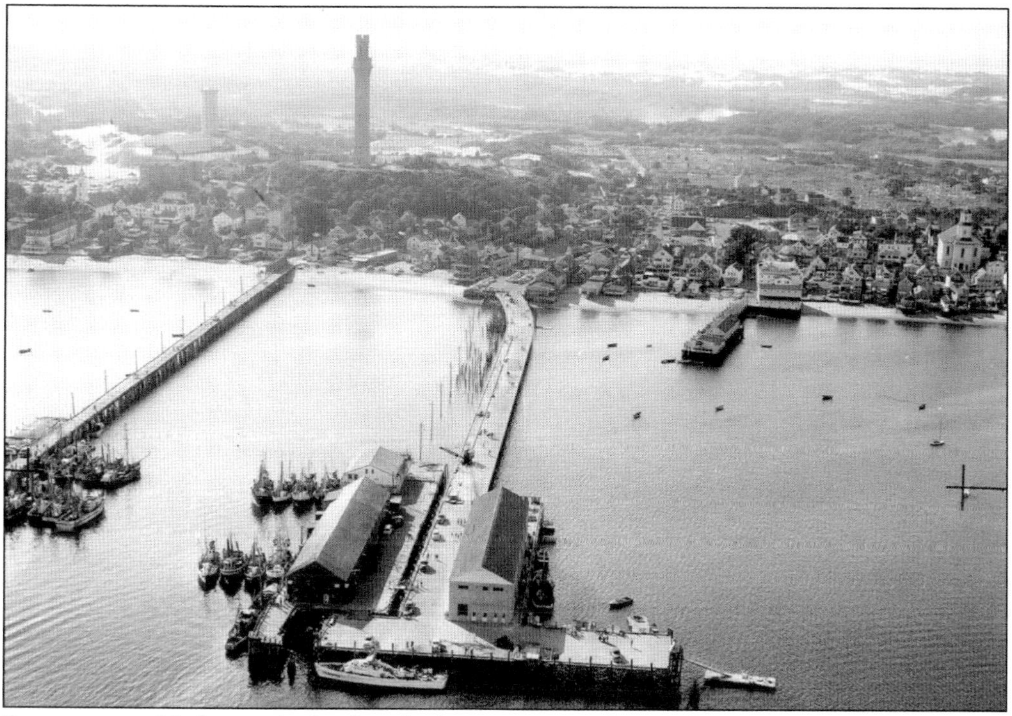

Provincetown Harbor and wharf, with the monument shrouded in fog, highlights this aerial view, shown above, in 1960. In the foreground is a Coast Guard cutter with the Provincetown fishing fleet alongside. The photograph below was probably taken during the low season. It is a clear aerial overview of the Provincetown Monument with few cars in the usually overflowing parking lot.

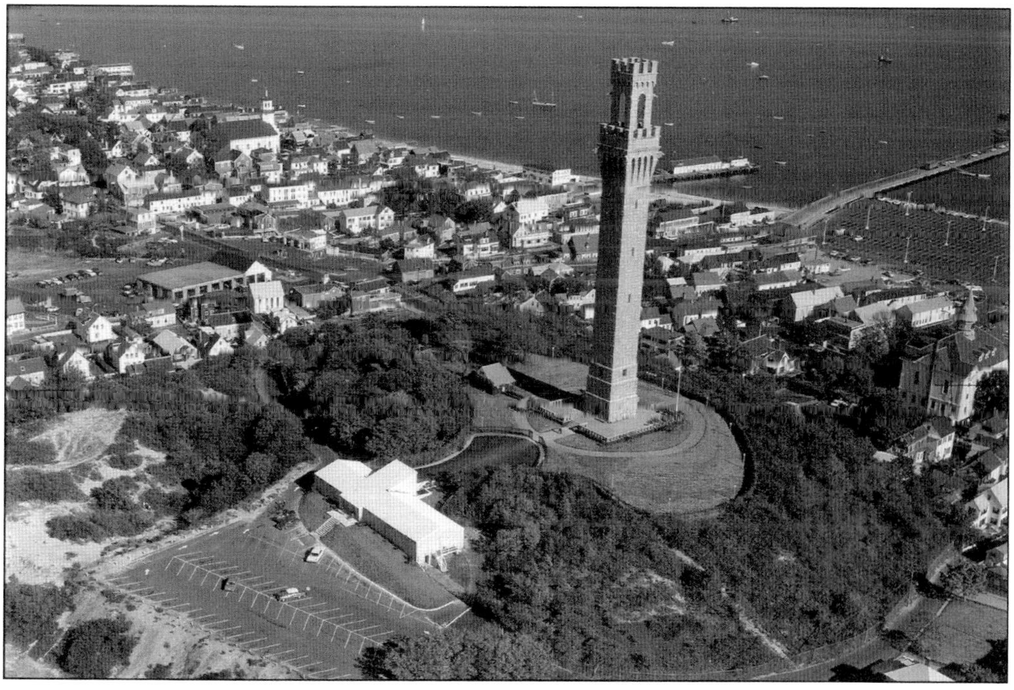

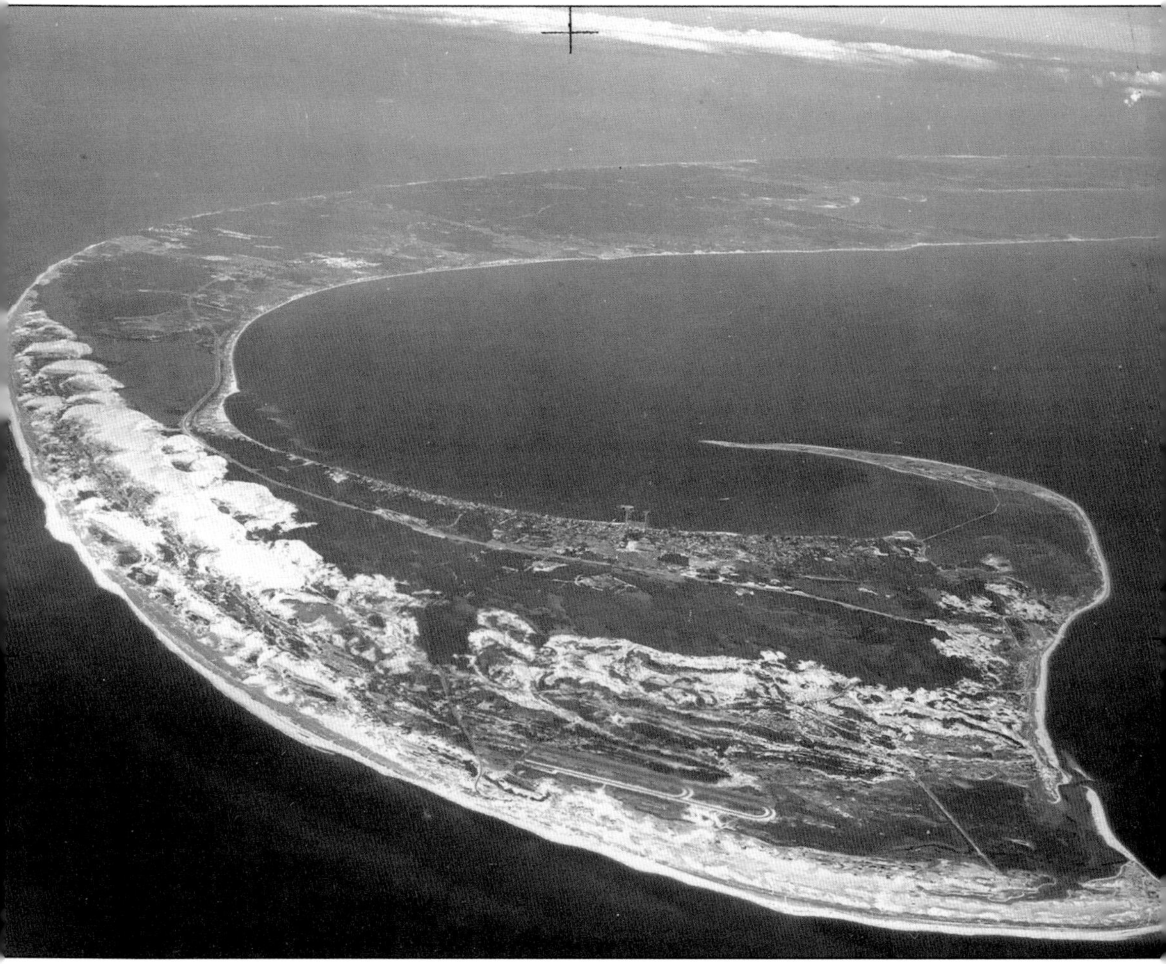

This is an aerial photograph of the point where land ends in Provincetown, a perfect hook showing the long stretches of beach from Race Point to Highland Light. This is just one of the magnificent aerials that characterized the mature photography of Richard Kelsey.

Two

Cape Cod Folks and Cape Cod Ways

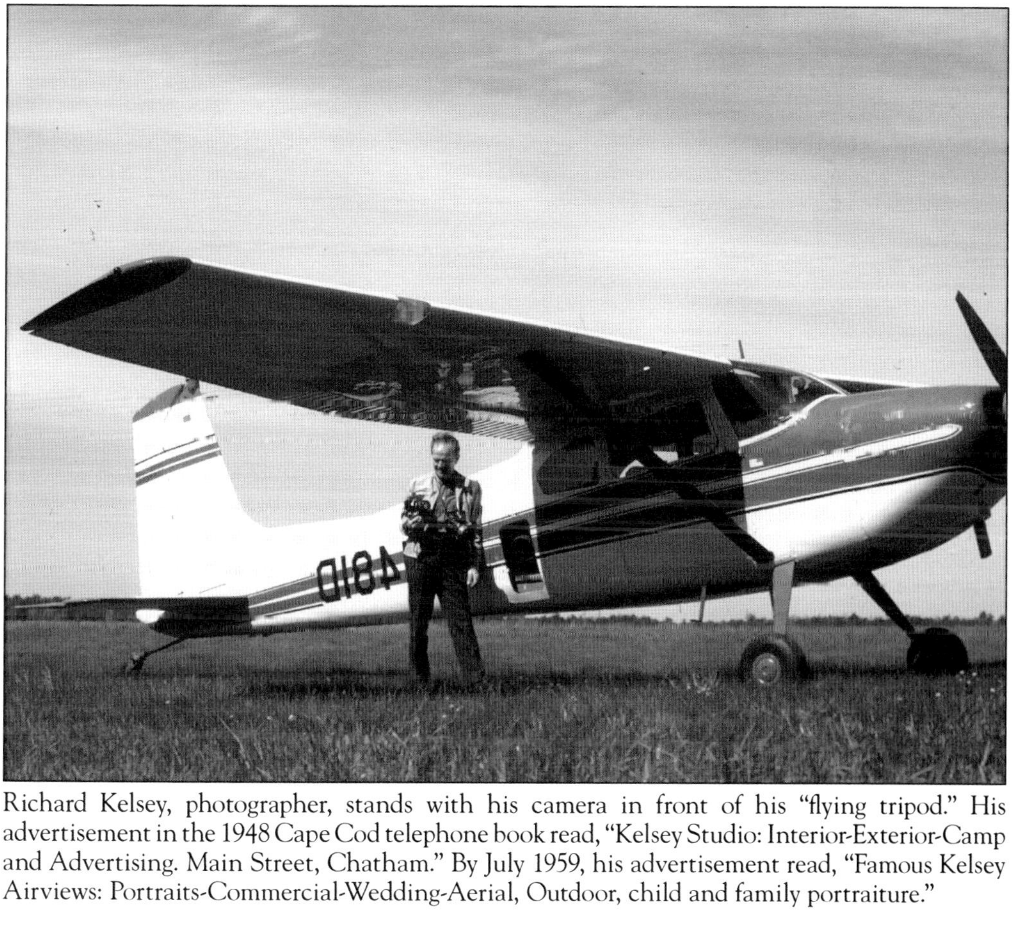

Richard Kelsey, photographer, stands with his camera in front of his "flying tripod." His advertisement in the 1948 Cape Cod telephone book read, "Kelsey Studio: Interior-Exterior-Camp and Advertising. Main Street, Chatham." By July 1959, his advertisement read, "Famous Kelsey Airviews: Portraits-Commercial-Wedding-Aerial, Outdoor, child and family portraiture."

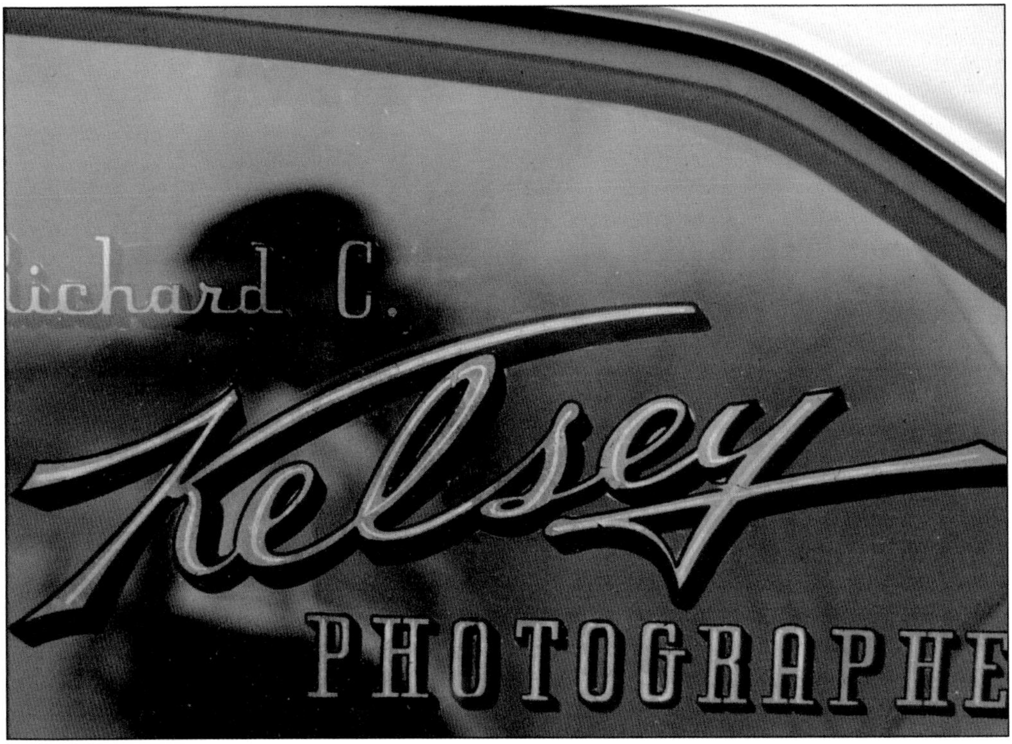

The Richard Kelsey signature that was his logo appeared on the verso of all his photographs and on the window of his plane. Also shown is the Kelsey Studio at 20 Heritage Lane, off 938 Main Street in Chatham.

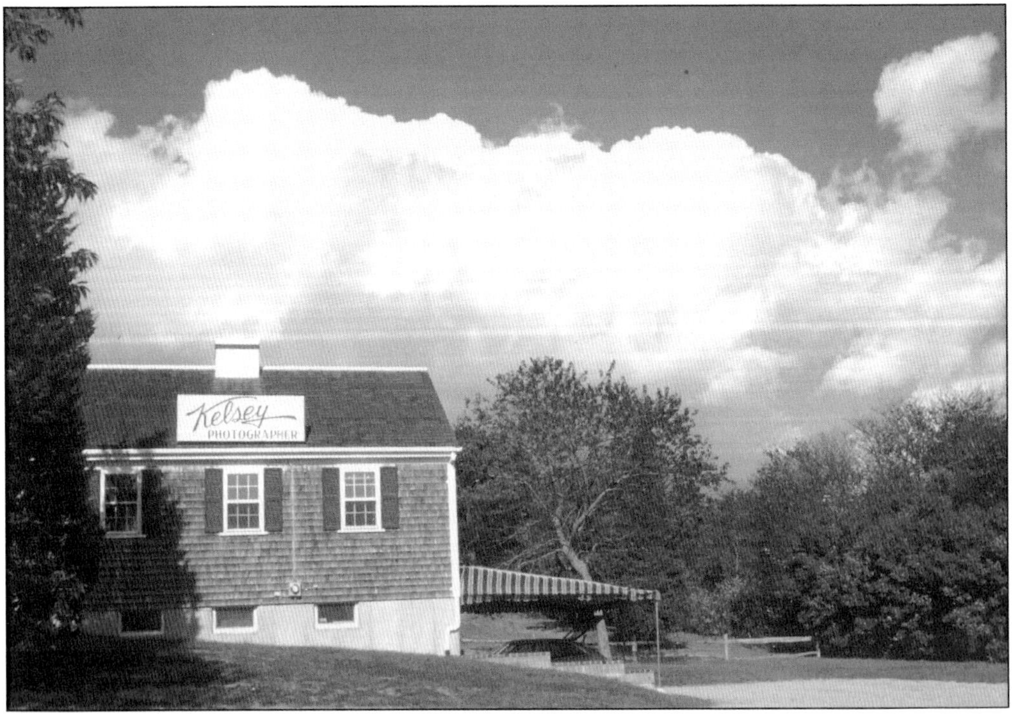

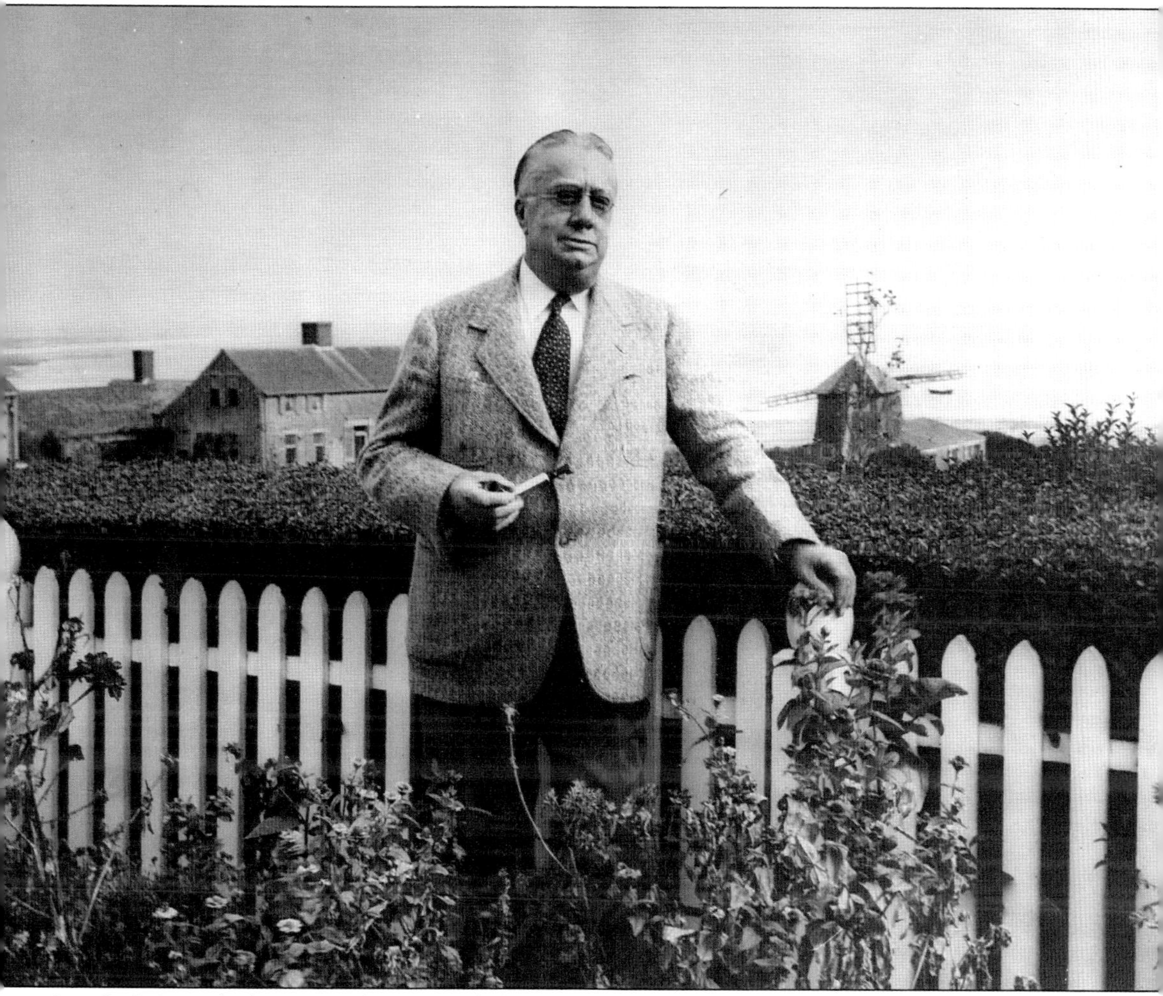

Joseph C. Lincoln (1870–1944), once called "the best PR man for Cape Cod," was quoted in the 1950 Cape Cod Chamber of Commerce brochure as saying "if one loves the sea and the clean, cool salt air, and the boating and fishing, both fresh and salt . . . if one drives through the pine and the oak woods by hundreds of lakes and ponds . . . for surf on still water bathing . . . why then Come to Cape Cod."

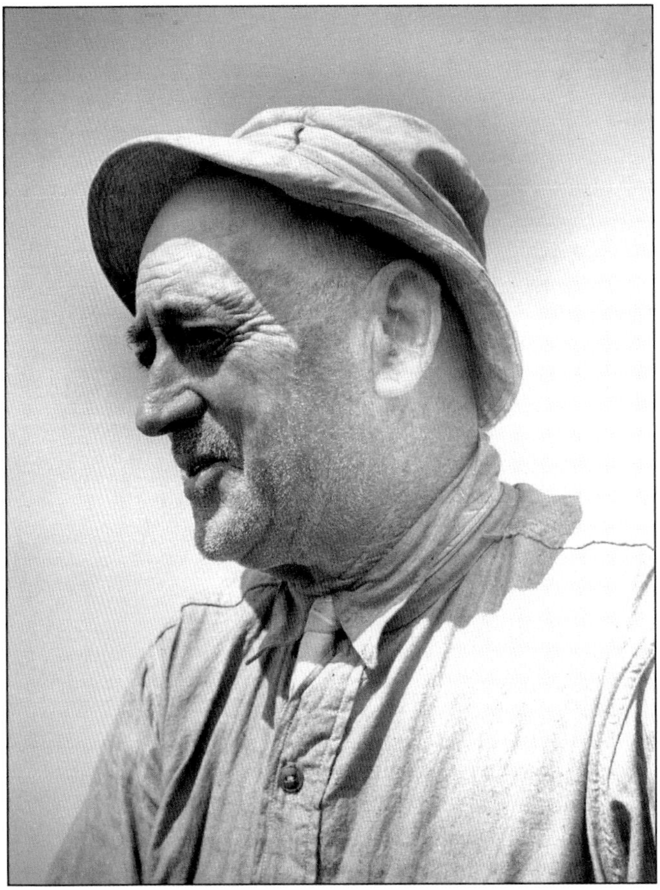

Pictured at left, "Good" Walter Watts Eldredge (1871–1955) has the weathered open face of a life by the sea. His old house, made from salvaged timber, stood on the beach near Harding's Lane. He was a whittler of ship models and an artist of local scenes. "Wicked" Walter Eldredge, shown below, was nicknamed by Andrew Harding to distinguish one Walter Eldredge from the other, with several living in Chatham. It was also said that the nickname was not particularly accurate. This Walter Eldredge, father of Luther Eldredge of Eastham, often taught Bible school classes but did not always attend church.

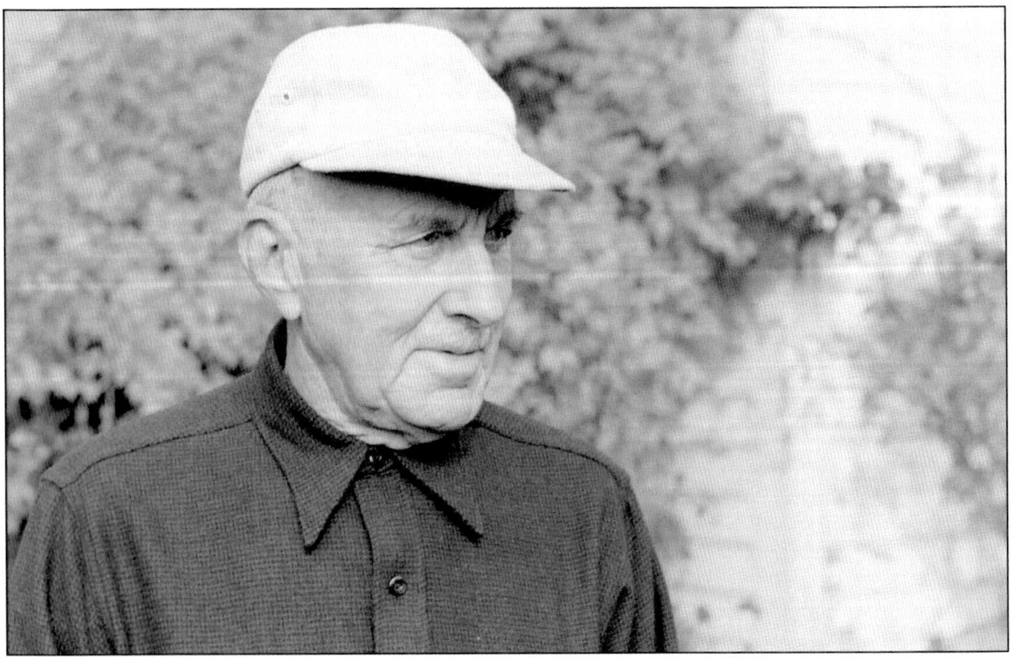

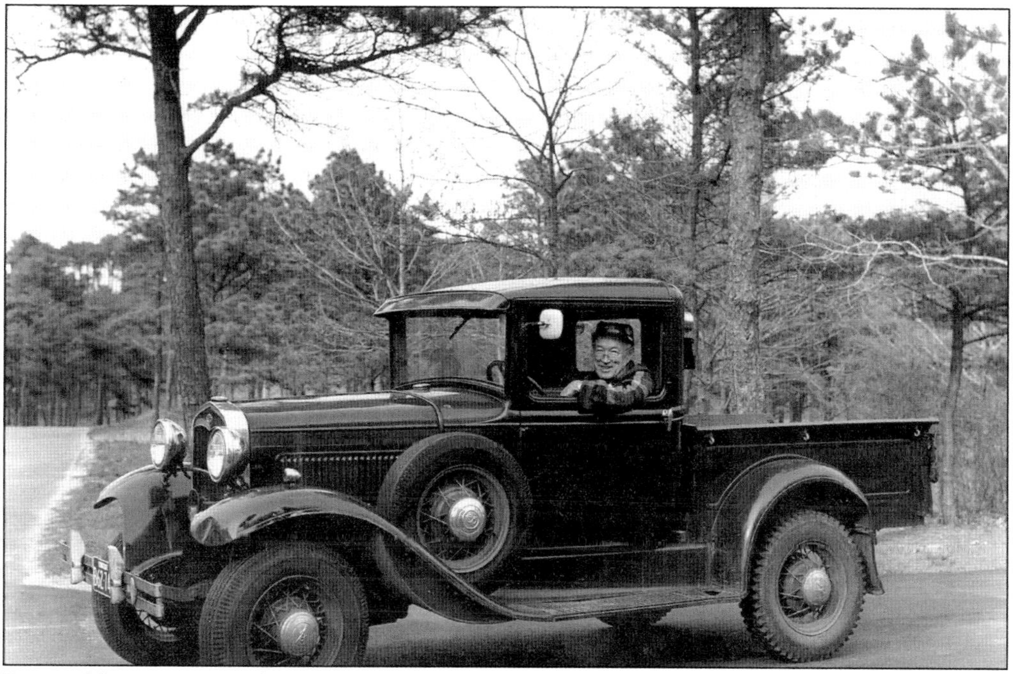

Pictured here are two classic Cape Cod characters. The above photograph shows Carroll H. Keene, "Doc" Keene, as he sits in his 1931 Model A Ford. This beloved physician and Boy Scout leader will always be remembered in Chatham. In the photograph below, Pat Cahoon poses in his perennial raccoon coat pictured on July 4, 1939. Cahoon lived in a shanty along the shore of Oyster River living on shellfish.

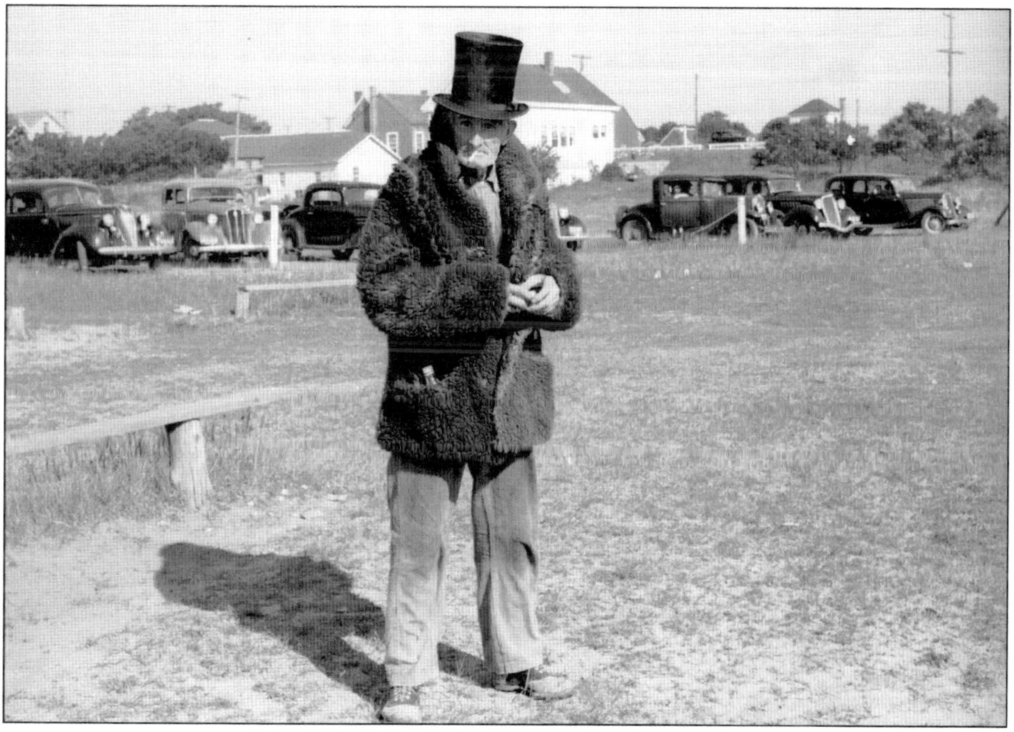

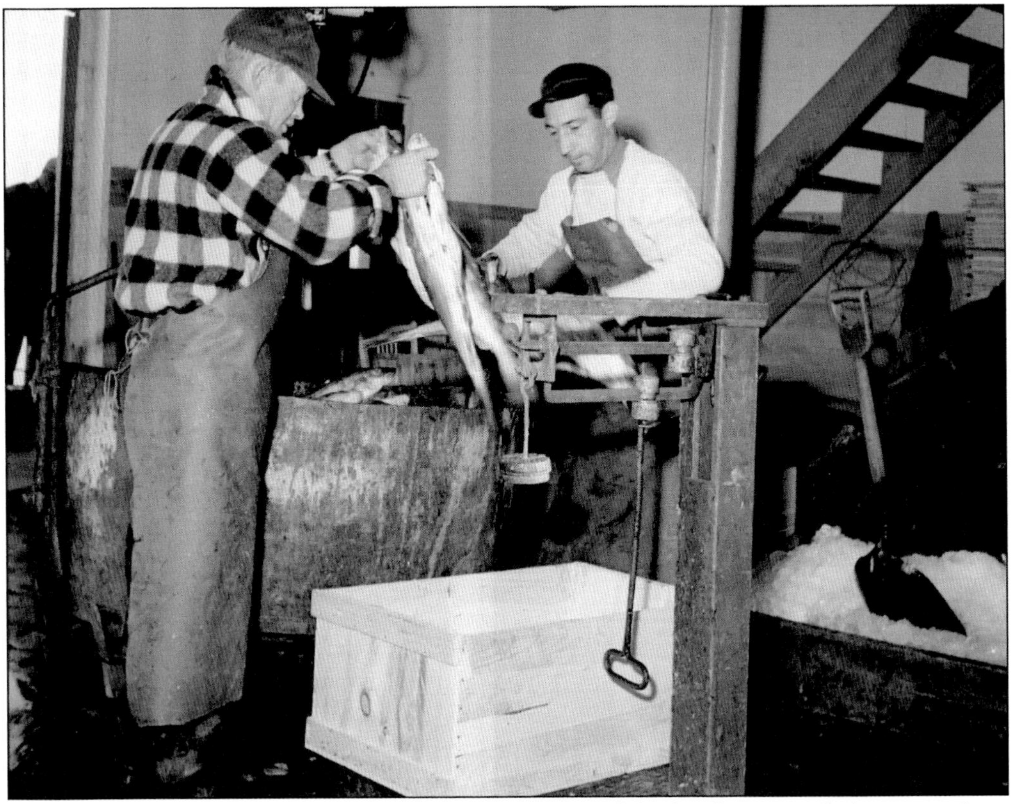

In the above photograph, "Tack" Young on the left, one of the local townies, helps out packing fish at the Chatham Fish Pier. Below, three fishermen haul fish with the aid of a winch. The new pilings by the Chatham Fish Pier with shanties visible in the background identify this photograph as from the late 1940s or early 1950s.

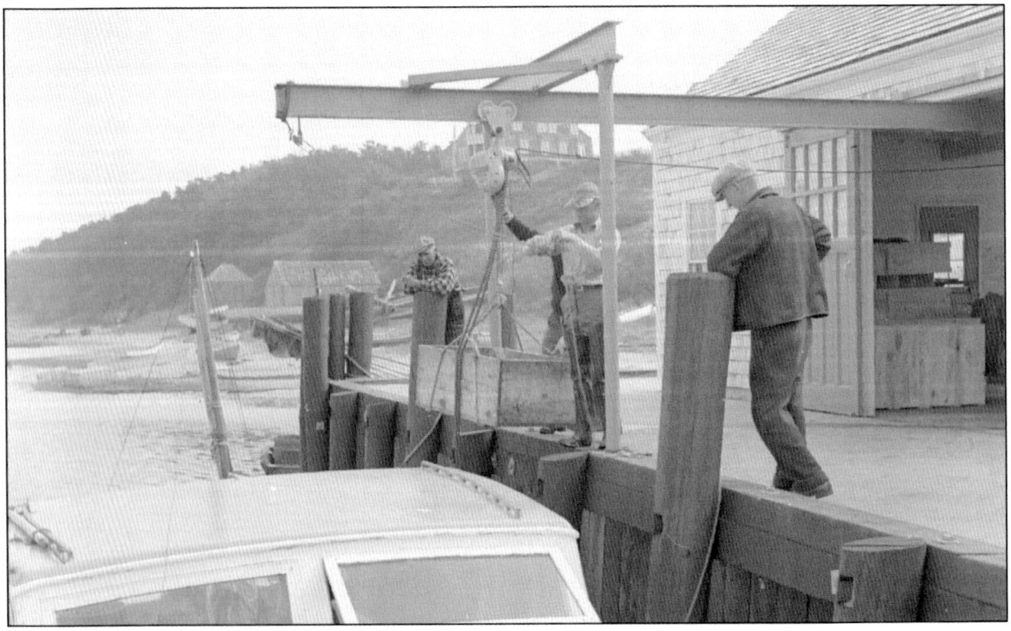

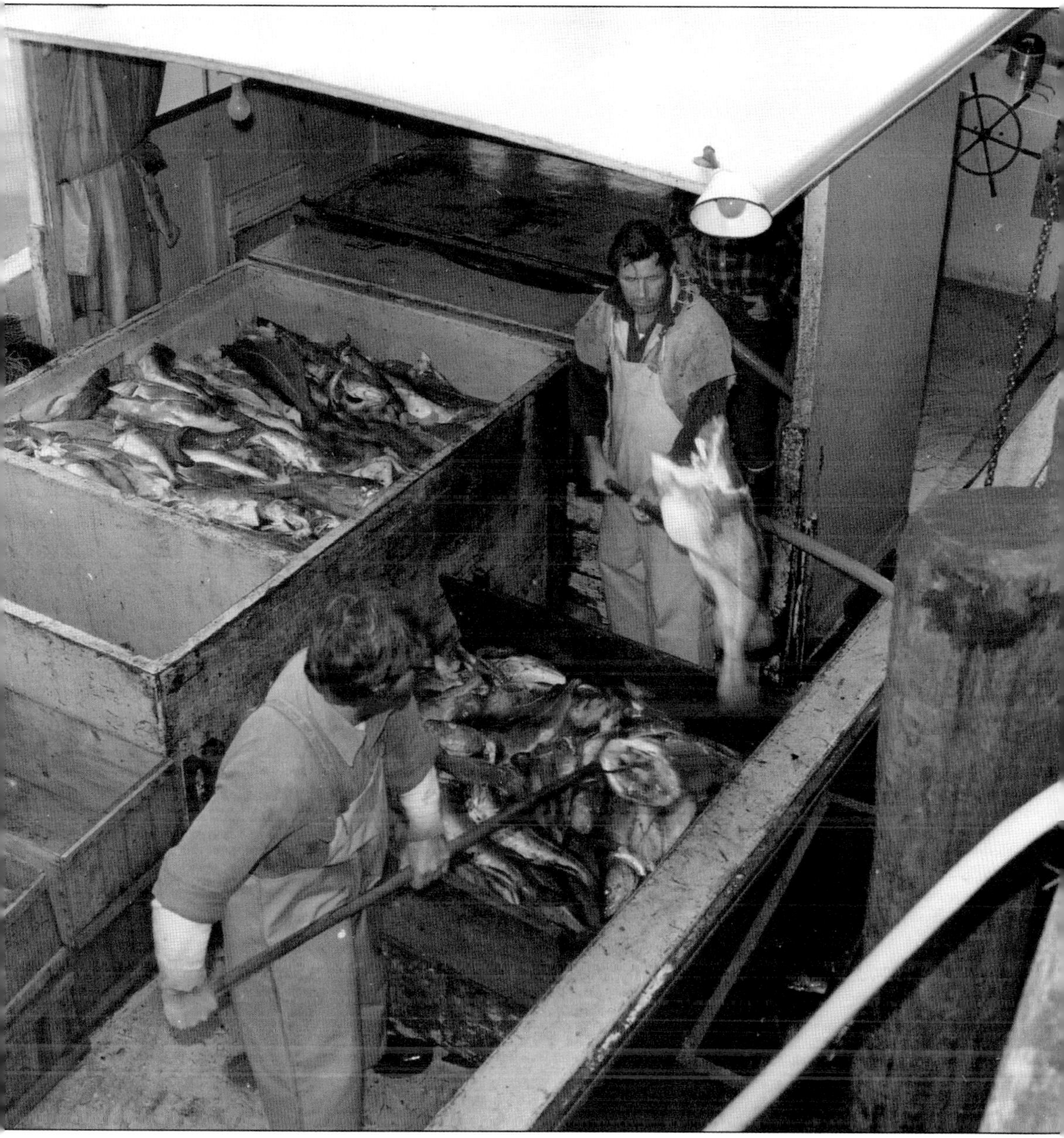

Dick Liska and Capt. Lee Tallman, all in their oilskins, aboard the fishing vessel *I'm Alone*, harvest the hook fishing codfish catch in the 1970s.

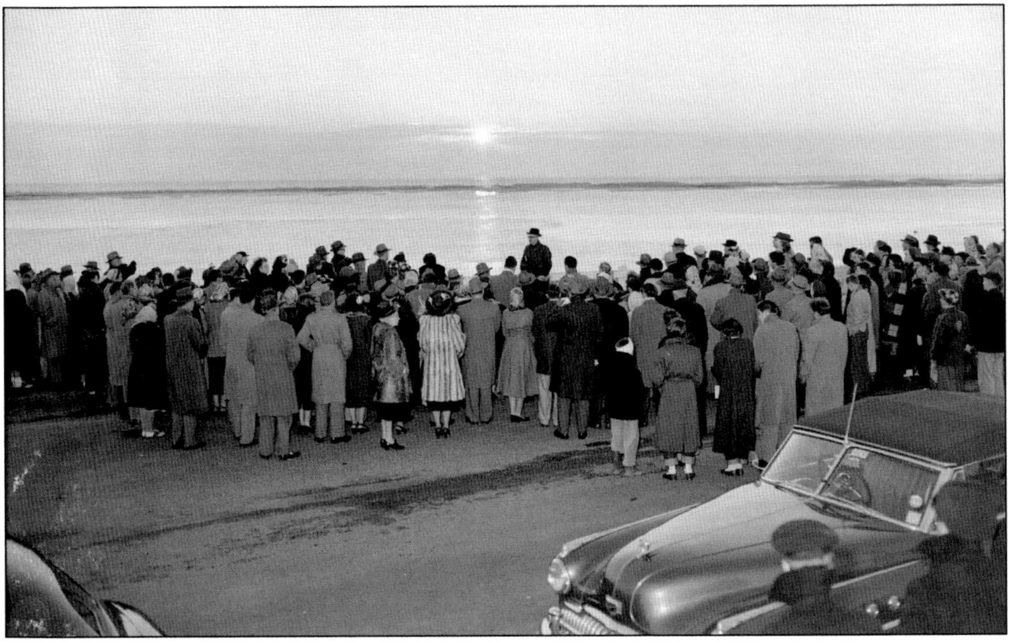

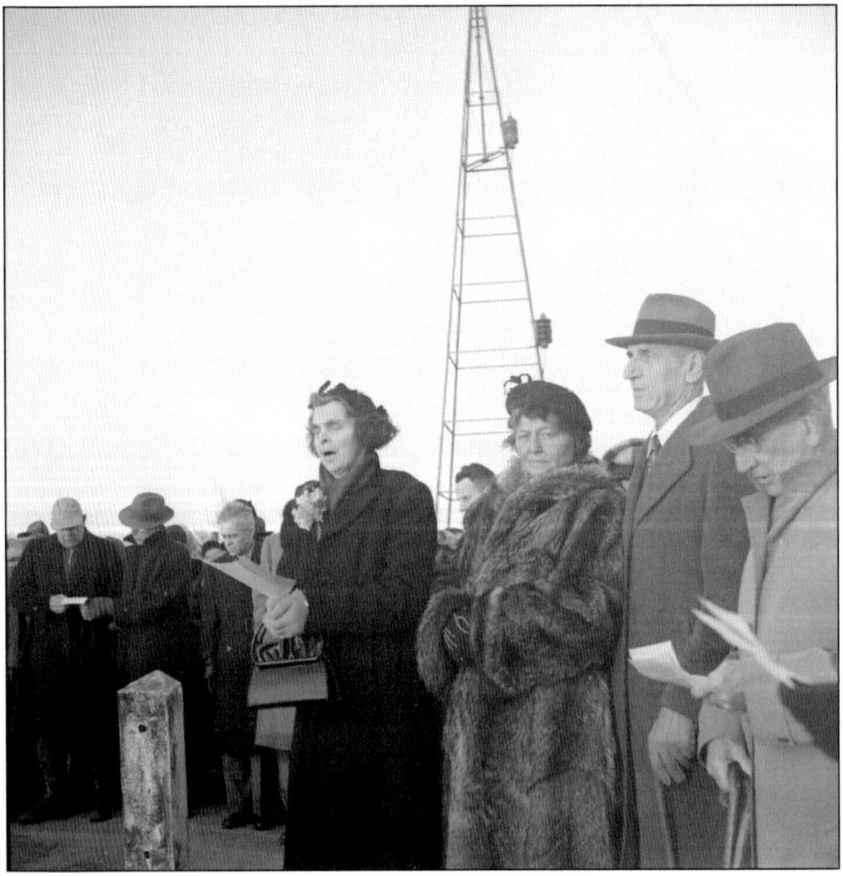

Pictured here is Easter sunrise service at Chatham Harbor on Easter Sunday in 1951. The choir and congregation carry on devotions on a chilled Easter morning, as a beautiful sunrise rewards their prayers. A vintage Buick is parked alongside the scene.

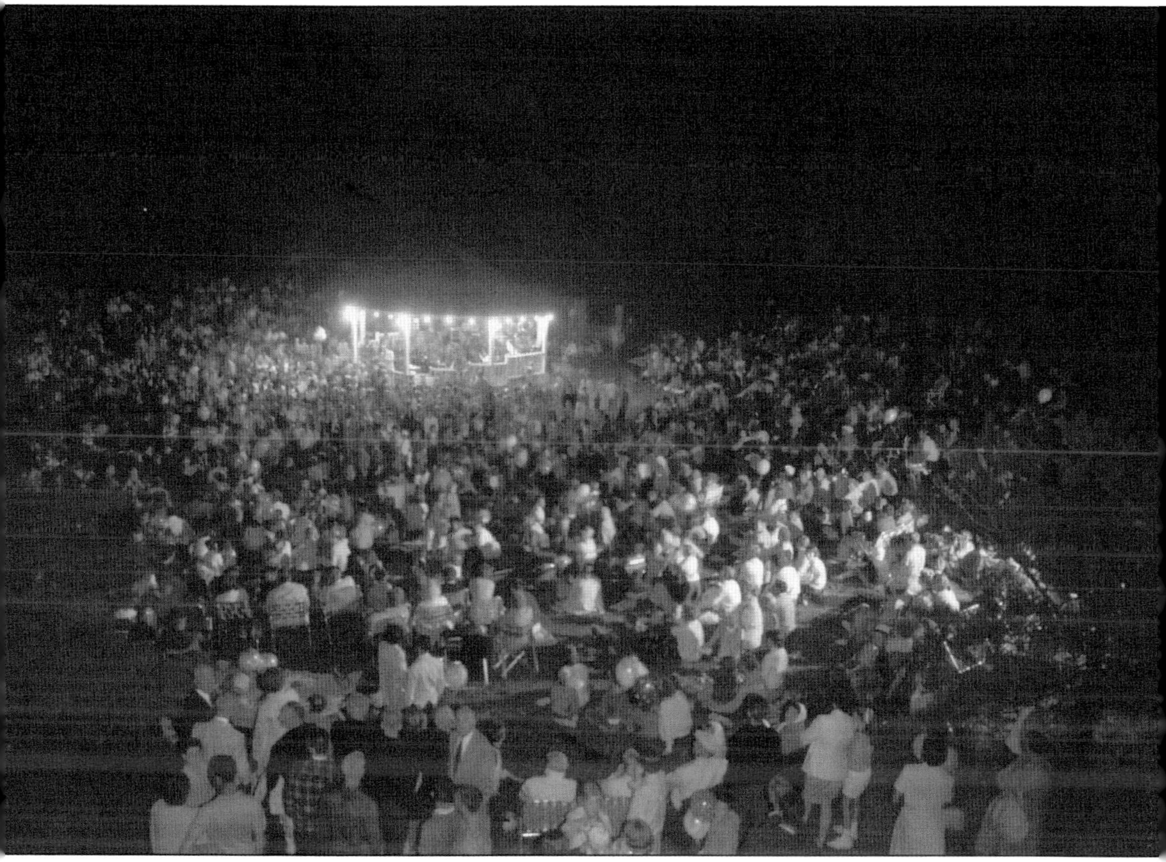

A classic way to spend a summer's evening on Cape Cod is to attend an outdoor town band concert held at a town park usually in a quaint gazebo. One of the most enduring traditions is the Chatham Band concert held on Friday evenings and led by Whit Tileston. Since 1948, Tileston led the concert in Kate Gould Park with his white bandmaster's uniform and a "hi-de-ho" greeting.

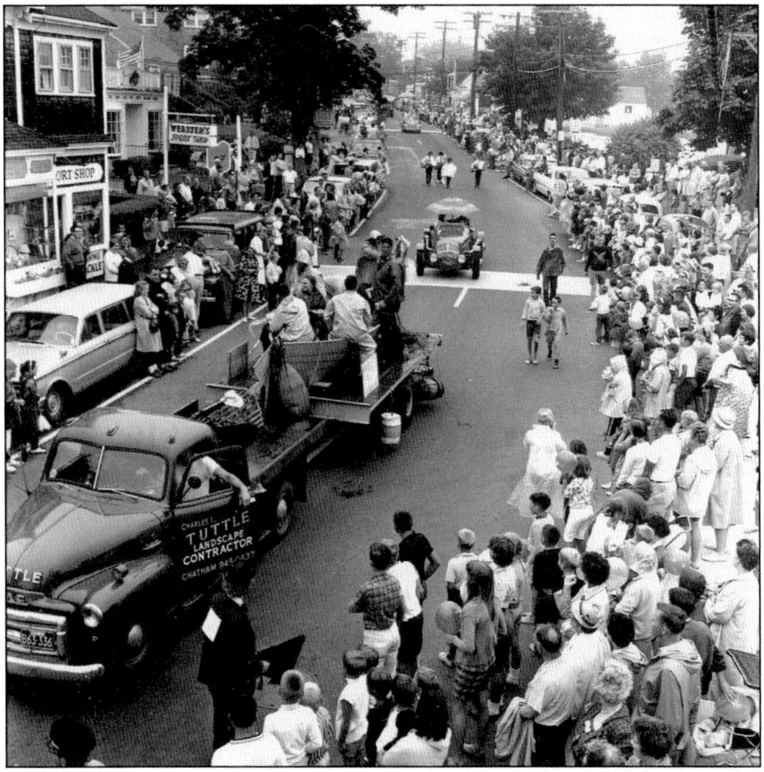

The Chatham Fourth of July parade is pictured here in the 1960s, as it heads down Main Street in Chatham by Webster's Sporting Shop. In the foreground of the top photograph is the fisherman's float pulled by Charlie Tuttle's Landscaping truck. Traditionally the fisherman's float would bail water into the onlooking crowd. The Miss Chatham Jaycee float, pictured below, follows behind in this somewhat rainy but spirited parade.

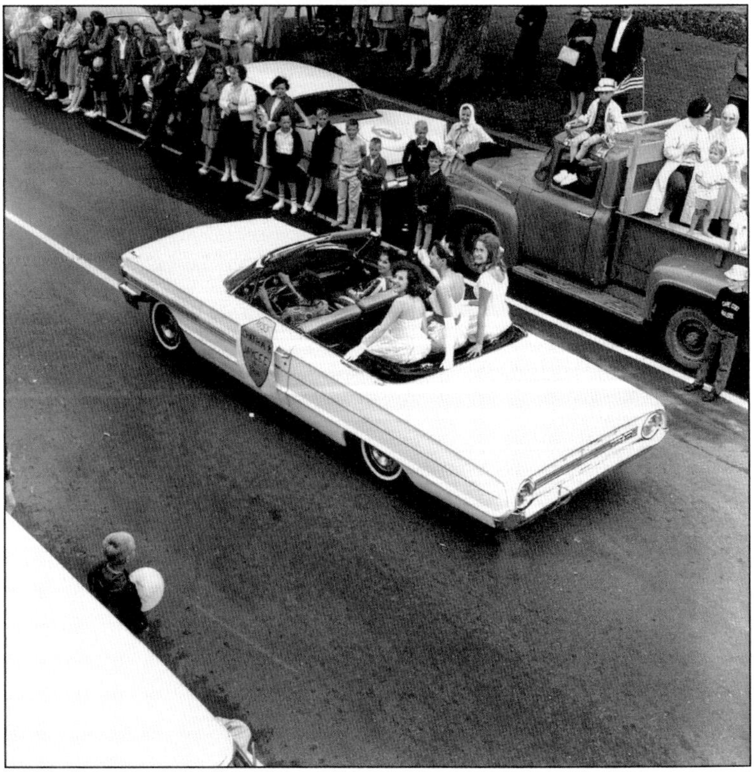

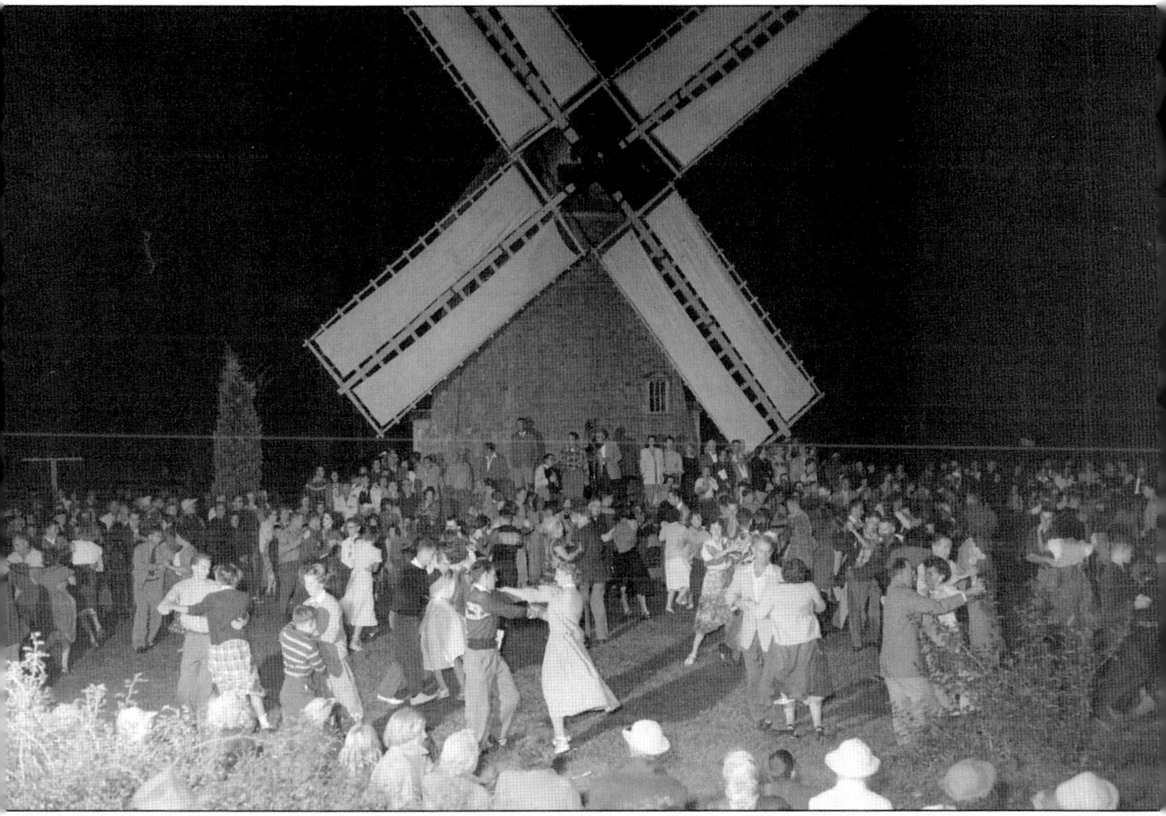

Couples swing at the popular Windmill Dance at Eastham with caller Jay Scofield on August 25, 1951. On this occasion they danced as part of the Eastham tercentenary that included a parade, concerts, pageants reenacting the founding of Eastham, and square dancing.

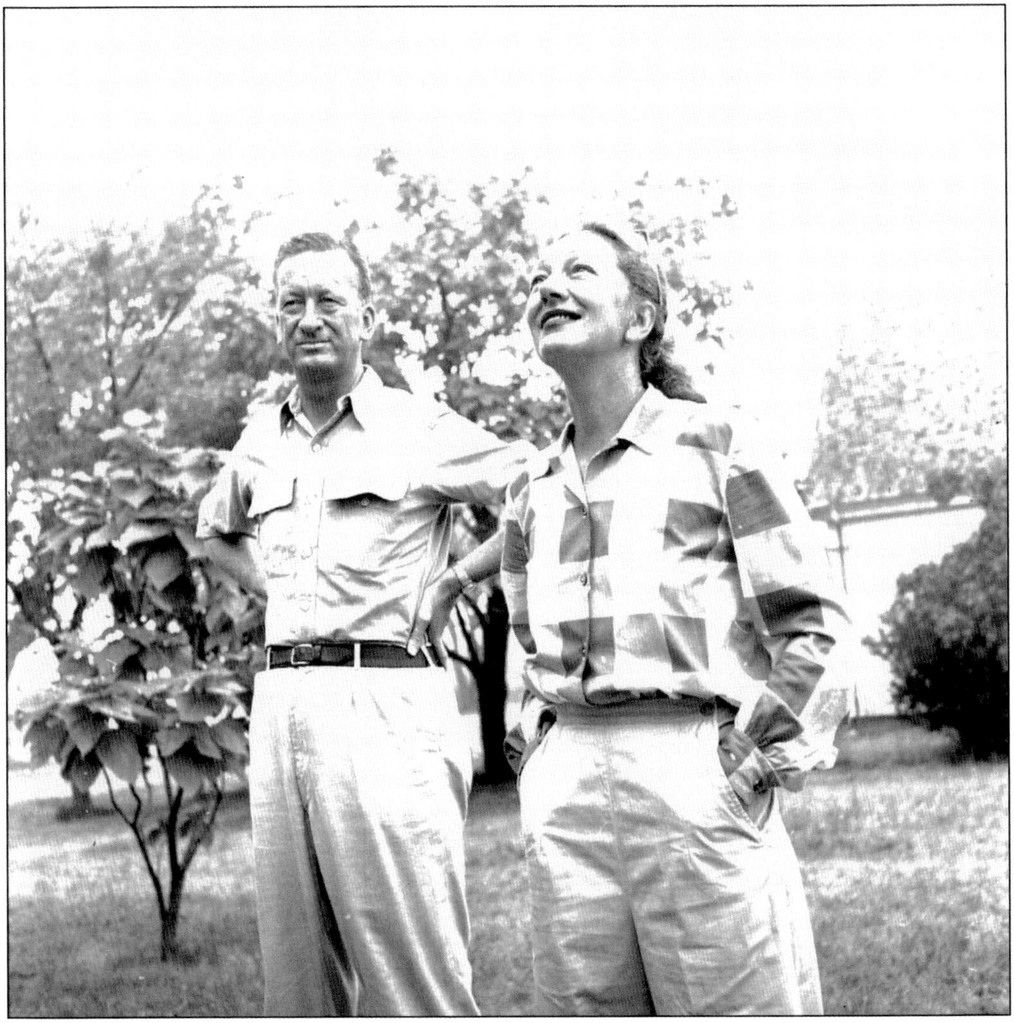

This rare photograph of Gertrude Lawrence and her husband, Richard Aldrich, in Dennis recorded a happy moment together in August 1952. They were the beautiful power couple behind the Cape Playhouse, "America's most famous summer theater." It was one of their last photographs, Gertrude Lawrence died suddenly on September 6, 1952, within weeks of this photograph. Upon her death, the lights of every theater and movie house on Broadway in New York blinked out in tribute.

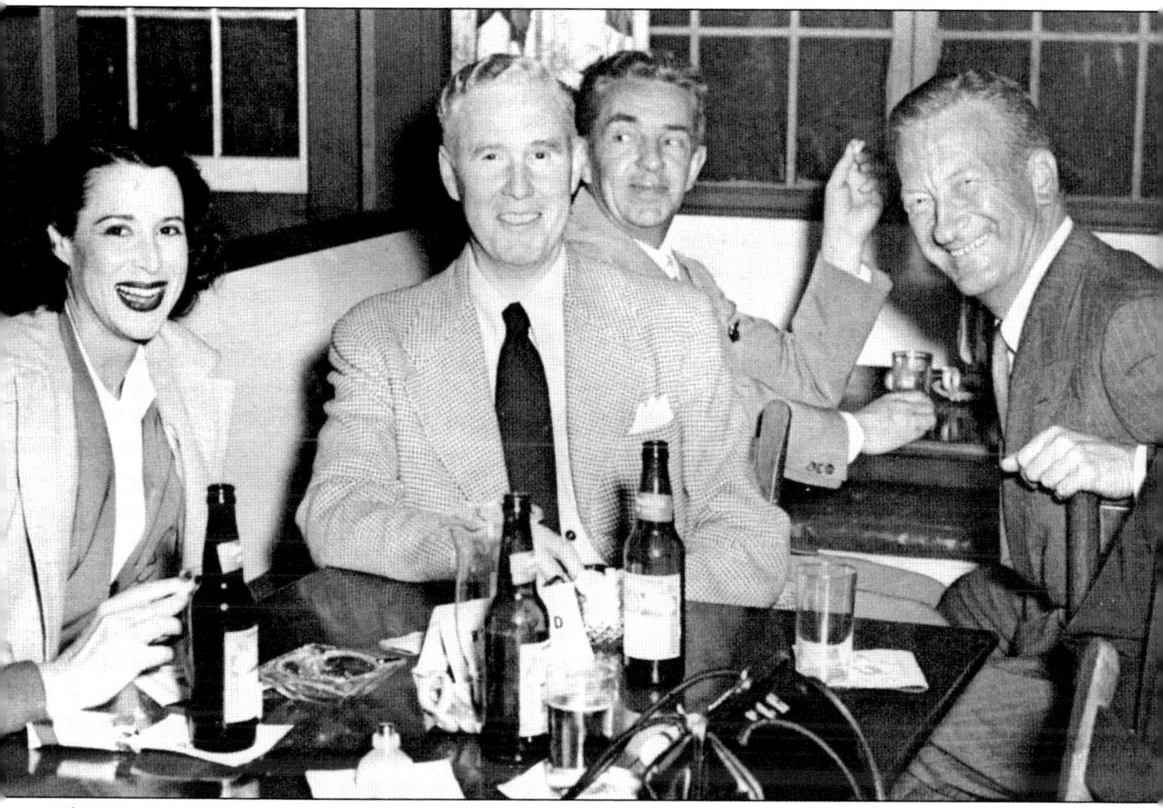

This extraordinary photograph credited to Richard Kelsey shows Kitty Carlisle after her performance in *Lady In the Dark* with drama critic Elliot Norton and Richard Aldrich, owner of the Cape Playhouse. Seated in back of them is Donald Trayser, author of several Cape Cod histories. The Cape Playhouse brought glamour and star power to Cape Cod.

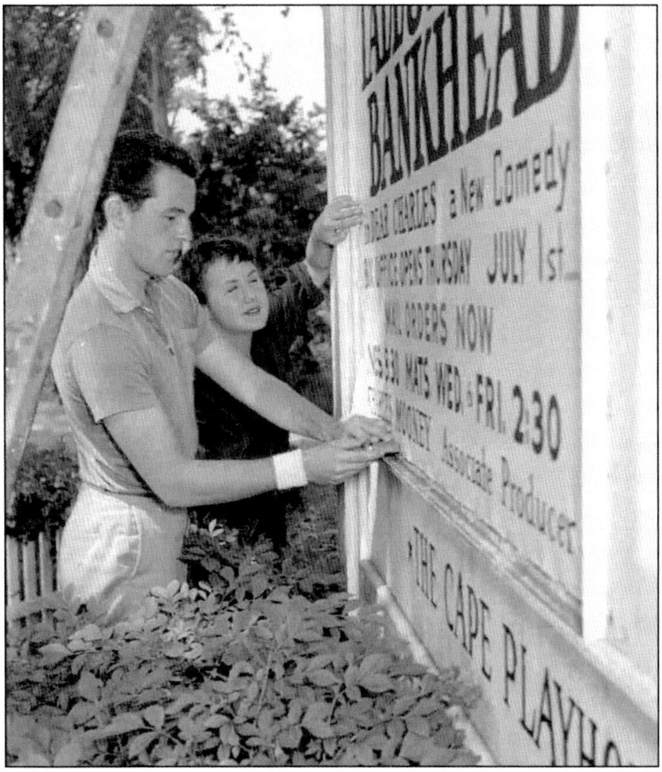

The Cape Playhouse in the early 1950s sponsored apprenticeship programs in the theatrical arts. In this photograph, two theater students set up the marquee for Tallulah Bankhead in the comedy *Dear Charles*.

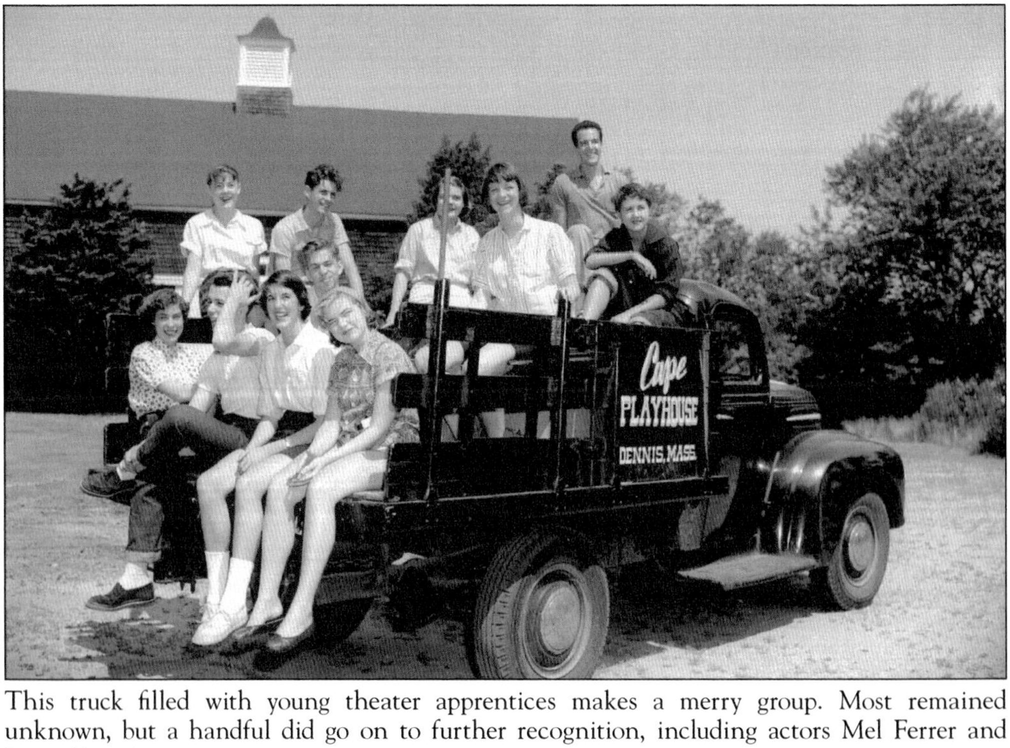

This truck filled with young theater apprentices makes a merry group. Most remained unknown, but a handful did go on to further recognition, including actors Mel Ferrer and James Franciscus.

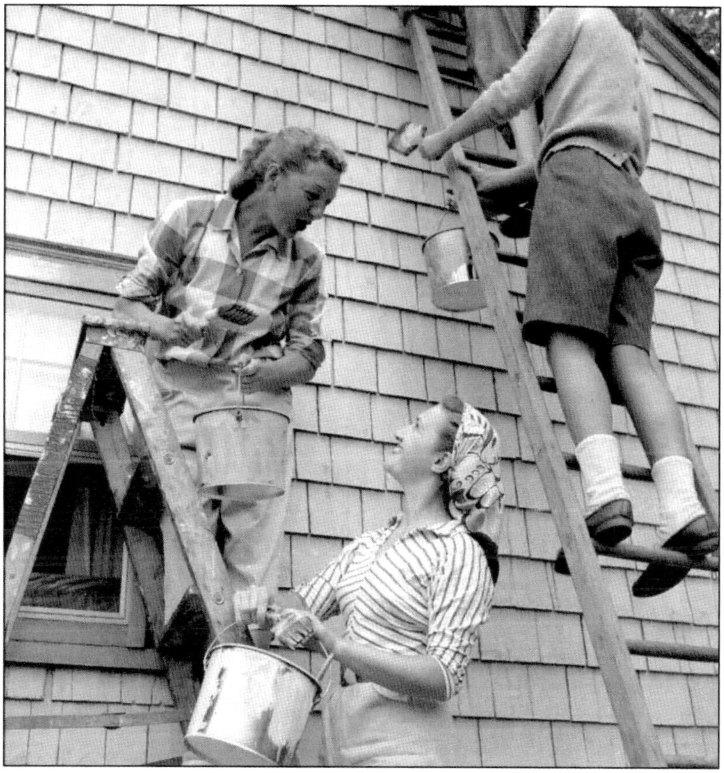

This close-up of Gertrude Lawrence with a group of apprentices shows her down-to-earth style in spite of her star status. She is shown below painting the house of Irene Fagan, the playhouse's costume mistress from 1932 through 1970. Fagan's dachshund pup Miss Anna, named from the production of *The King and I*, is held by her owner.

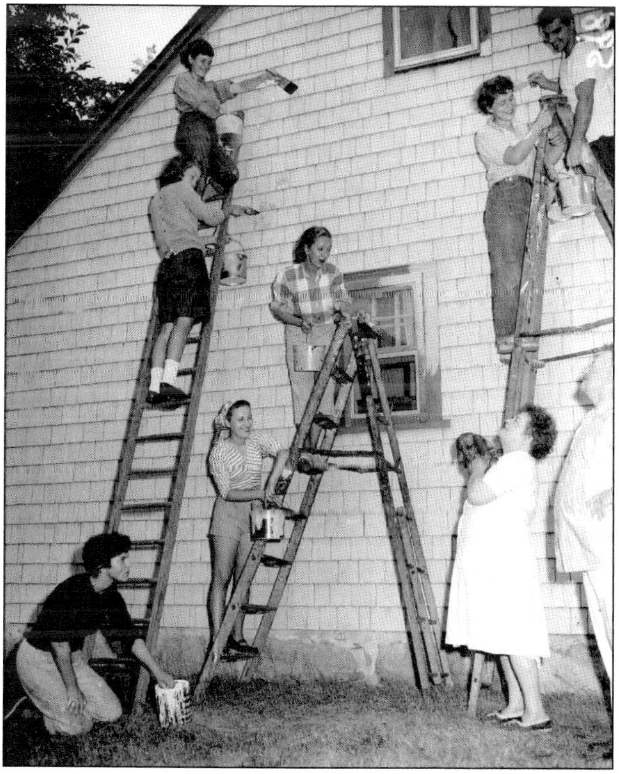

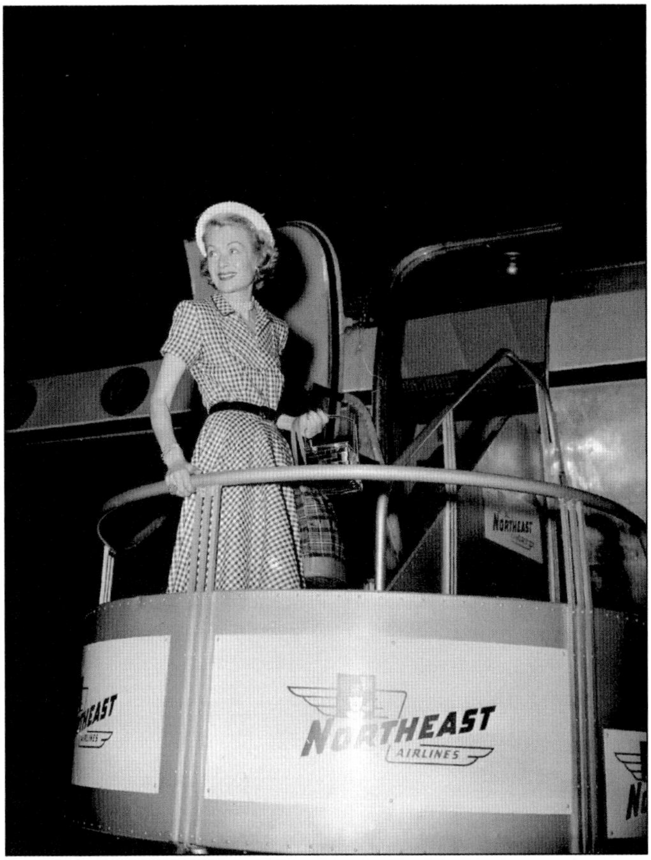

Two stars of the Dennis Playhouse are shown in these photographs. Constance Bennett arrives by Northeast Airlines for a production of *I Found April* in the 1952 season, and Butterfly McQueen is shown in rehearsal for the 1951 production of *Summersault*.

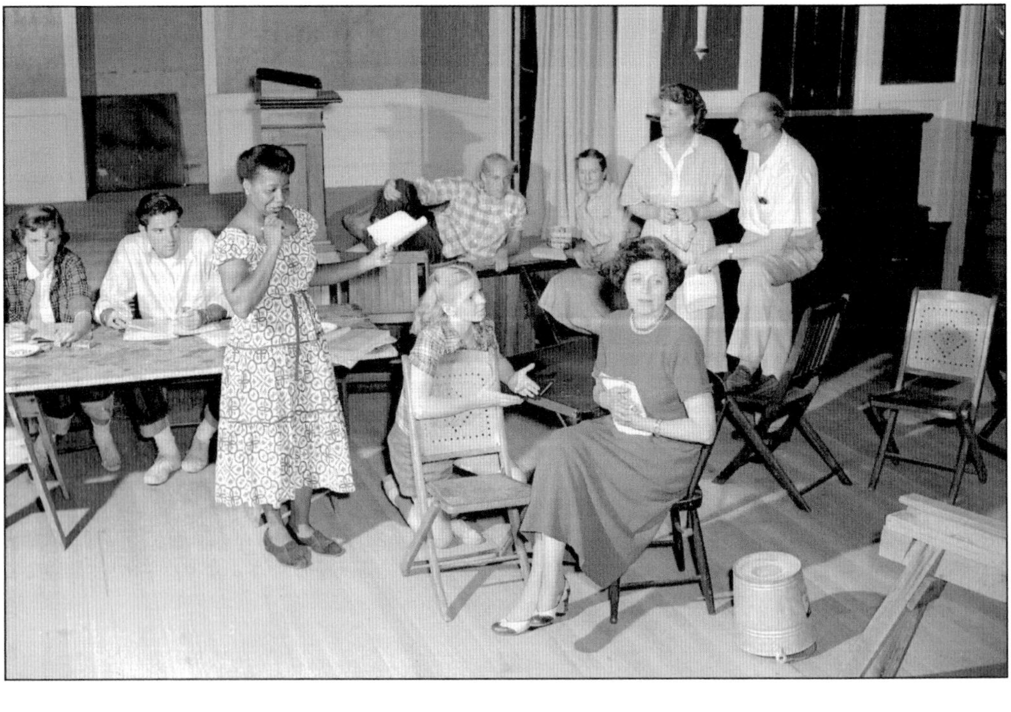

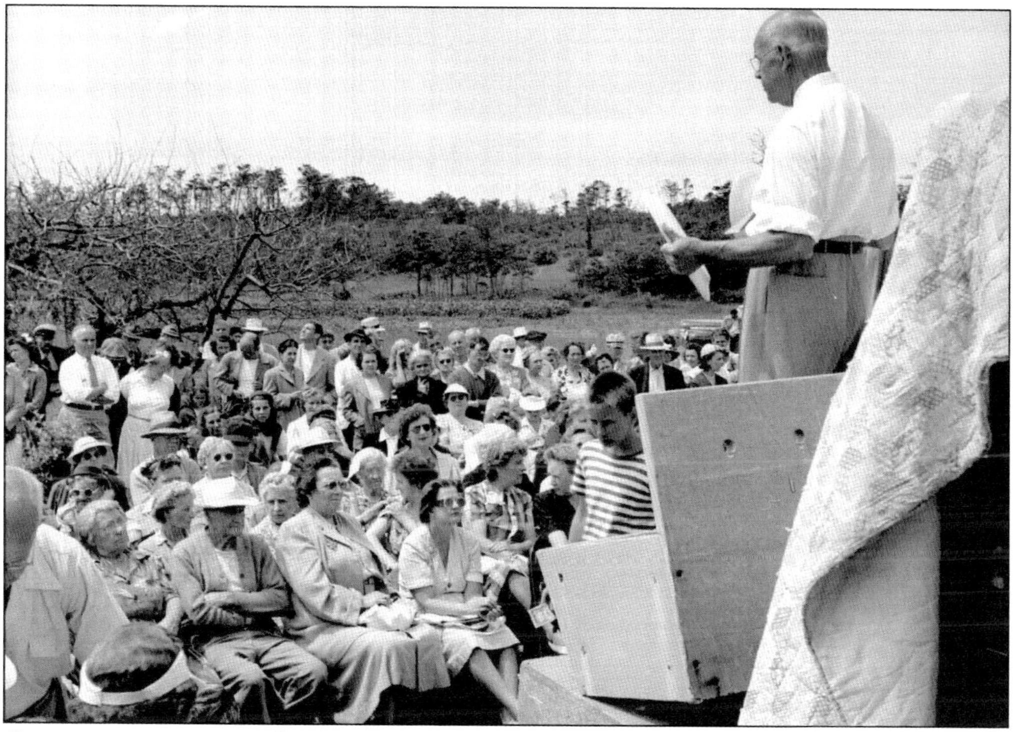

Country auctions were a frequent entertainment and sometimes necessity in Cape Cod in the 1940s. Croquet bedspreads, braided rugs, ships in bottles, hand-painted seashells, Cape Cod novelties, and heirlooms were dragged from attics and auctioned. This rousing outdoor auction in 1946 drew a large neighborhood crowd.

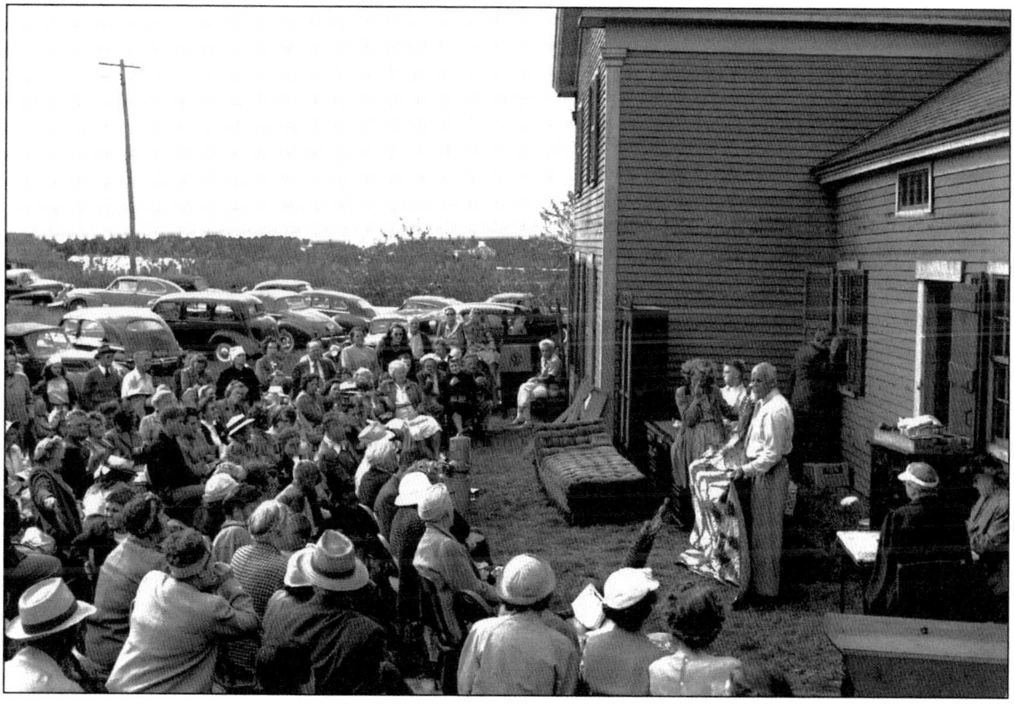

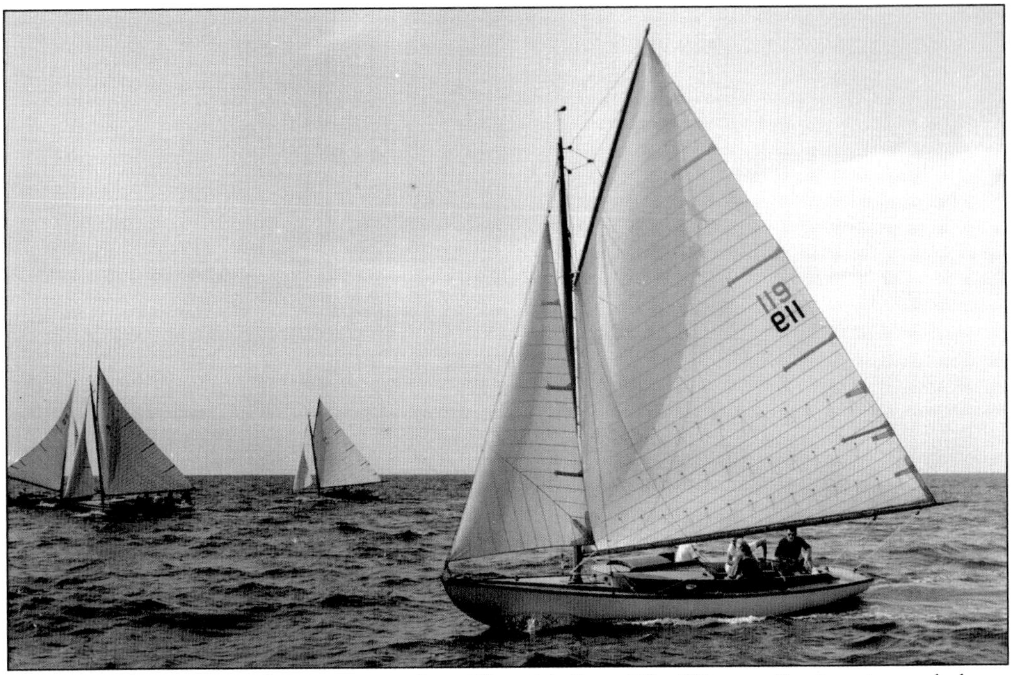

Boating enthusiasts are shown racing along Harwich Port. The Wianno Senior pictured above takes part in a 1948 race while beautiful sailboats tack by Wychmere Harbor by the jetty. Wianno Senior racing off of Hyannis, Hyannisport, Harwich, and Bass River has been a fairly common occurrence since 1930.

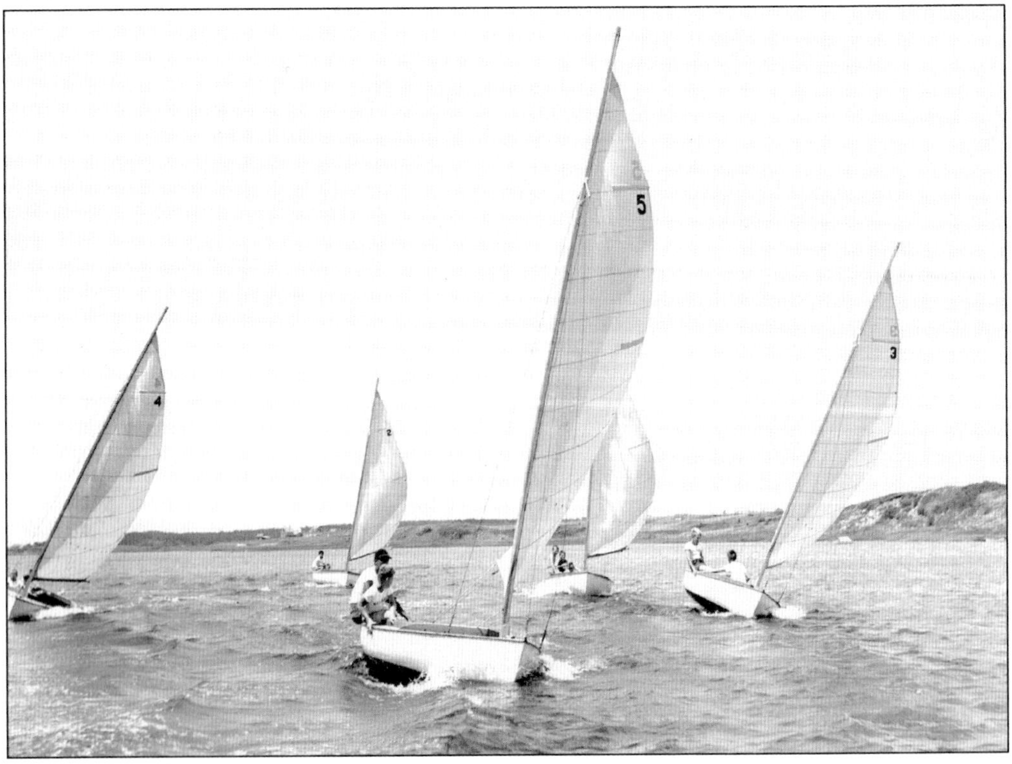

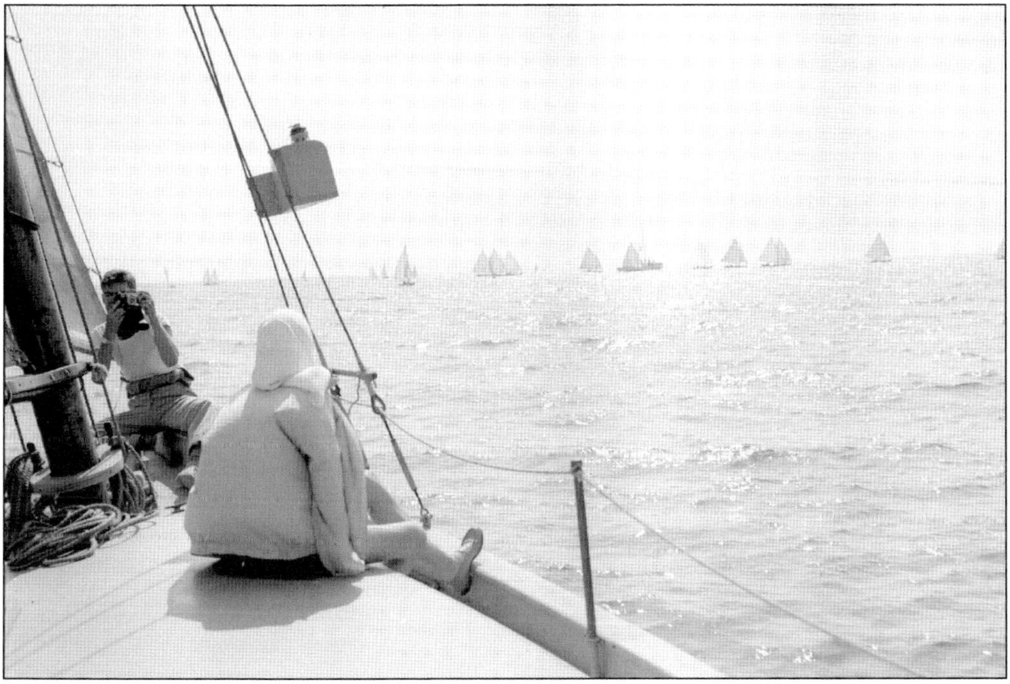

Knockabouts race alongside a gentleman and lady sailor as they pose for pictures by their scenic view of ocean and sails. Below, Malabar Woodpussies in 1948 head out as part of a boating school exercise.

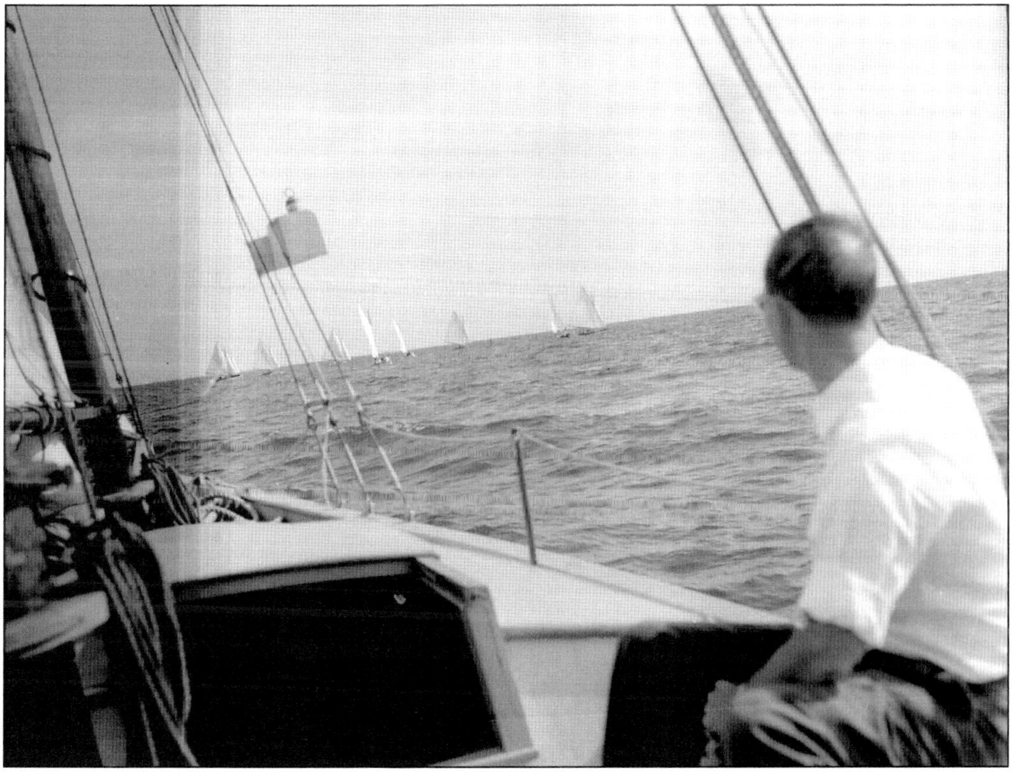

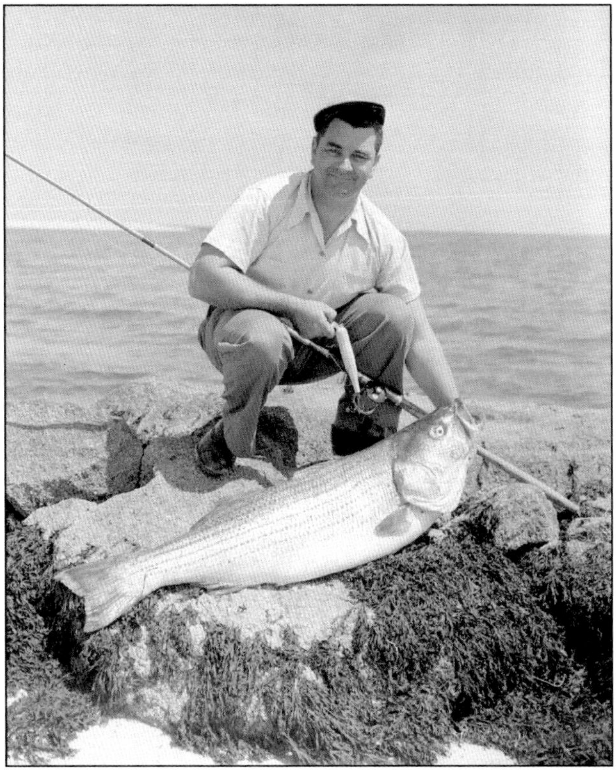

Richard Kelsey must have loved the drama of fishing because he took many photographs of tournament winners proudly displaying their catch. Here Bob Williams and Fred Hollis pose by their bass catches. Fishing tournaments were a regular event on Cape Cod. The *Sportman's Guide to Cape Cod* states, "on Cape Cod the fisherman not only experiences the joy of indulging in his chosen sport but gets added zest from the excitement of competing for the many trophies and awards offered for prize catches."

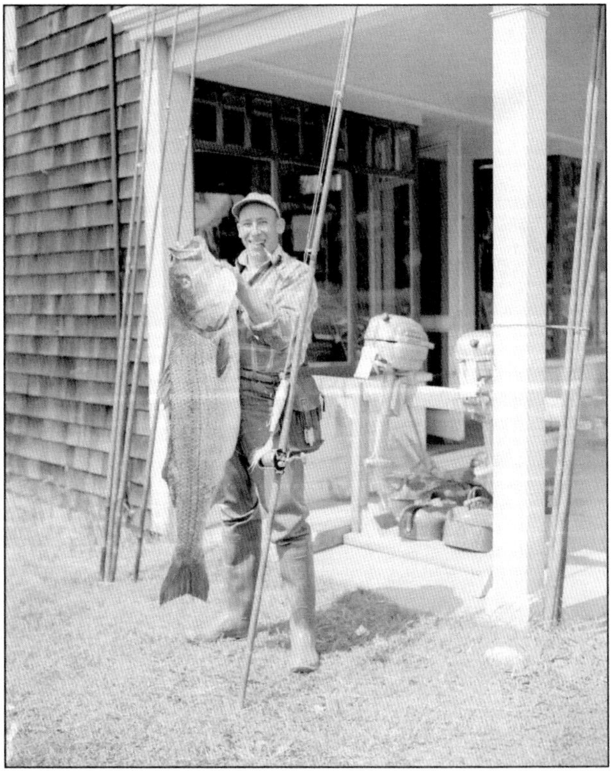

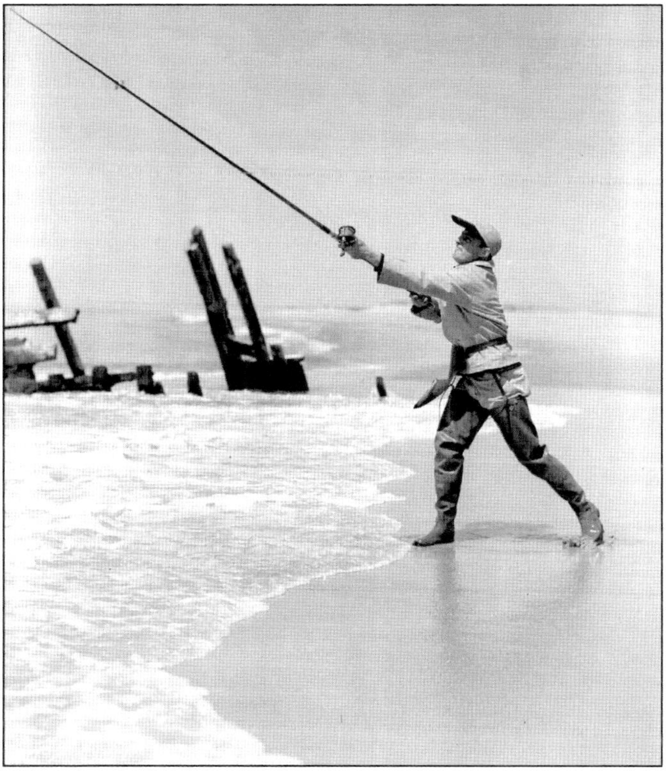

Surf casting is as much art as an athletic sport among the enthusiasts at Nauset Inlet. Hand-rigged beach buggies with catch baskets were seen all along Chatham Inlet, Orleans, and Eastham. These shots are from the season of 1947.

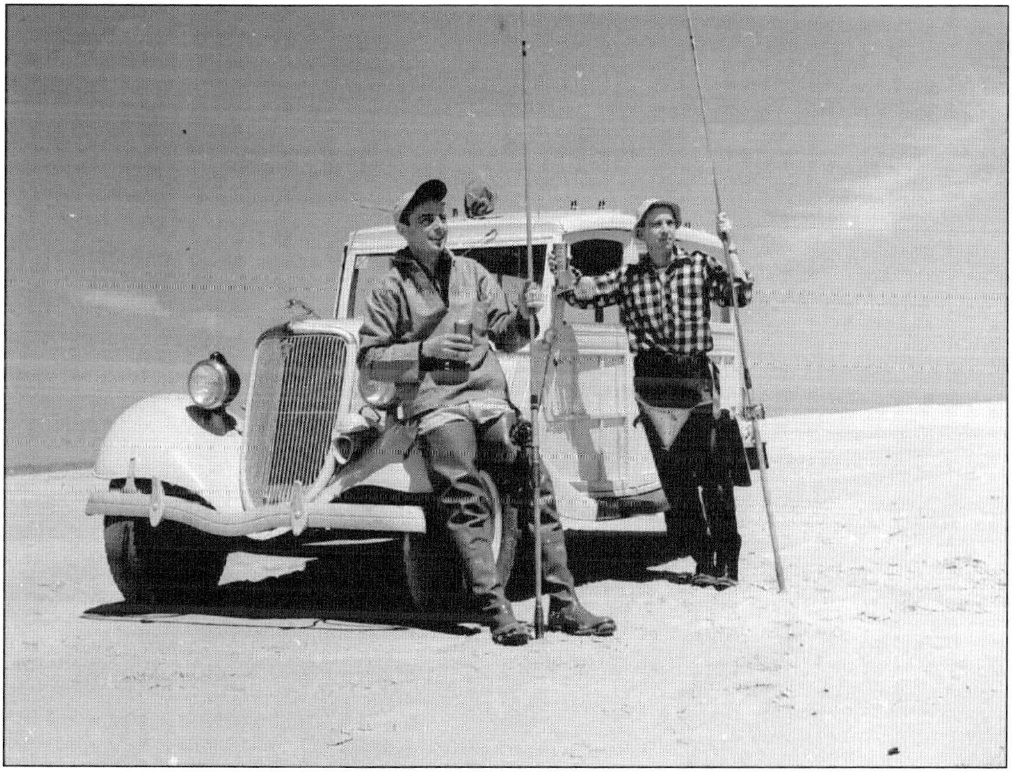

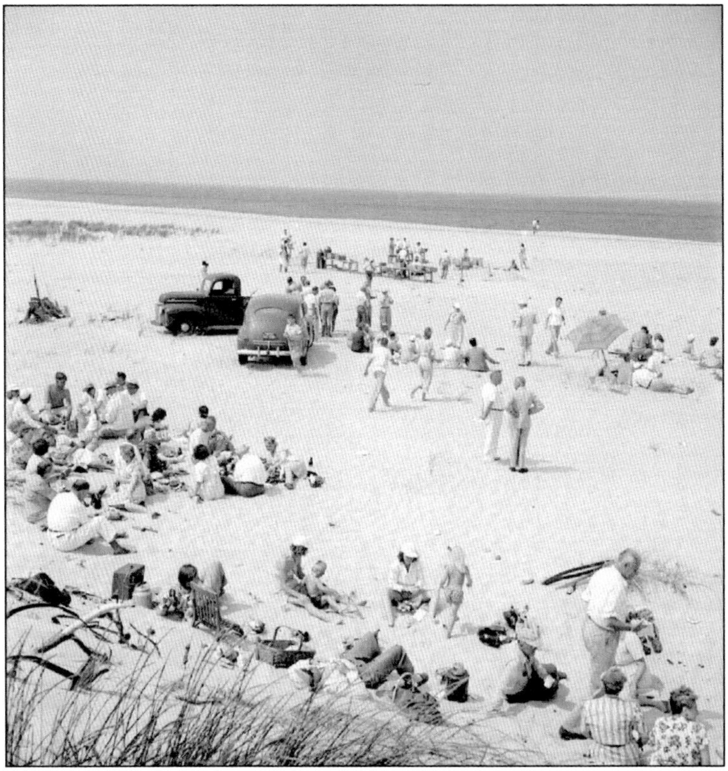

An irresistible picnic takes place on the beach in the 1940s. Although the occasion is a bit formal with dresses and soft hats, the feast included lobster, steamers, and beverages from the Whistle Bottling Company, New Bedford.

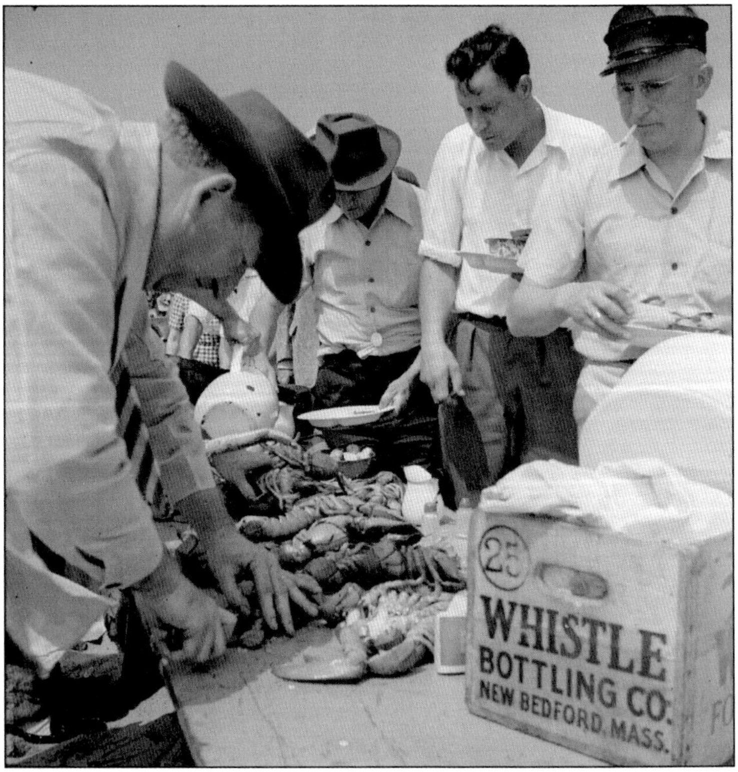

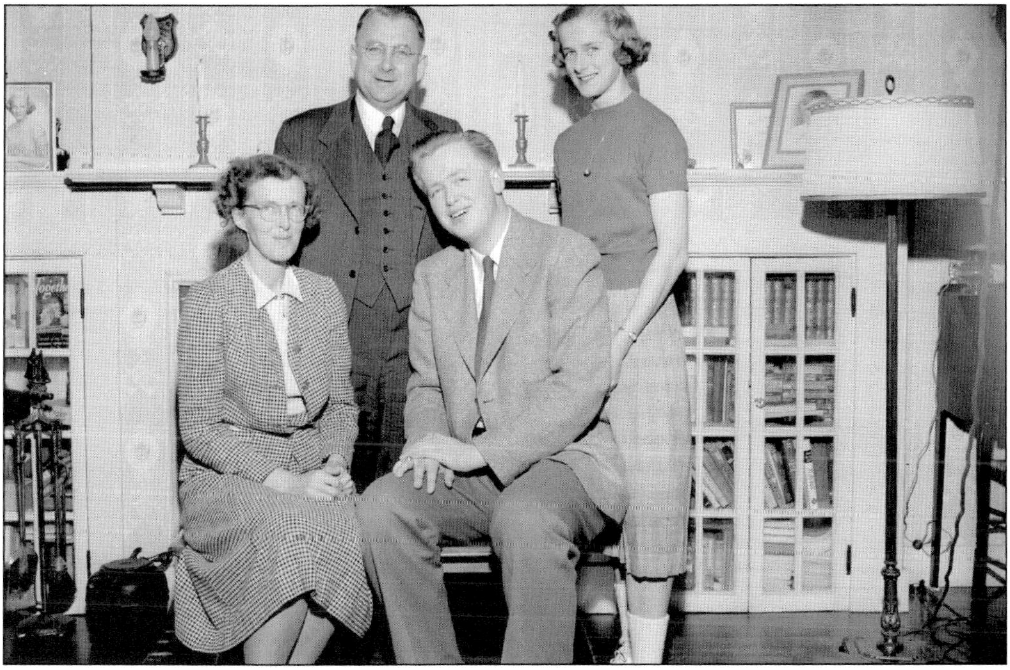

Two reverends of Cape Cod are posed in these formal portraits taken by Kelsey Photographs. The above family portrait is of the Schultzes. The Reverend Dr. Carl Fearing Schultz of the Federated Church in Hyannis is shown with his family, which includes his wife, son, and daughter. Reverend Schultz is known for opening the first drive-in church at Hyannis and was called "the marrying preacher" for all the weddings he performed on the cape. The Reverend Wyeth Willard (right) of Forestdale is shown in 1956. Reverend Willard was a missionary who established a Christian youth camp on Cape Cod, Camp Good News in Sandwich.

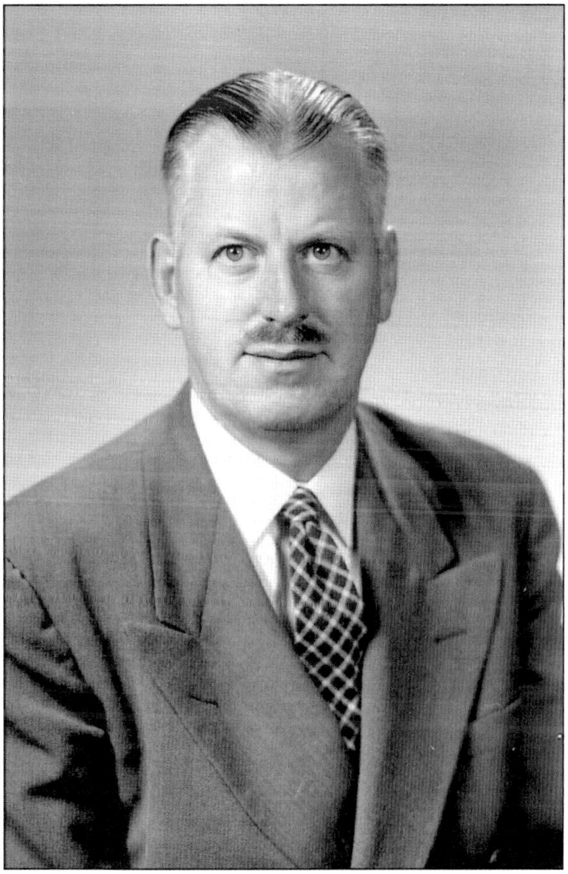

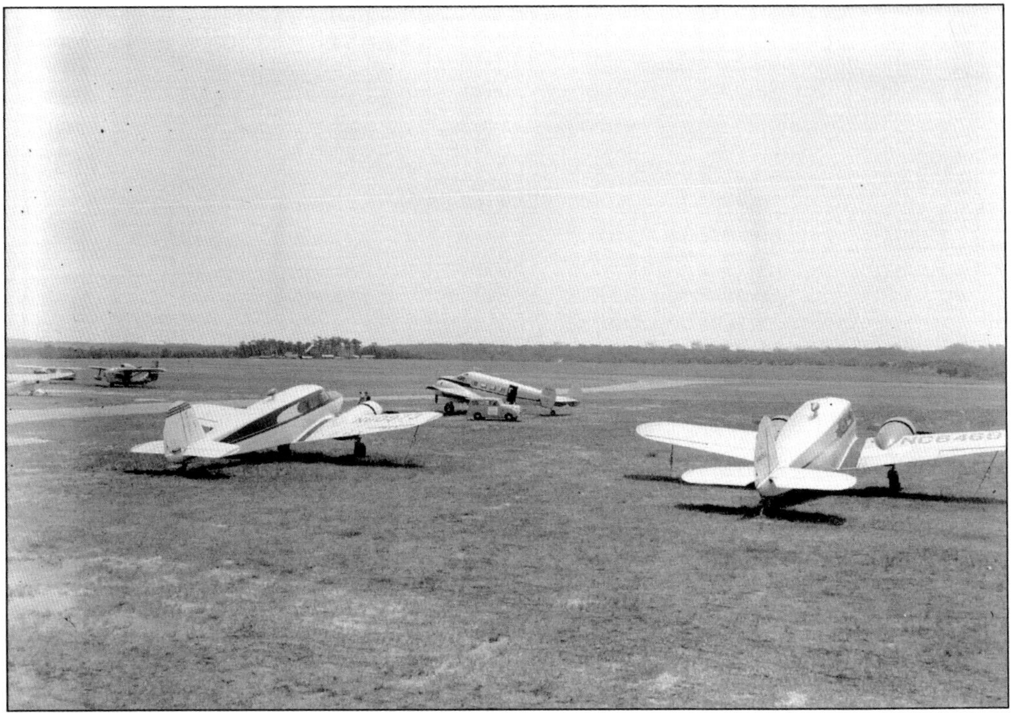

Chatham Municipal Airport was Richard Kelsey's second home. This photograph shows an exhibition of models and planes on this grass landing airport.

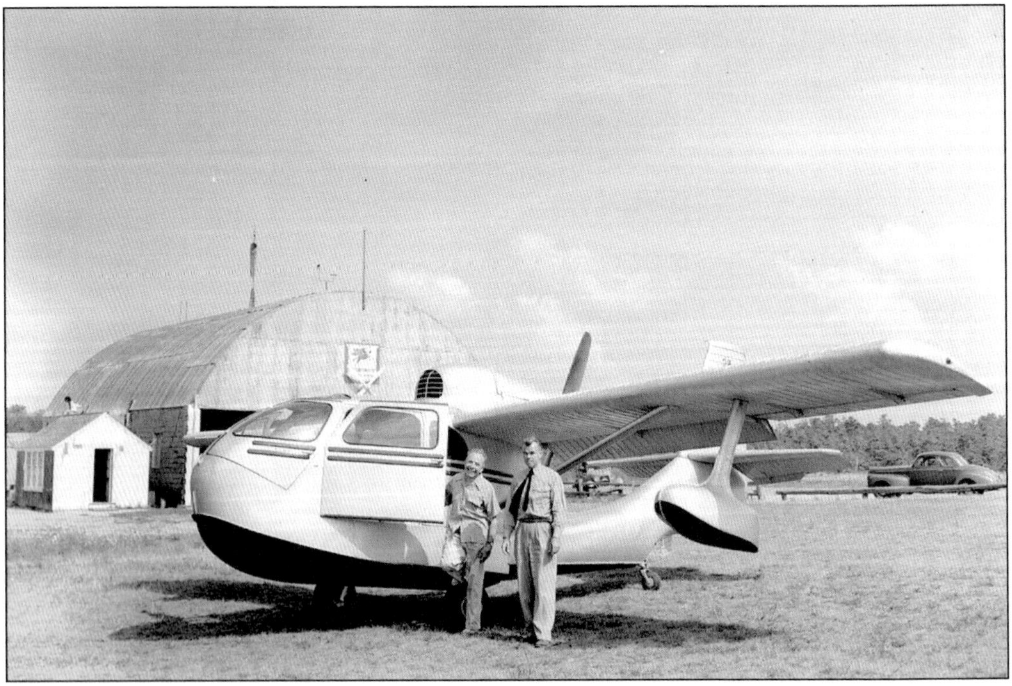

Frank Joy is shown leaning on his airplane, a RC-3 Seebee on floats. Joy was manager of the Chatham Municipal Airport for a number of years and is one of the early pioneers of Cape Cod aviation.

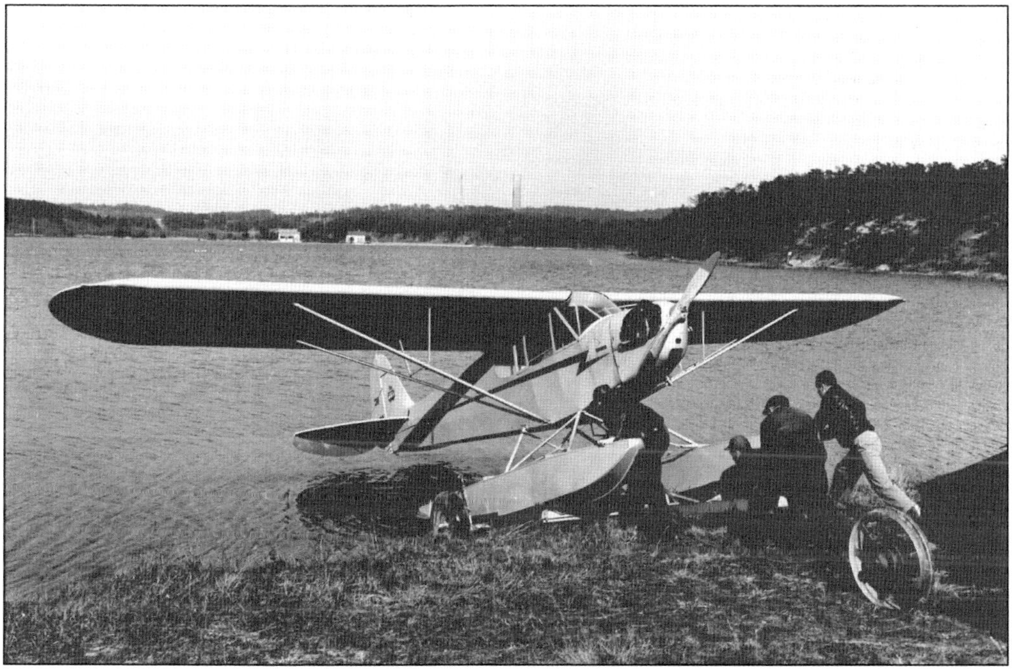

In the photograph above, the Piper Watercraft Seaplane is launched in 1946 on a Cape Cod cove. In the photograph at right, it is modeled by an attractive Cape Codder.

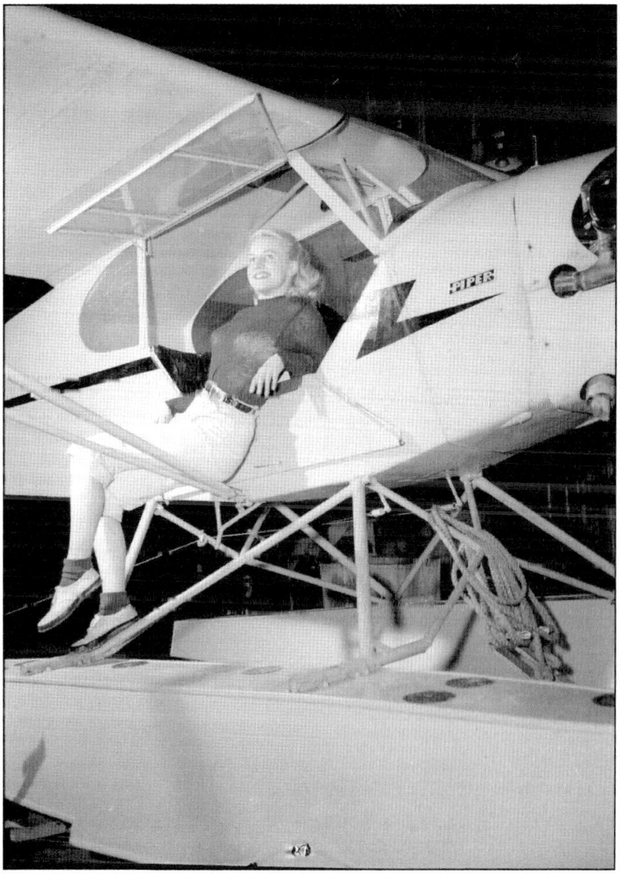

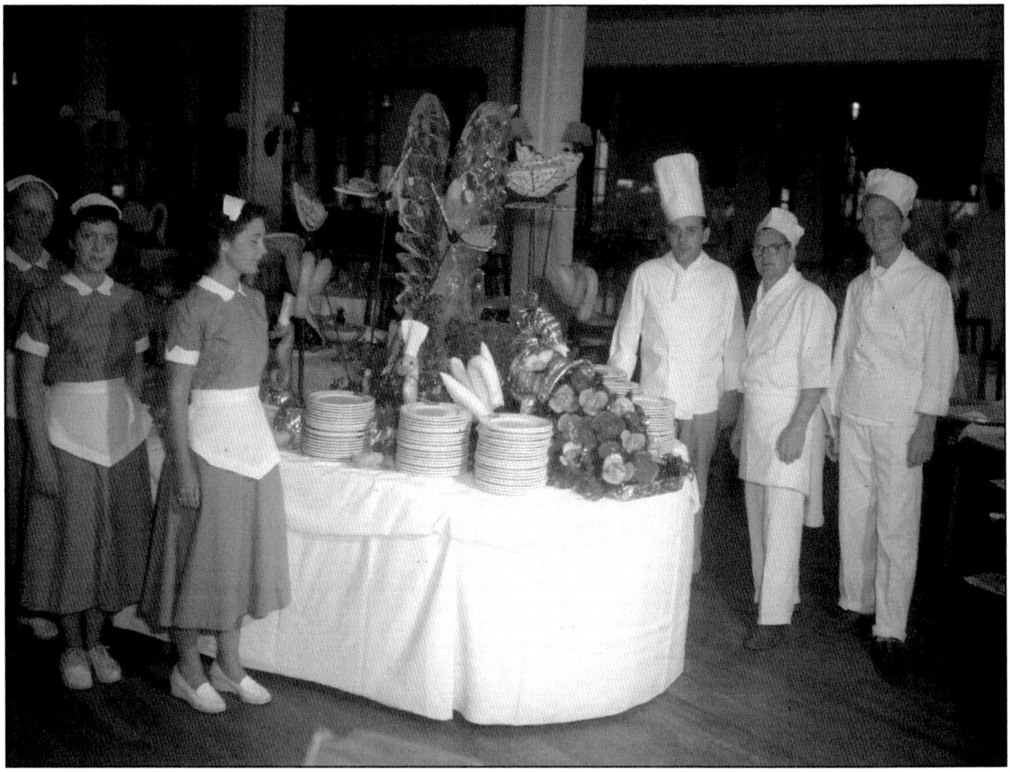

The Chatham Bars Inn, one of the grand plan resorts, opened its doors in 1914 and remains the ultimate room with a view on Cape Cod. The waitstaff at Chatham Bars Inn display an elaborate and elegant buffet with an ice sculpture and cornucopia.

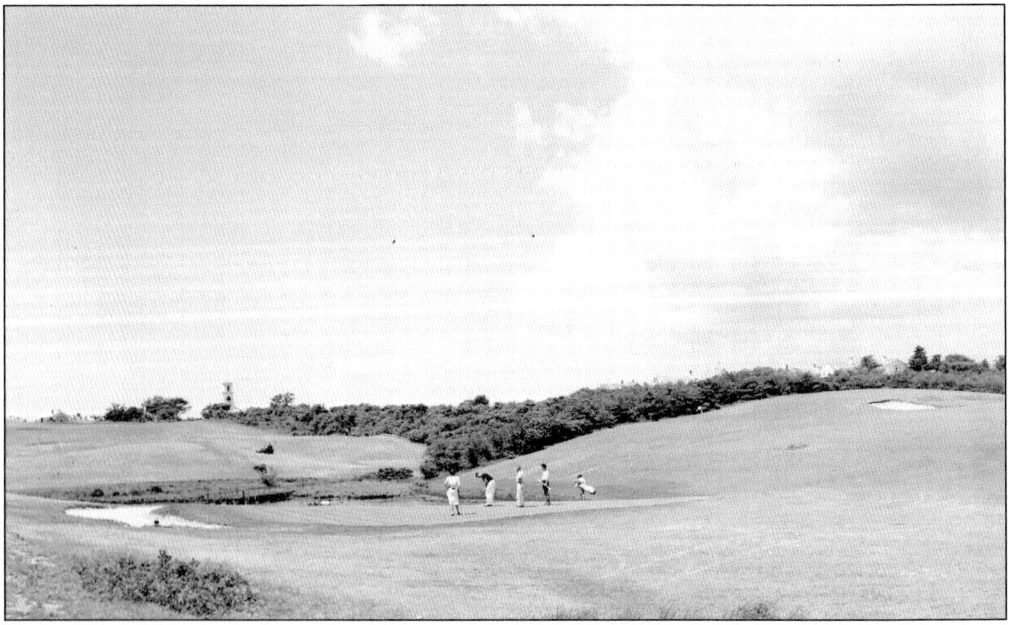

A scene from the golf course once owned by the Chatham Bars Inn in 1947 shows in the background the unmistakable steeple of the First United Methodist Church.

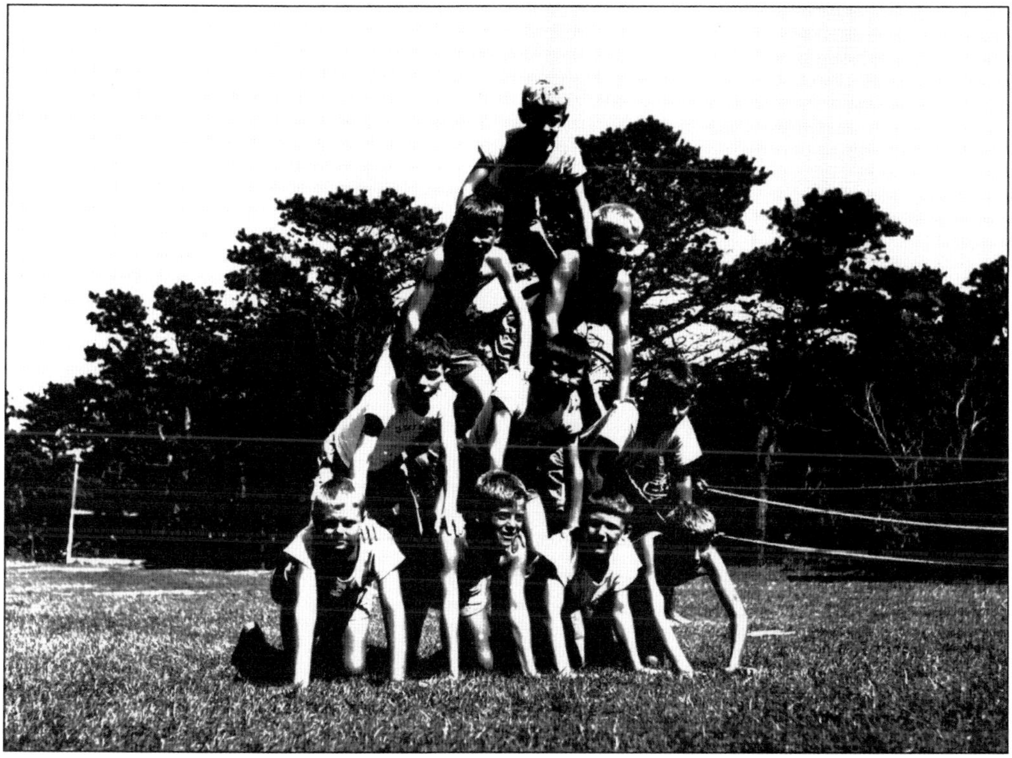

Camp Viking (1929–1984), a boy's camp, was situated at the head of Little Pleasant Bay in Orleans. Although the camp emphasized boating and seamanship, there were other activities such as boxing and gymnastics. In the photograph below, a full compliment of counselors is shown when the enrollment of the camp was probably at its highest.

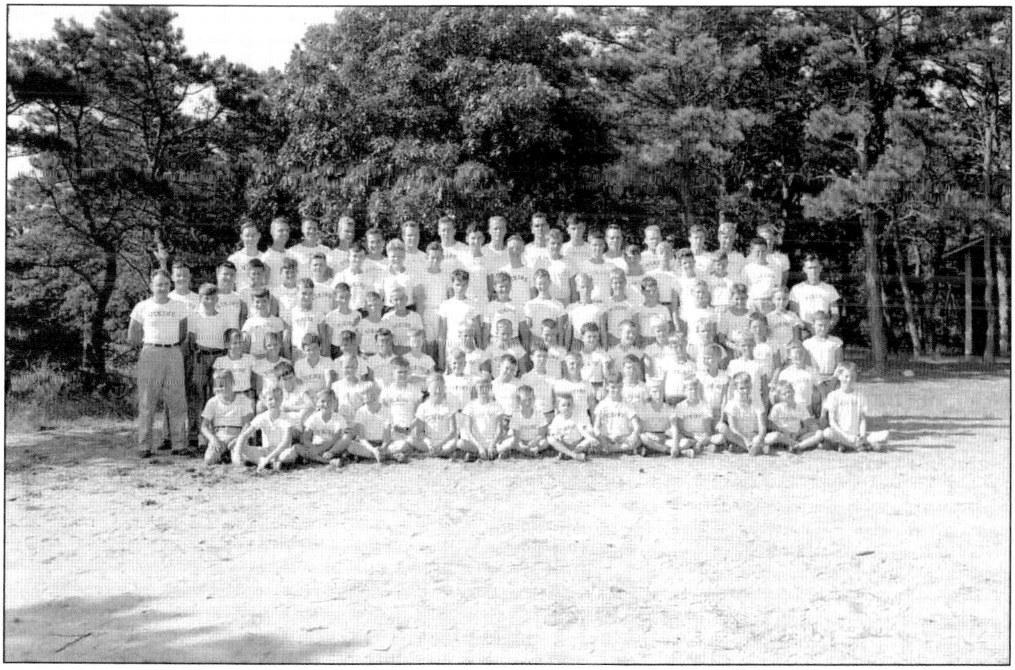

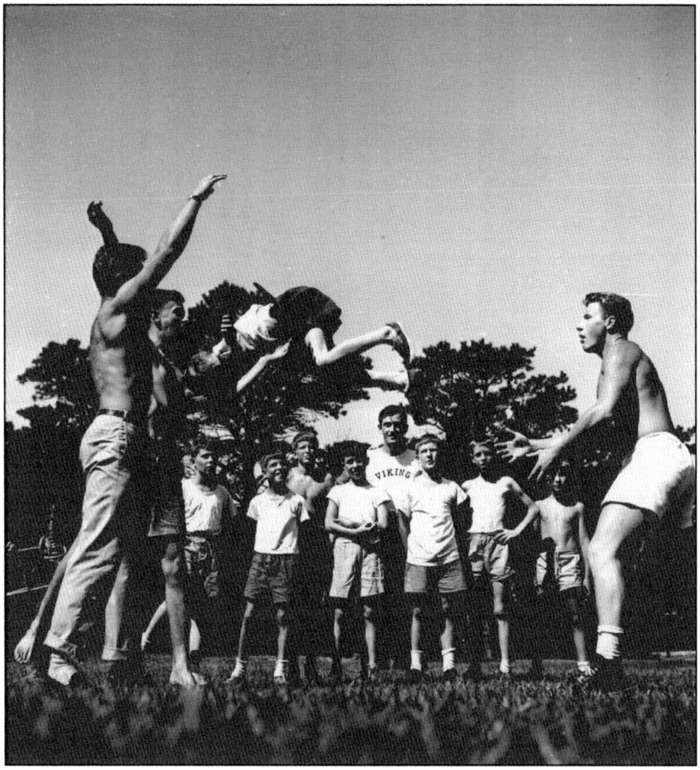

The camp credo was stated in an early catalog as "successful handling of the individual is of greater importance than any other camp activity."

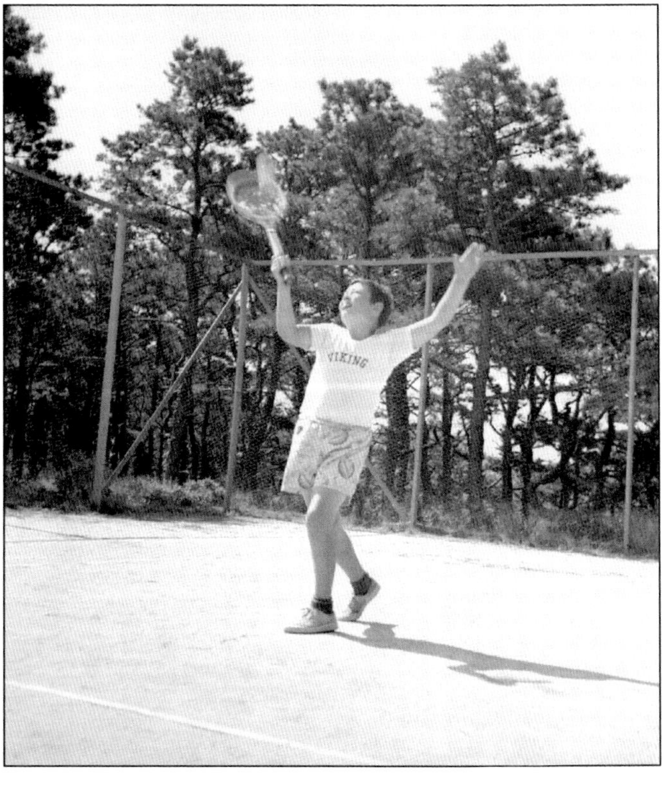

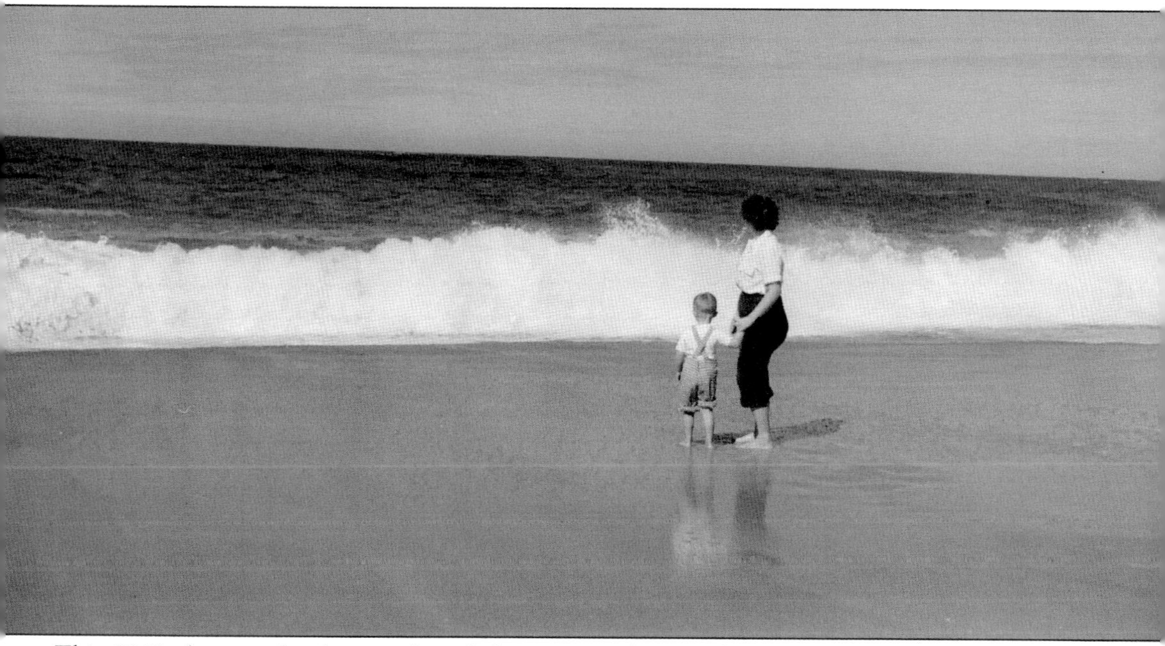

This 1948 photograph of an unidentified woman and young boy in front of the wild surf at Nauset Beach shows them wandering alone on this great beach without crowds. As Thoreau noted, "I do not know where there is another beach in the Atlantic States, attached to the mainland, so long, and at the same time so completely uninterrupted."

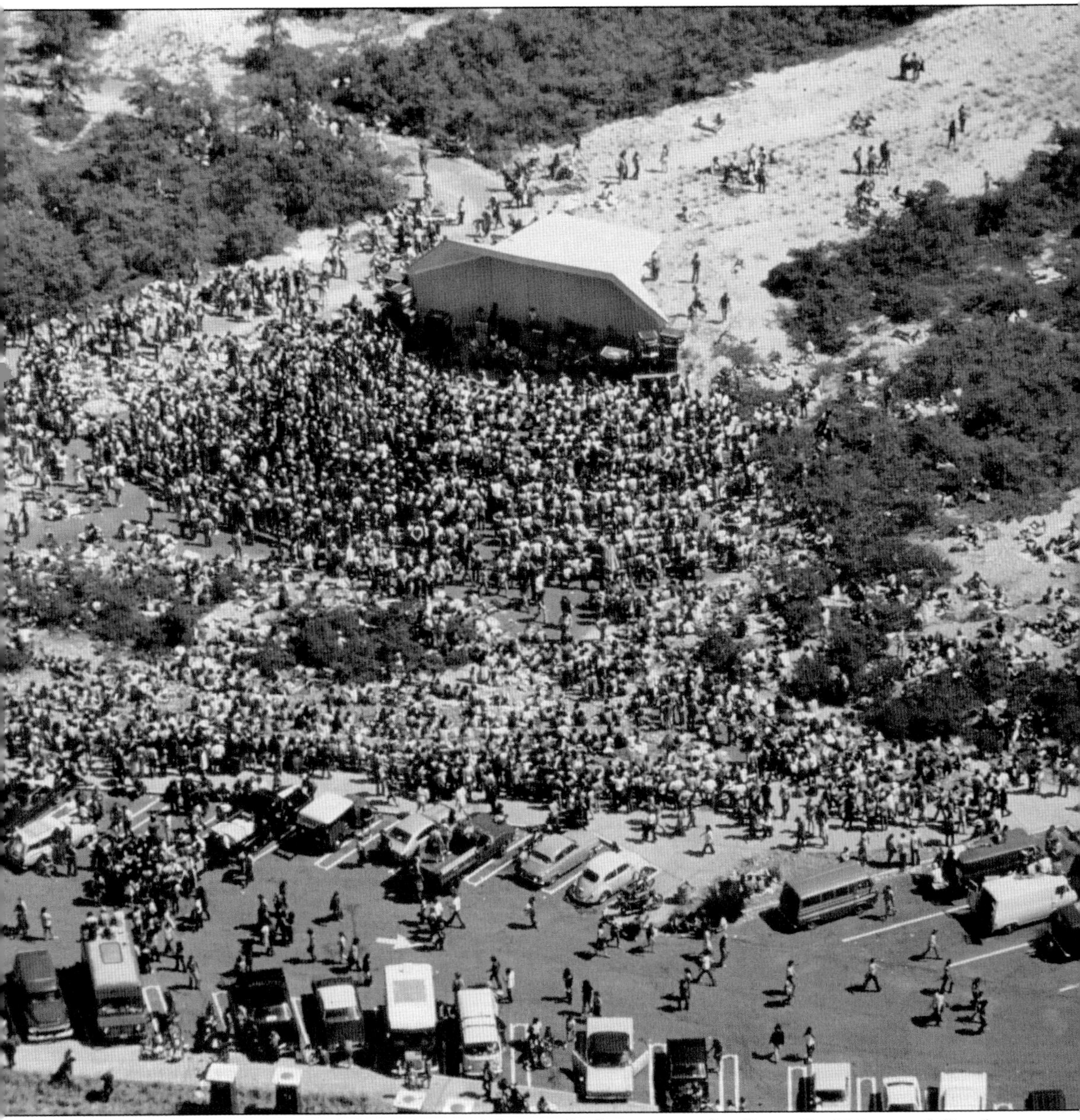

Contrasting is this aerial shot of one of the amphitheaters in the Cape Cod National Seashore. The National Seashore was dedicated on May 30, 1966, and many of the official program photographs were taken by Richard Kelsey.

Three

Storms, Shipwrecks, and Rescues

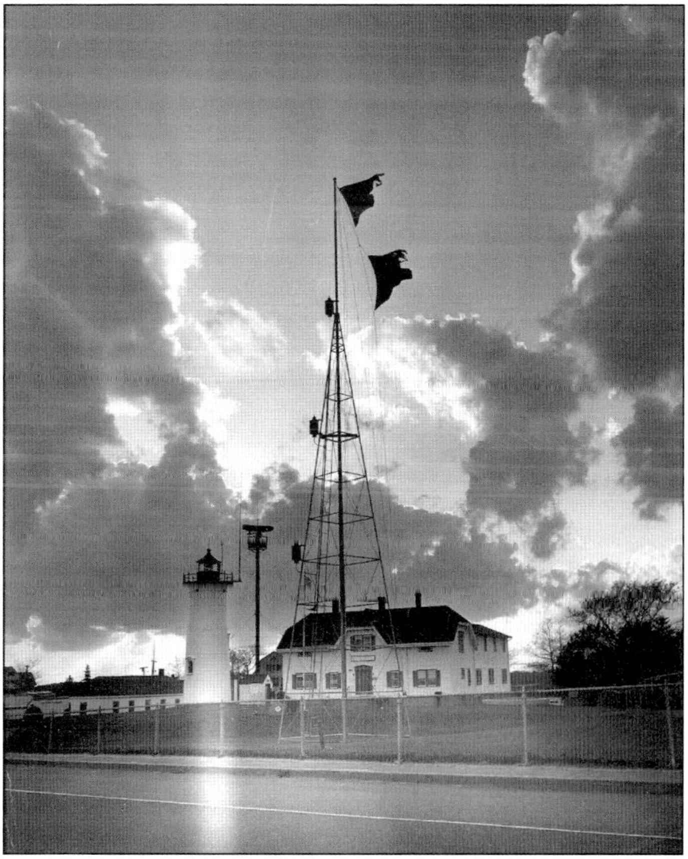

This dramatic photograph shows gale warnings in full force at Chatham Coast Guard Station. The station's flags indicate a severe storm is on the way. Cape Cod's history has been punctuated by storms, hurricanes, gales, nor'easters, and natural forces that have changed landforms and events. Beginning in December 1626, when the ketch *Sparrowhawk* shipwrecked off Nauset Beach, Cape Cod has a long chronology of storms, shipwrecks, and rescues.

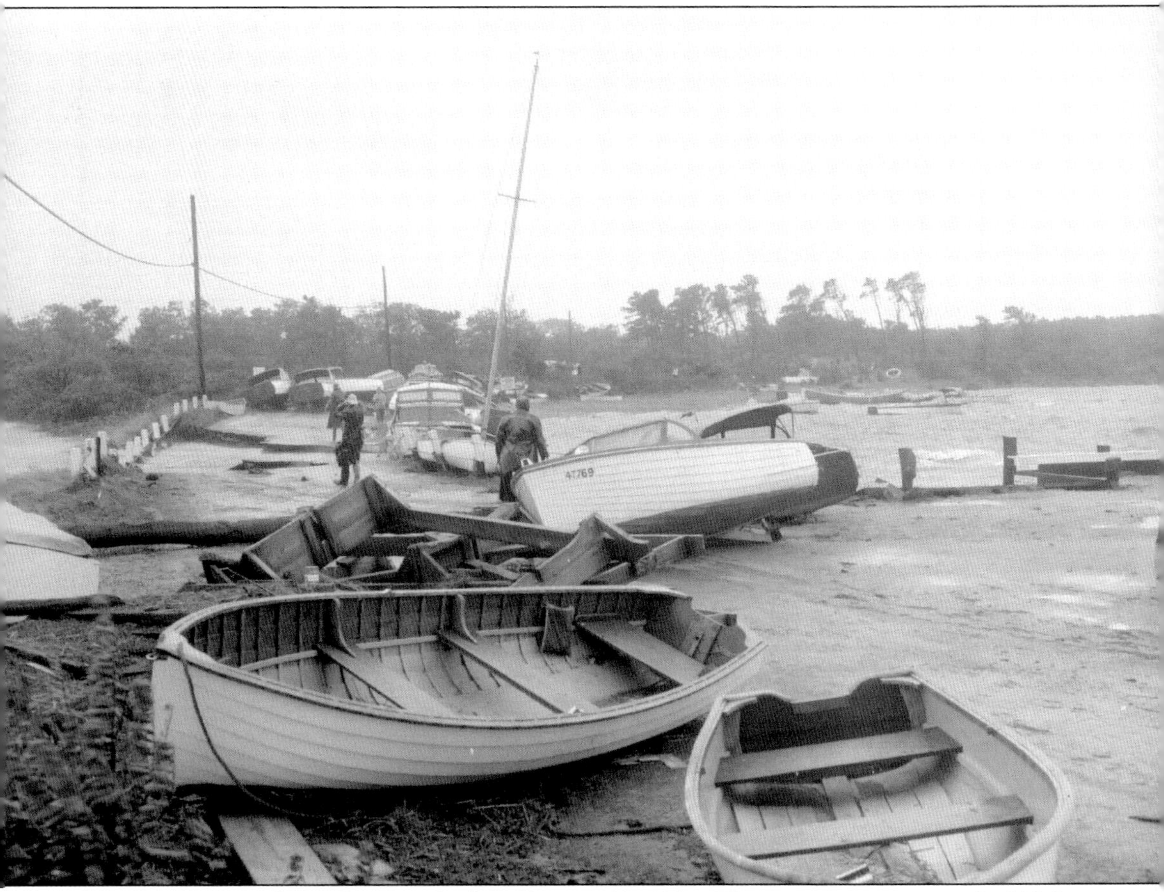

Hurricane Carol struck Cape Cod on August 31, 1954. There were approximately 200 boats moored at Allen Harbor in Harwich. Rupert Nicoles, owner of the boatyard, recalled the boats coming loose one by one, then drifting onto the marsh, and eventually ending up on Route 28.

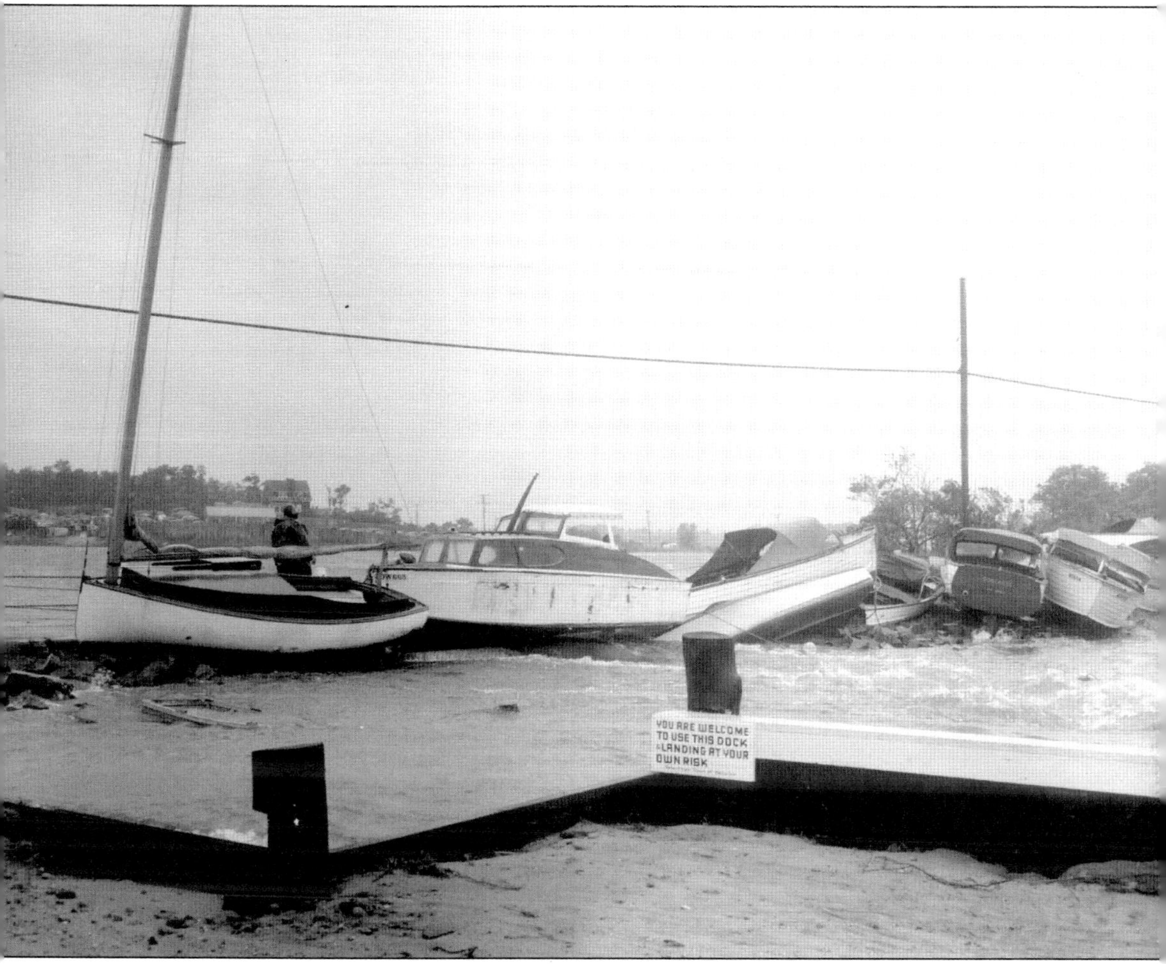

This is another view of Allen Harbor showing Lower County Road. The sign reads, "you are welcome to use this dock and landing at your own risk." The headlines for September 1, 1954, however, tell the real story: "Upper Cape area hit hard by storm; 3 are dead, property loss in millions."

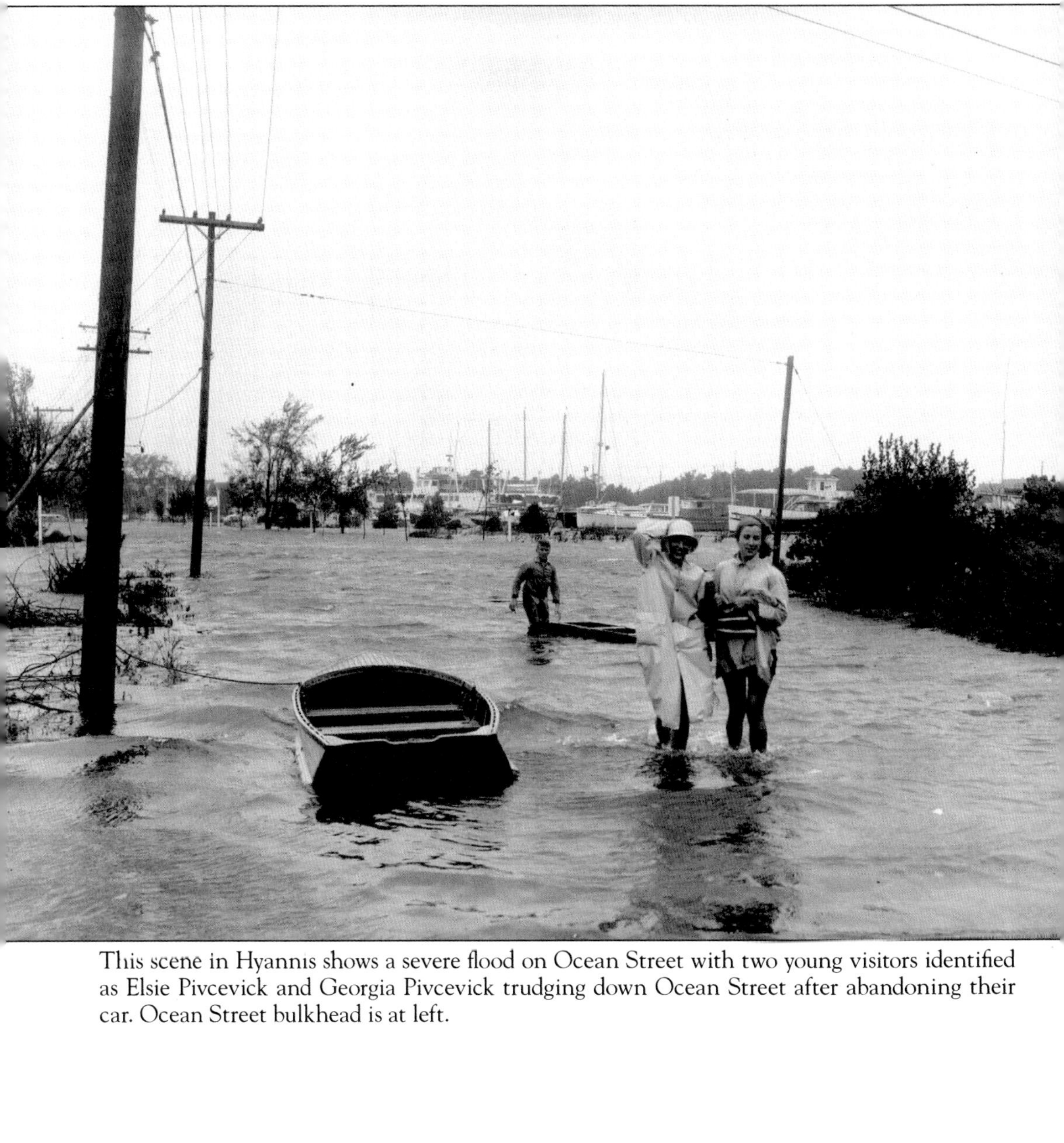

This scene in Hyannis shows a severe flood on Ocean Street with two young visitors identified as Elsie Pivcevick and Georgia Pivcevick trudging down Ocean Street after abandoning their car. Ocean Street bulkhead is at left.

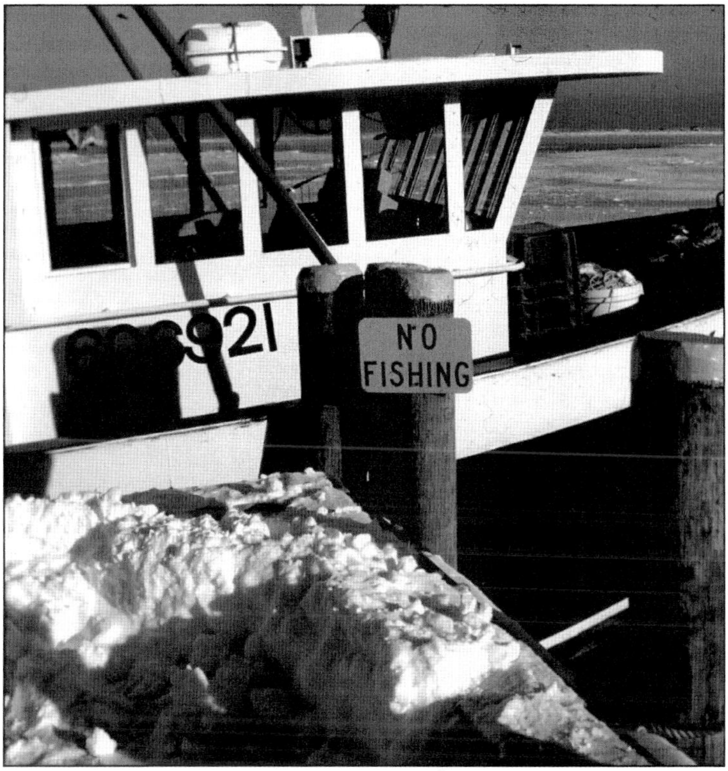

Snow scenes in Chatham Harbor prove that although known for its temperate climate, the myth that it never snows on Cape Cod was never a serious claim. Too many nor'easters, high tides, and great surfs have too frequently visited Cape Cod.

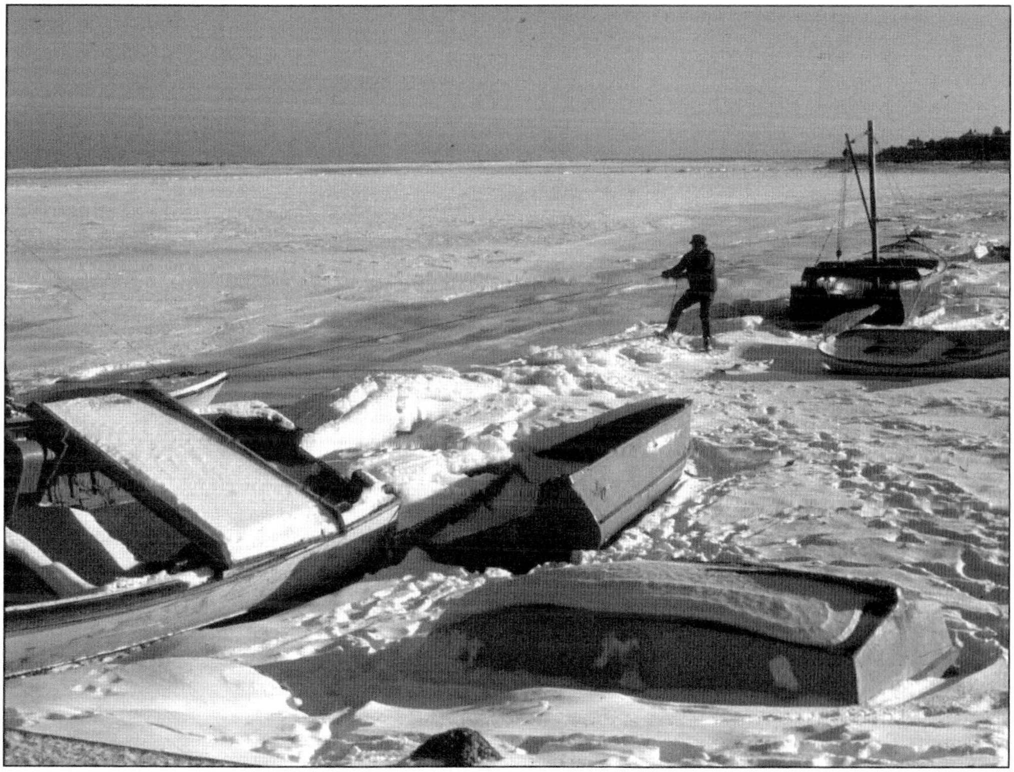

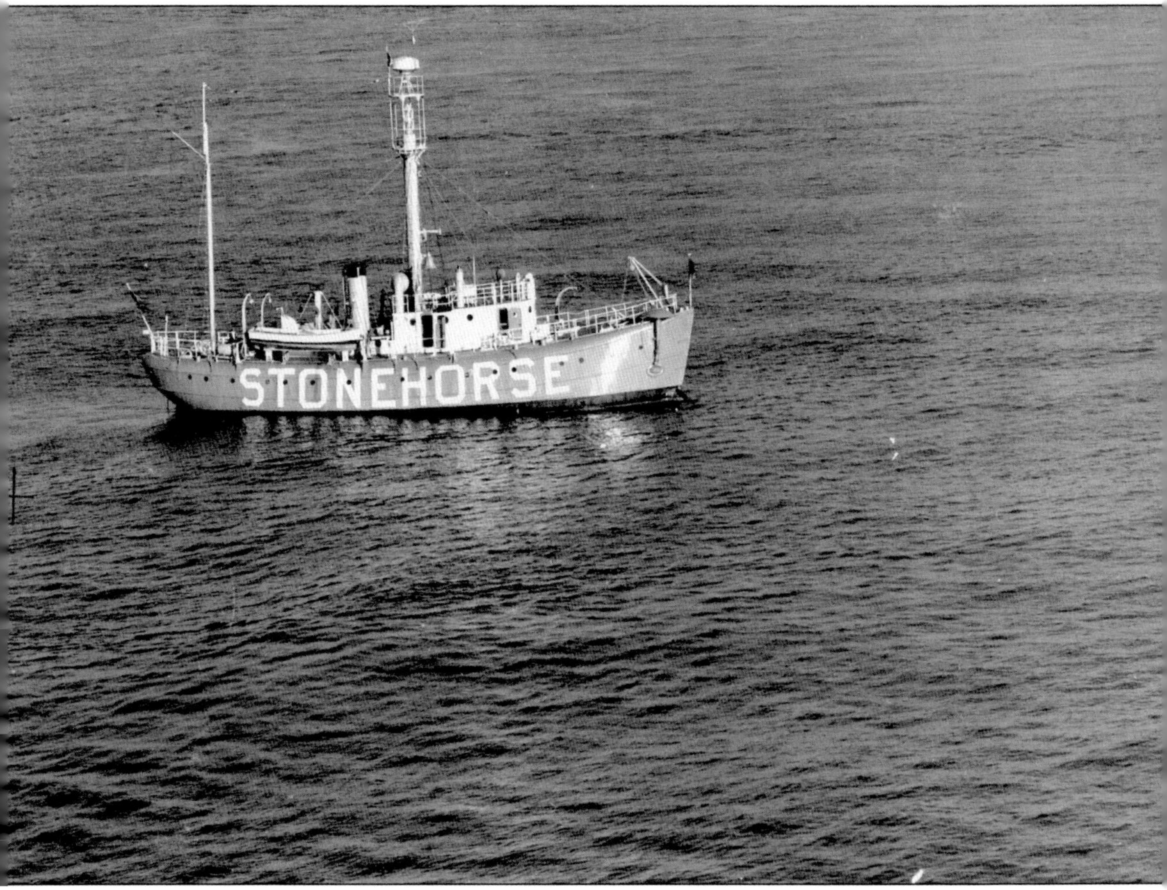

Cape Cod was once one of the most populated lightship areas in the county, having 12 stationed in Nantucket Sound and Buzzards Bay at the beginning of the 20th century. The *Stonehorse* lightship stood looking northwest across Monomoy Island onto Cape Cod. On October 5, 1963, this lightship was withdrawn and replaced by buoys. Many a harrowing tale of violent storms and World War II German U-boat encounters followed in the wake of these sterling ships.

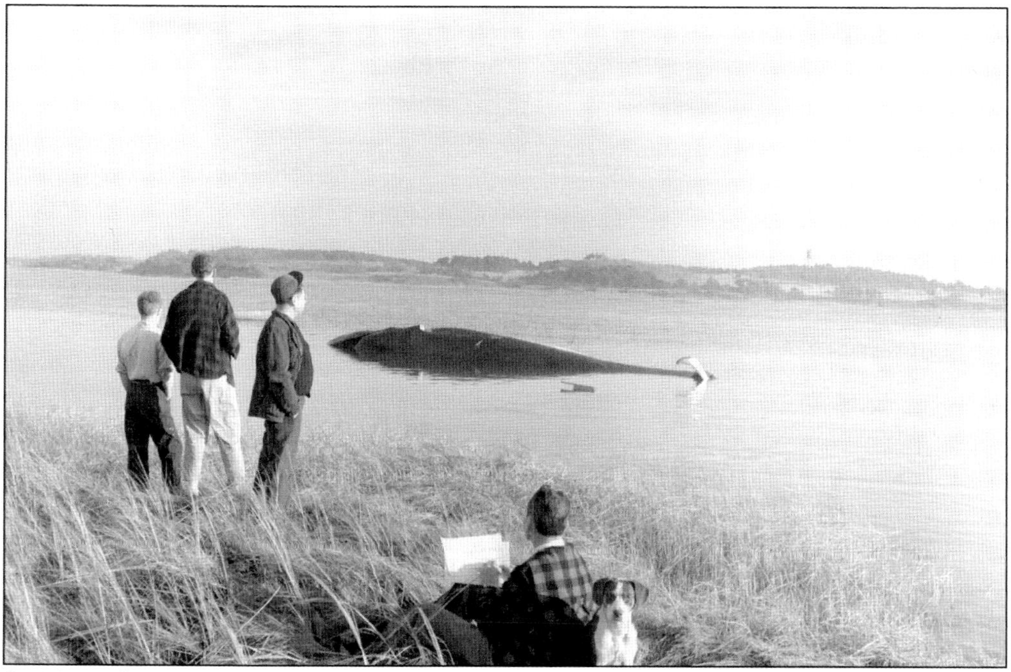

On November 19, 1946, the *Cape Cod Standard-Times* had the front page headline "Slain whale being towed to Chatham for salvage." The following series of photographs gives a chronology of a rescue of sorts, not for resuscitating the whale but for the recovery of parts for oil and bone. The dead whale is seen floating off of Ryder's Cove in Chatham. This recovery became a family and community event.

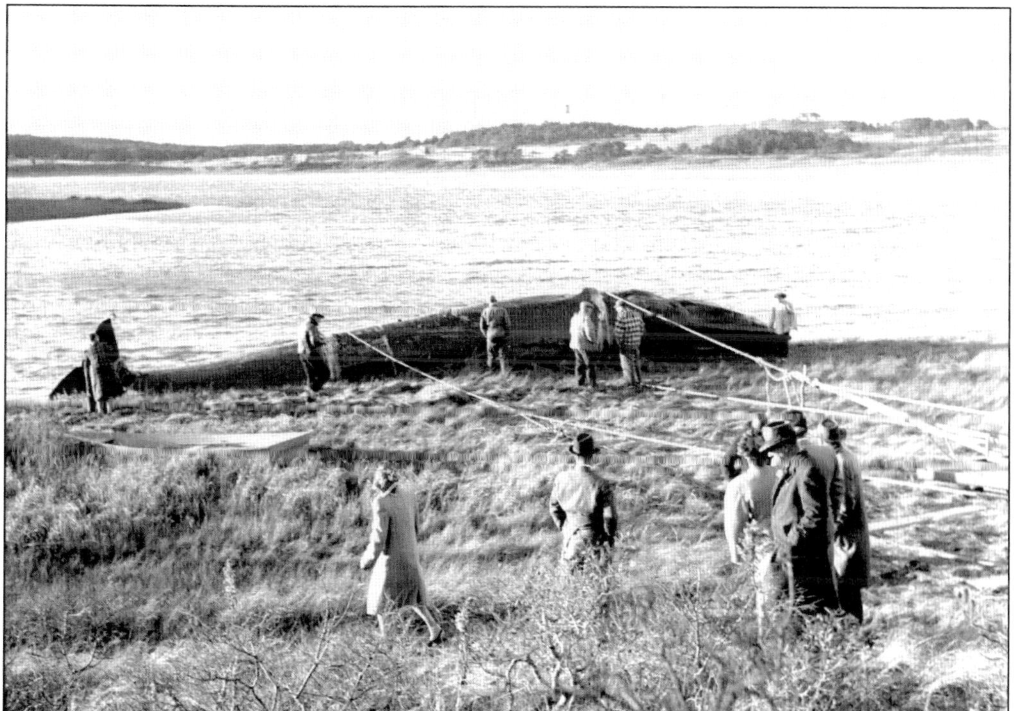

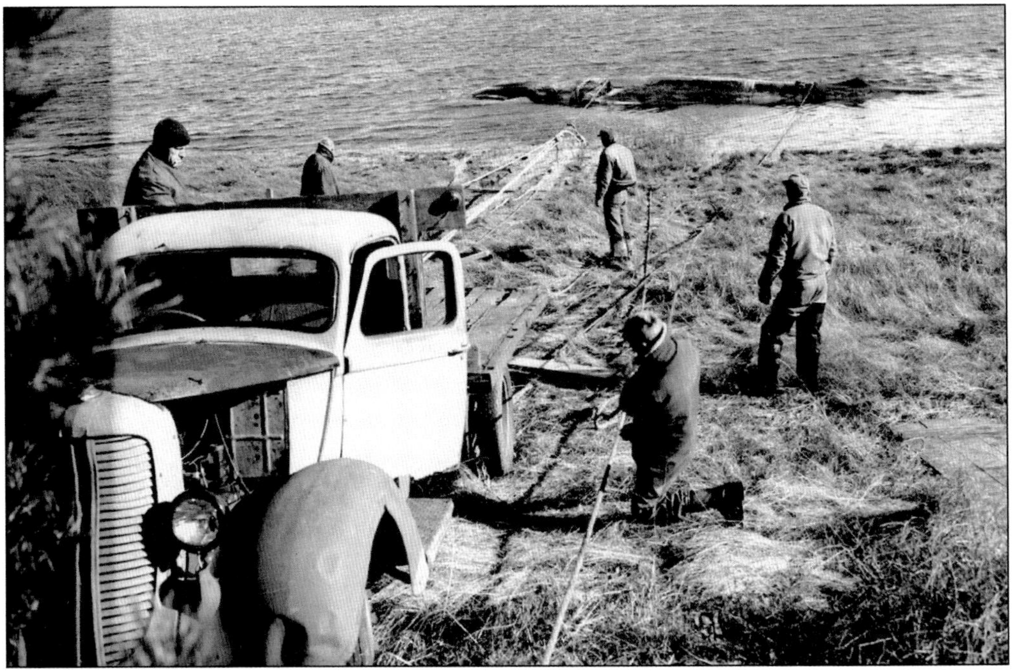

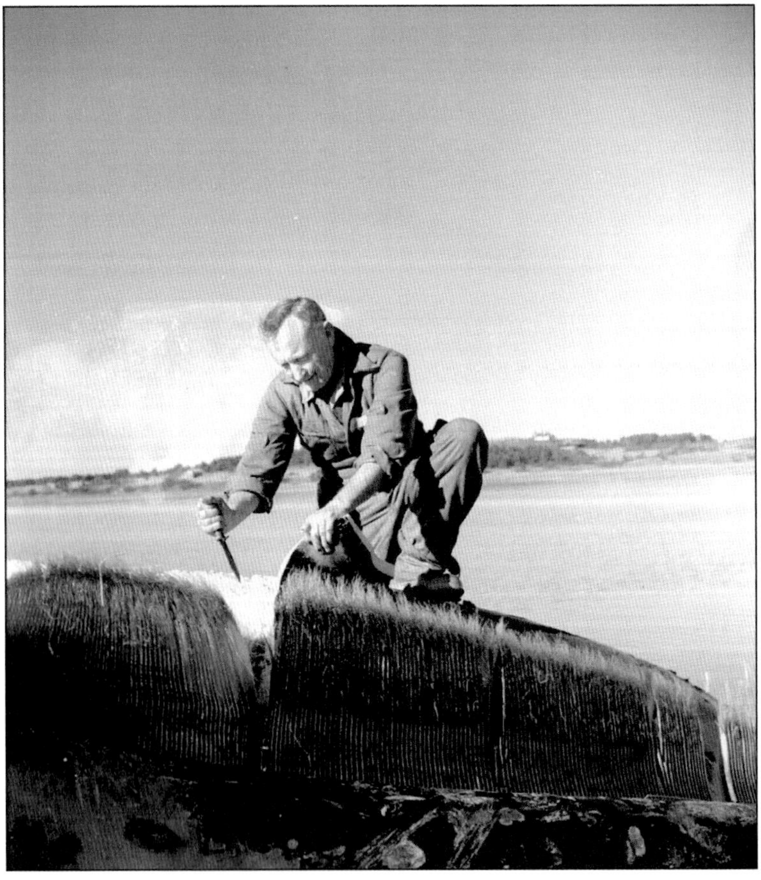

Dr. Floyd E. Rowland claimed the whale and had his sons and family tow the whale with winch from Ryder's Cove. In the image below, Dr. Rowland cuts into the baleen of the 40-ton whale. Standing networks and rescues would not happen until several decades later.

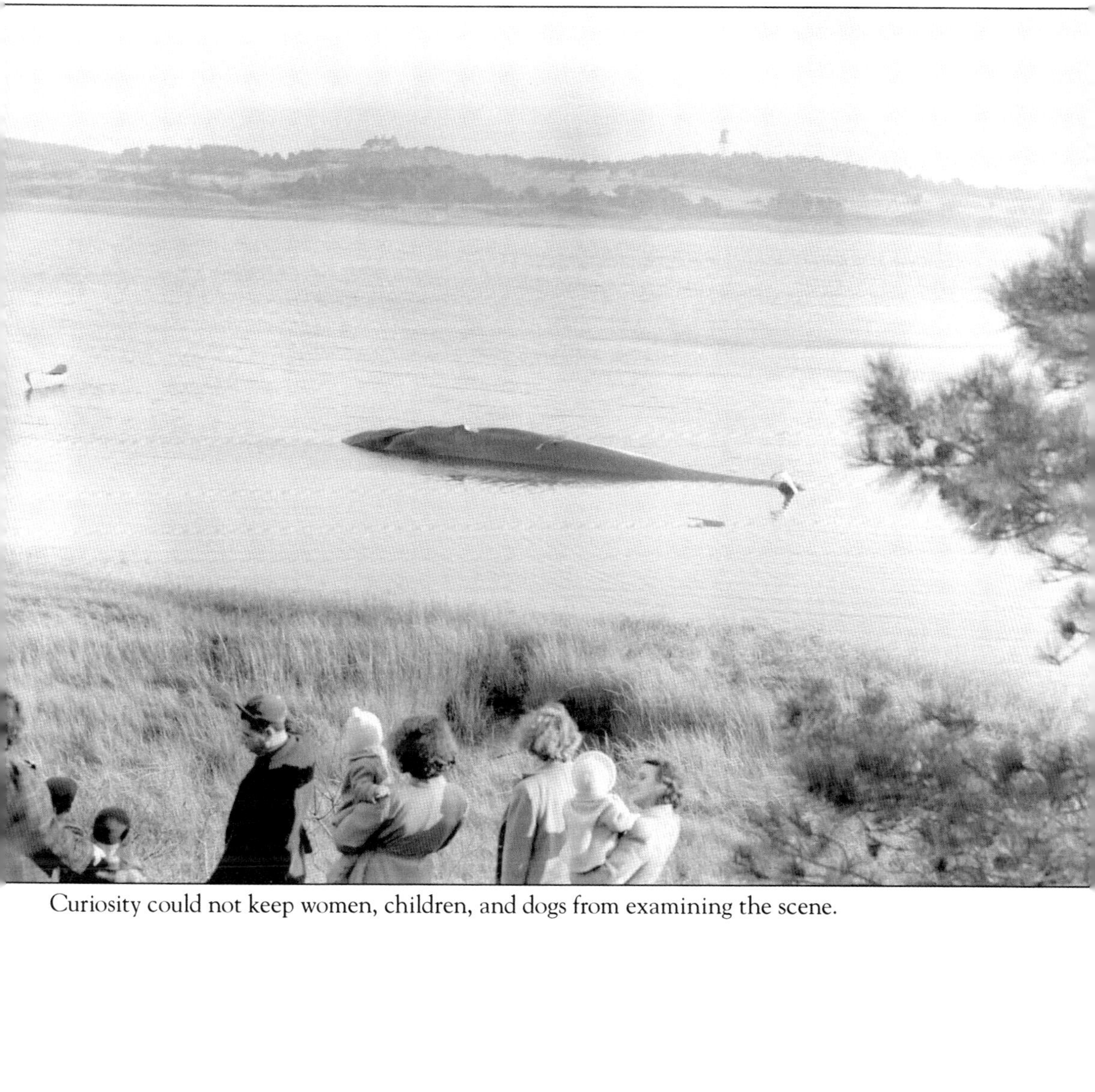

Curiosity could not keep women, children, and dogs from examining the scene.

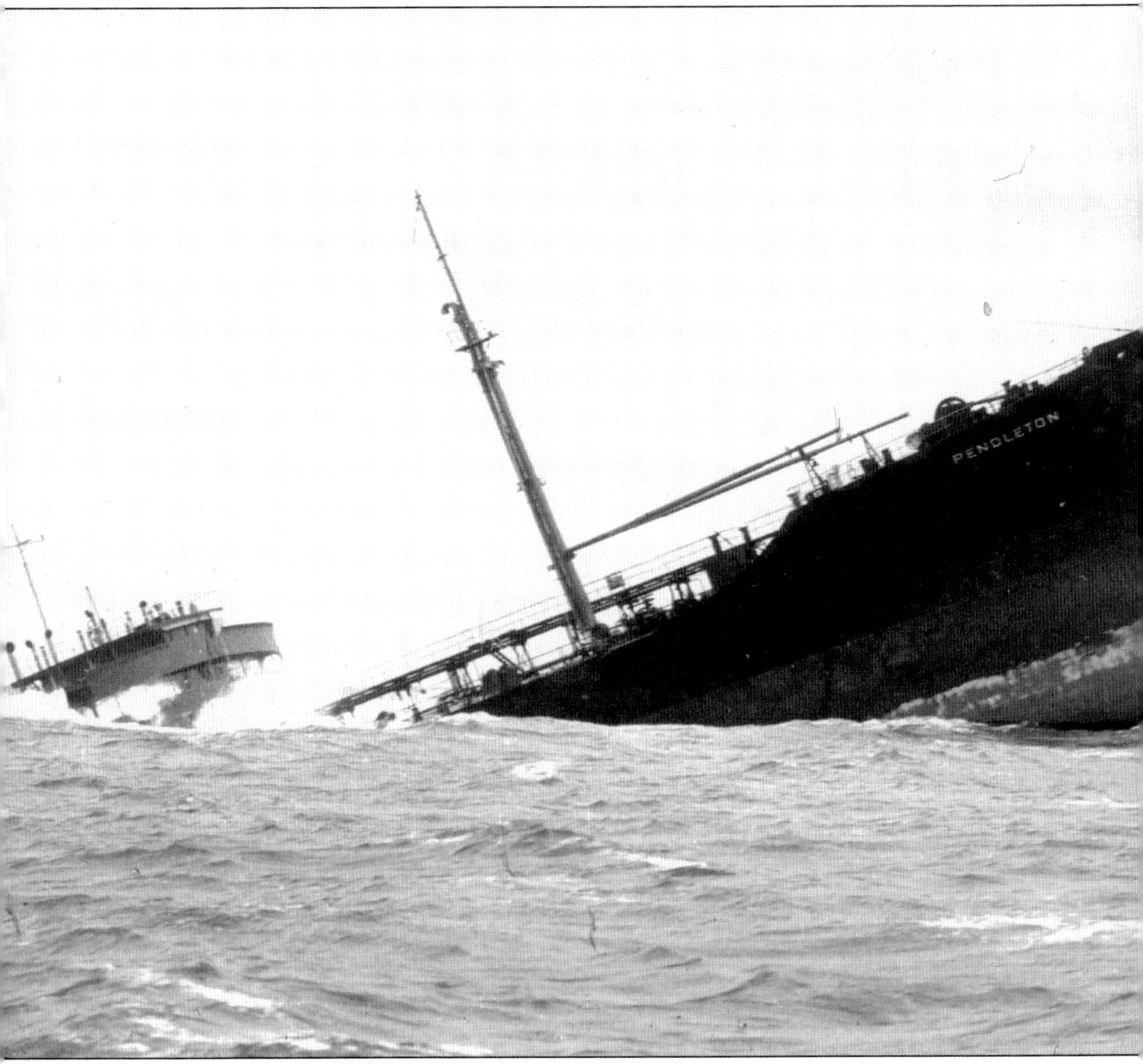

Oil tankers *Fort Mercer* and the *Pendleton* were both caught in a nor'easter off Chatham on February 18, 1952. The *Pendleton*, a 504-foot tanker, split in half during that severe storm, and the following series of photographs tell the dramatic story of the rescue of 32 members of the crew of the *Pendleton* by the Chatham Coast Guard. Richard Kelsey was one of the first on the scene, and these photographs are valued for capturing the raw terror of that night off the Chatham Fish Pier.

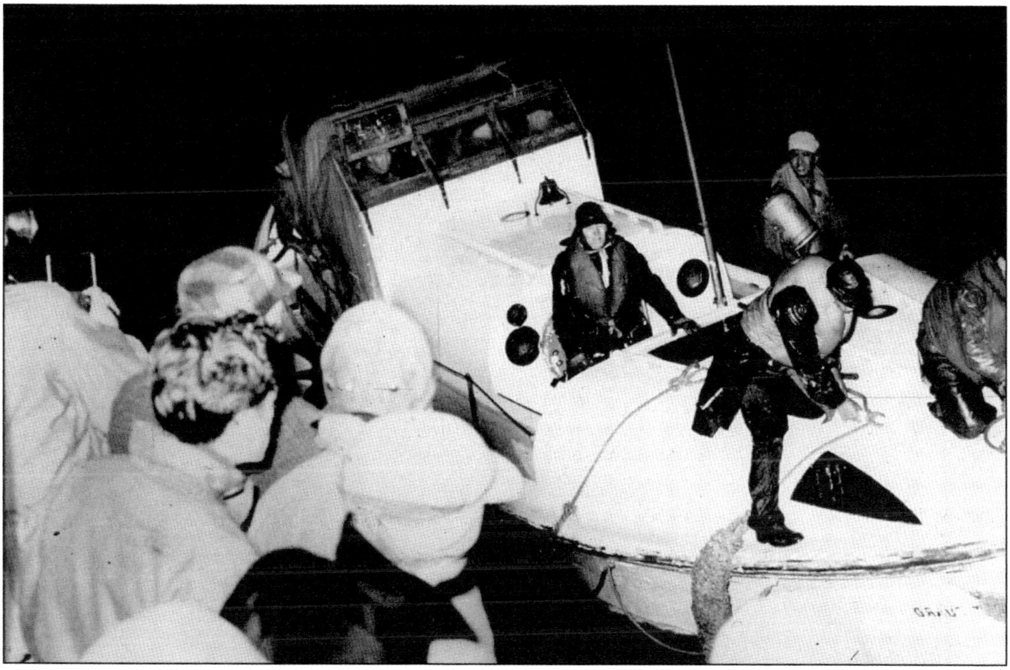

Pictured here is the first sighting of the 36-foot Coast Guard motor lifeboat CG36500 at the Chatham Fish Pier, captained by Coast Guardsman Bernie Webber. The exhausted crew with Andrew Fitzgerald at the bow receives help docking while an eager crowd of townspeople awaits word of the *Pendleton* crew.

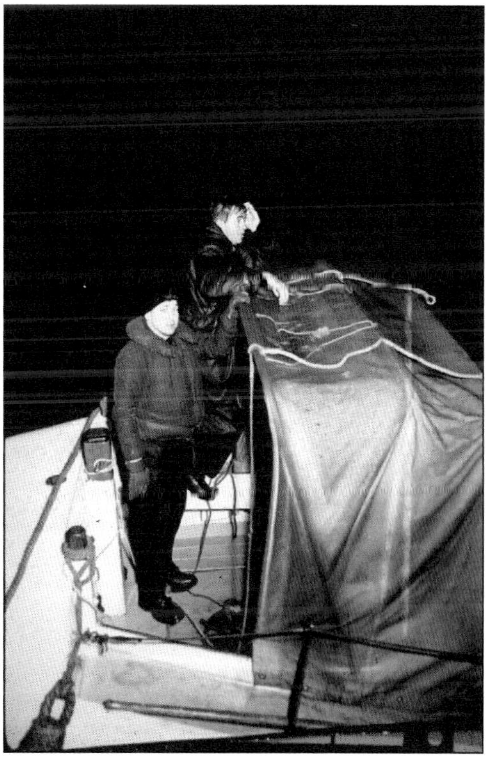

Webber (left) and seaman Irving Maske both look wet and exhausted as they secure the vessel. Webber was hailed as hero of the rescue and later received the Award of Merit.

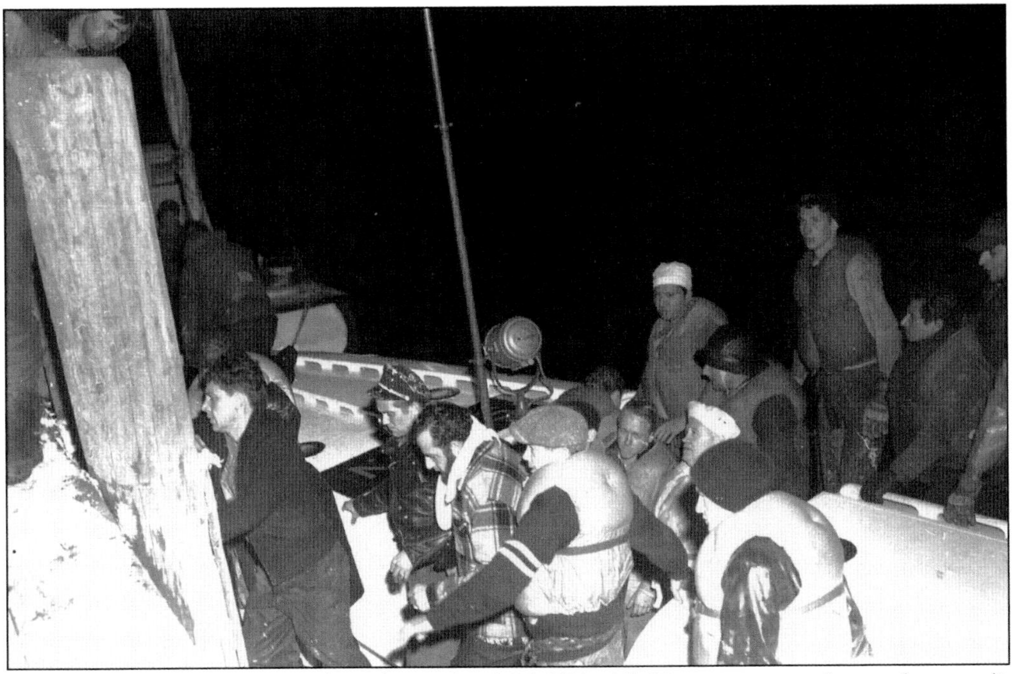

The crew of the *Pendleton* rush to leave the CG36500. All 32 were squeezed into the vessel's tiny compartments.

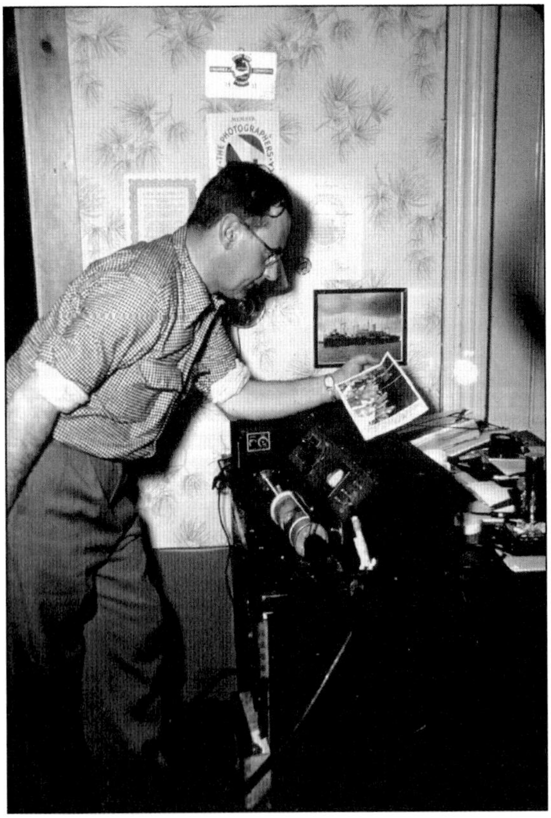

As the world awaited word on the seamen's fate, Richard Kelsey's photograph of the rescue is seen being sent to the Associated Press from his office.

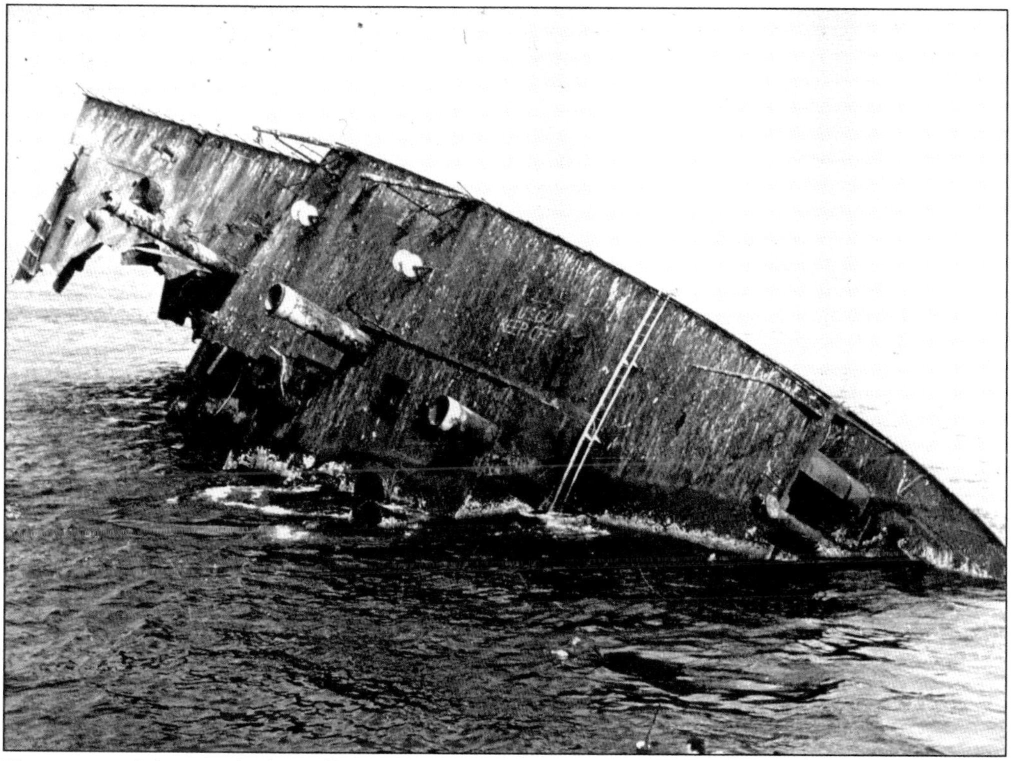

Two views of the wrecked *Pendleton* are seen here. It became somewhat of a motorboat tourist's attraction off Monomoy until it was demolished.

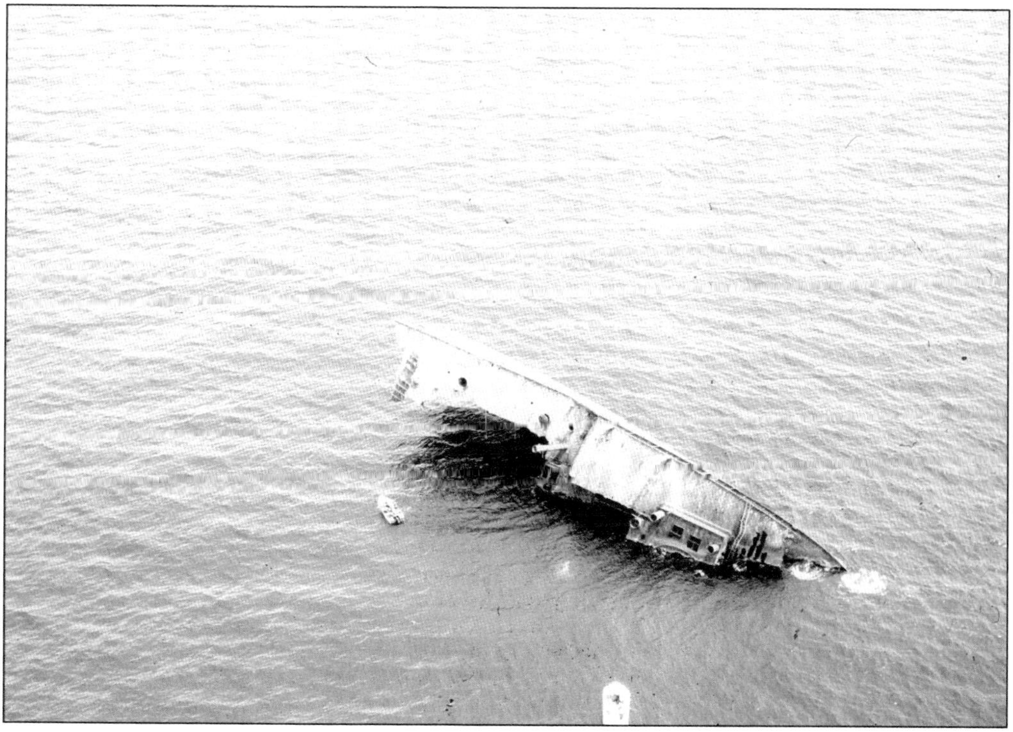

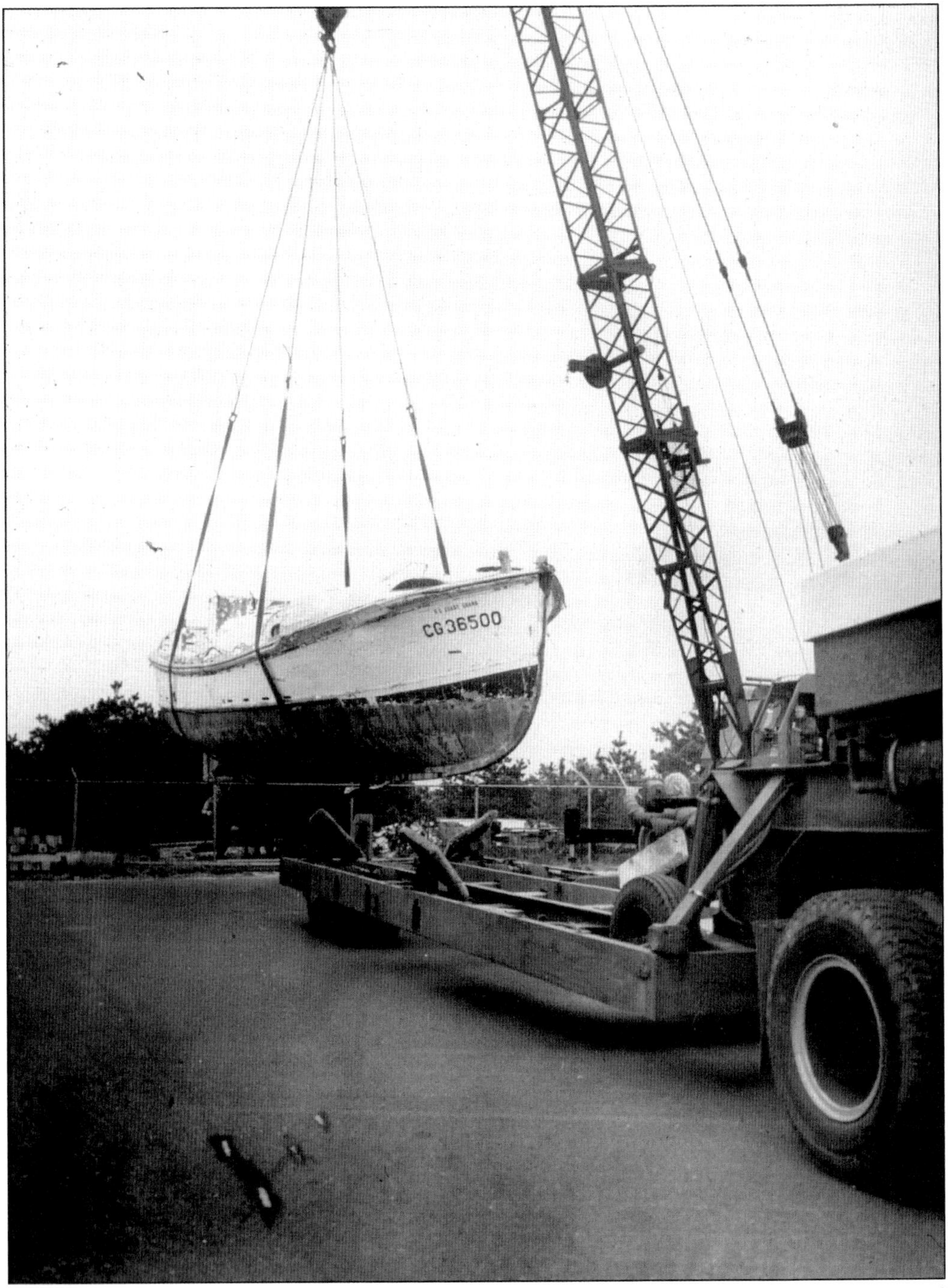

As a fitting regard for its heroic past, the *CG36500* was restored by the Orleans Historical Society. Today this Coast Guard vessel lies in Rock Harbor with tours and the retelling of the *Pendleton* story.

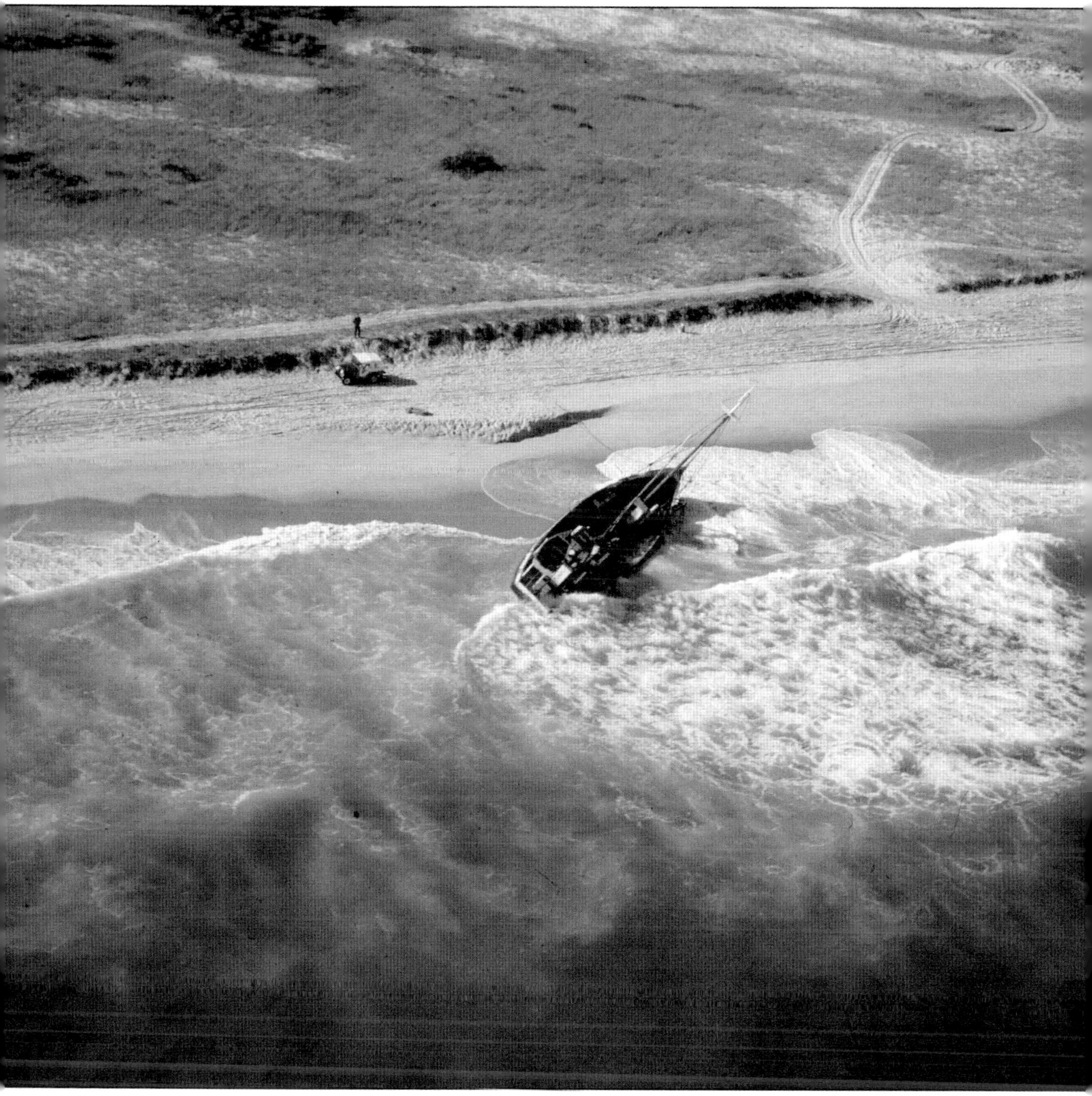

This 1965 stranding of a vessel that strayed too close to the Atlantic shoreline is captured here with spectacular clarity

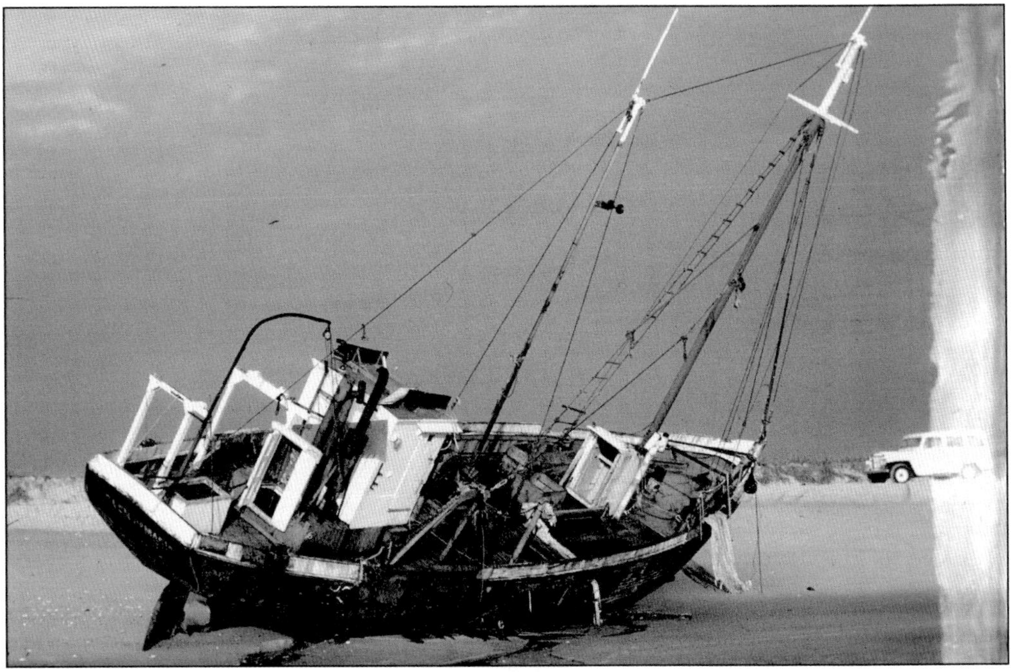

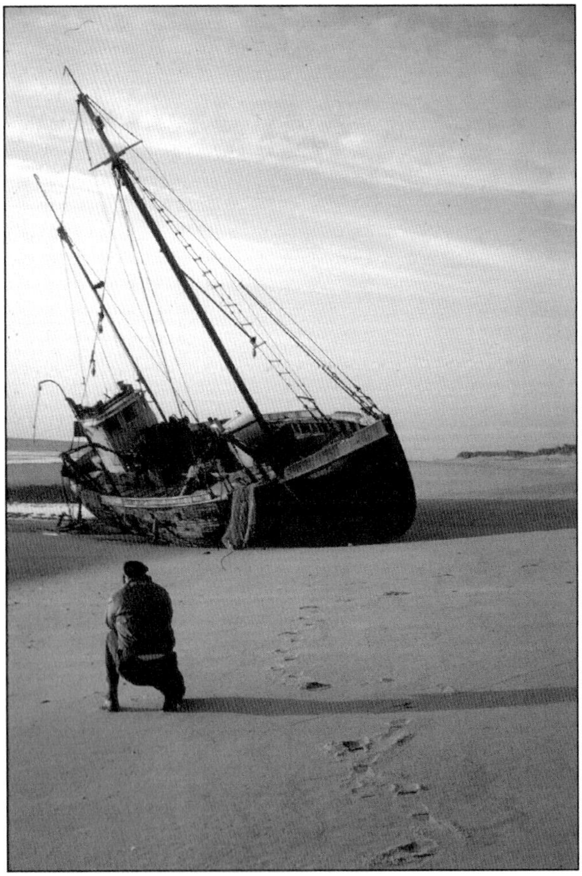

This is a close-up of the wreckage and an amazing photograph opportunity along this sometimes forbidding coast.

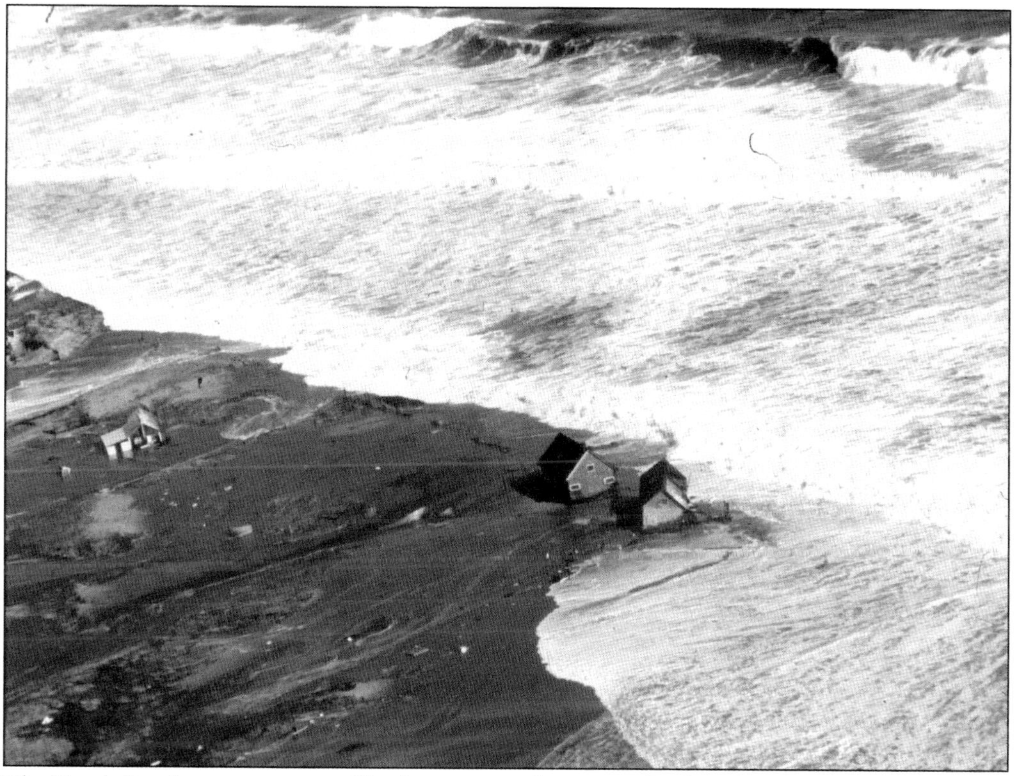

The North Beach community in Chatham received a great setback in the powerful storm of 1978. Here are shown the final sequences of these tiny cottages on the shoreline being methodically swept away with violent fury.

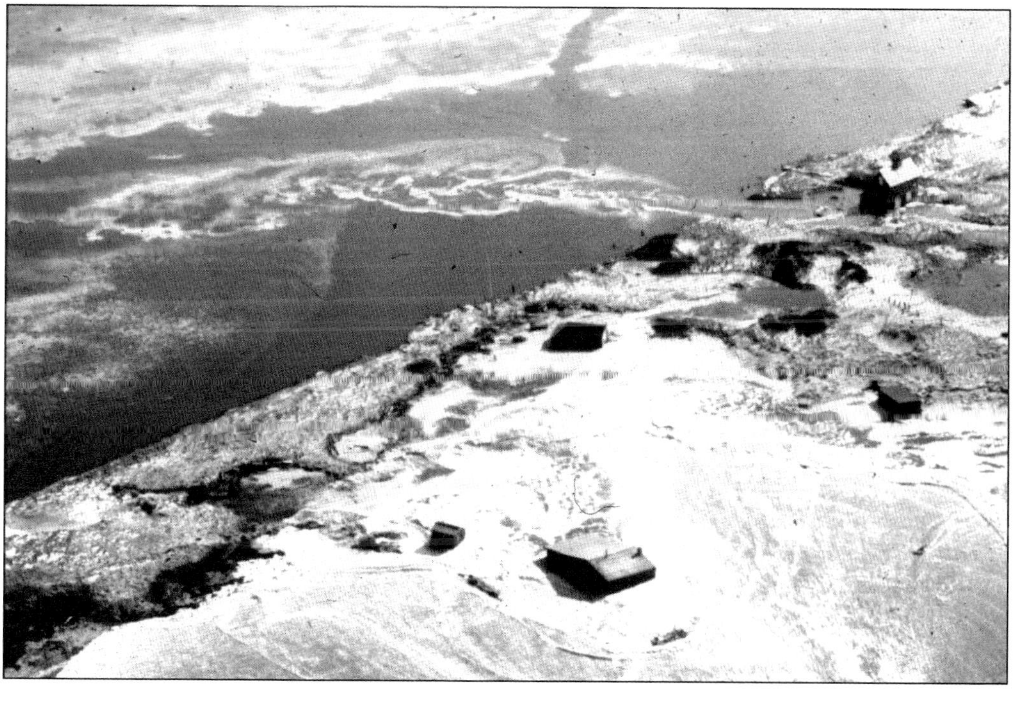

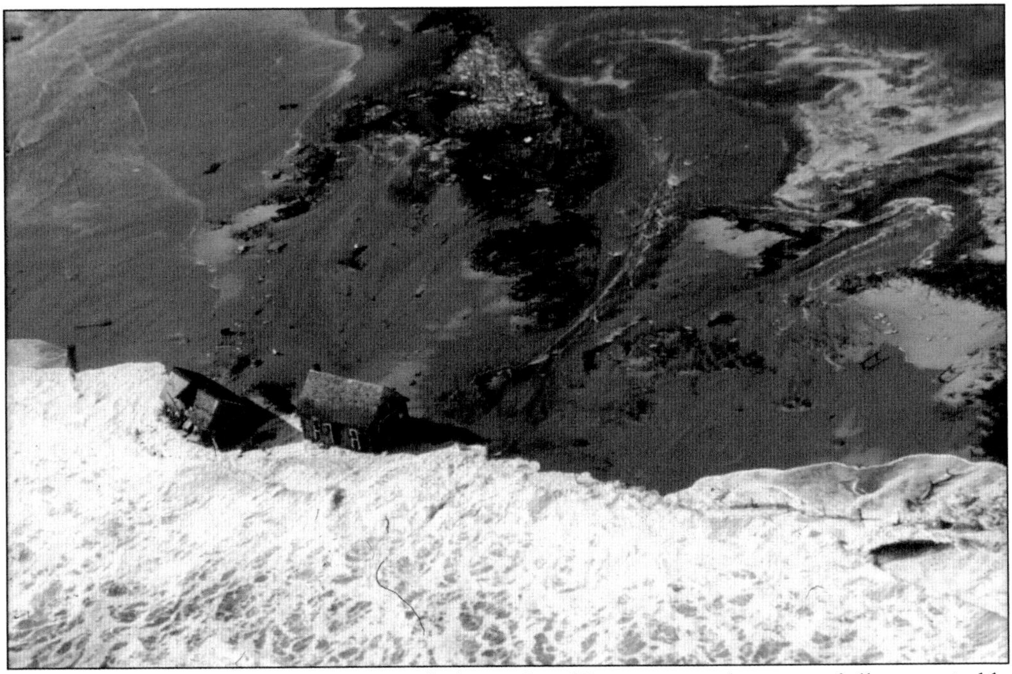

The final outcome of this storm, once called "two fisted," was a great cleansing of all recognizable structures, including the loss of Henry Beston's Outermost House in Eastham. It was Richard Kelsey's photographs that told the story of sudden desolation to the world.

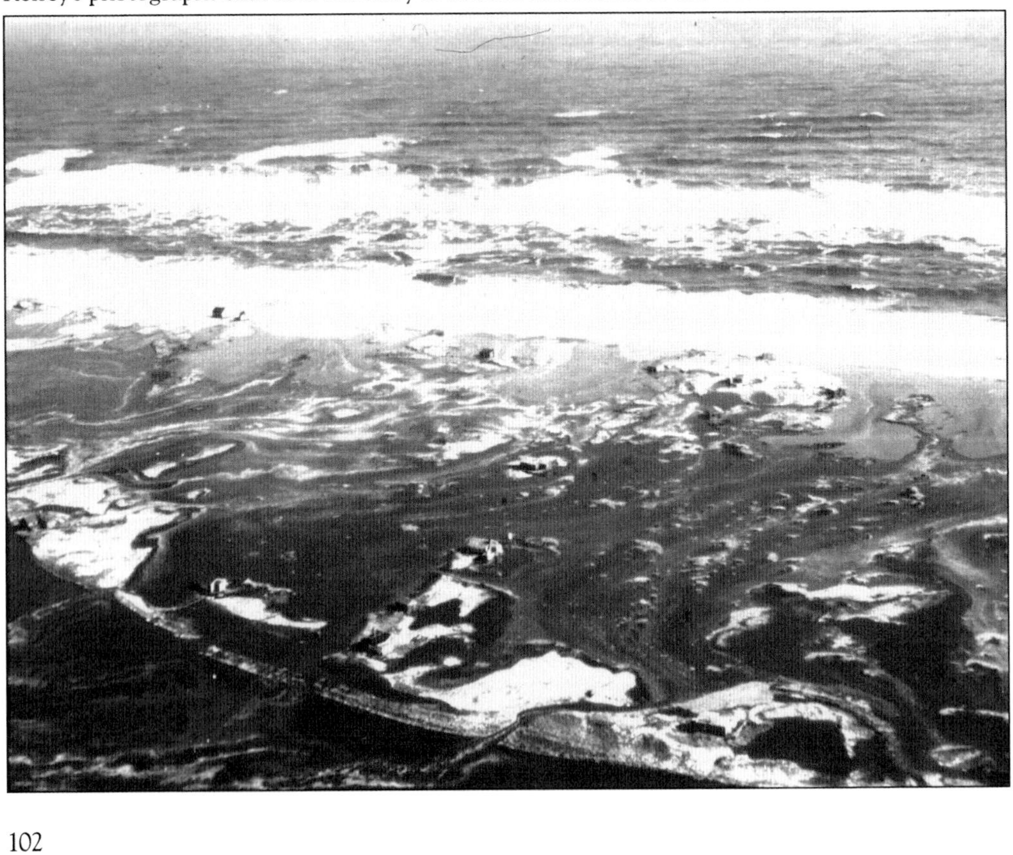

Four

EARLY AERIALS AND BEYOND

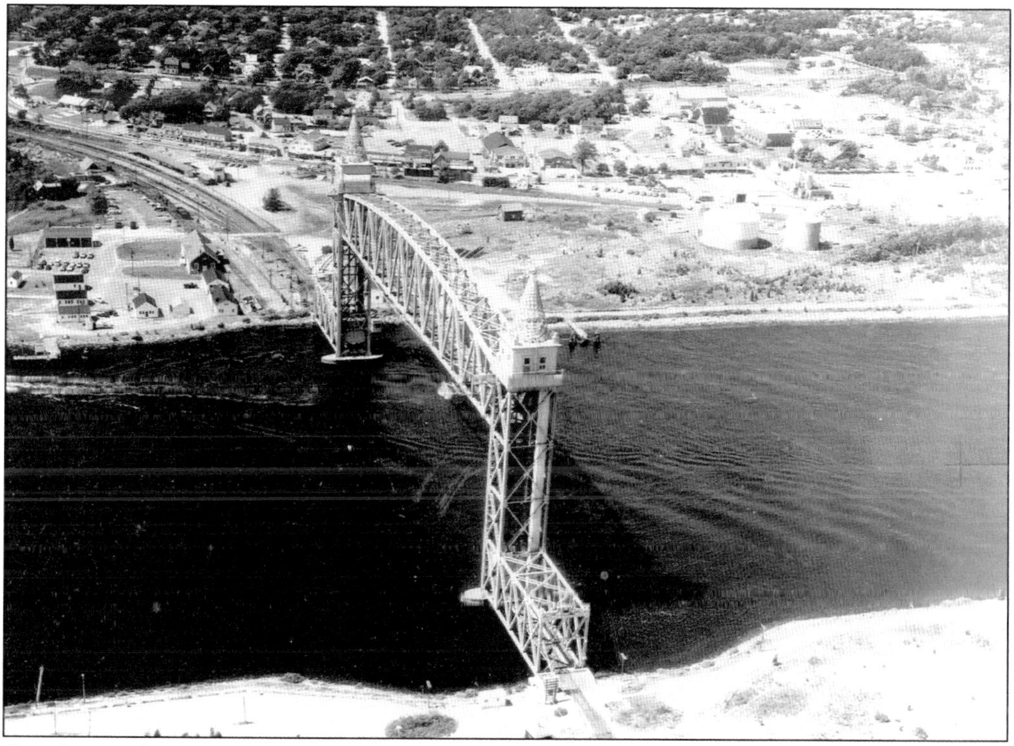

Aerials are the signature Kelsey photograph. Shown here is the vertical lift railroad bridge in downtown Buzzards Bay in the late 1960s. The Buzzards Bay bypass road is visible in the background, and in the foreground are the defunct oil tanks once used as storage bins for Grossman Lumber Company. Also shown in the upper left is the railroad station with canopy.

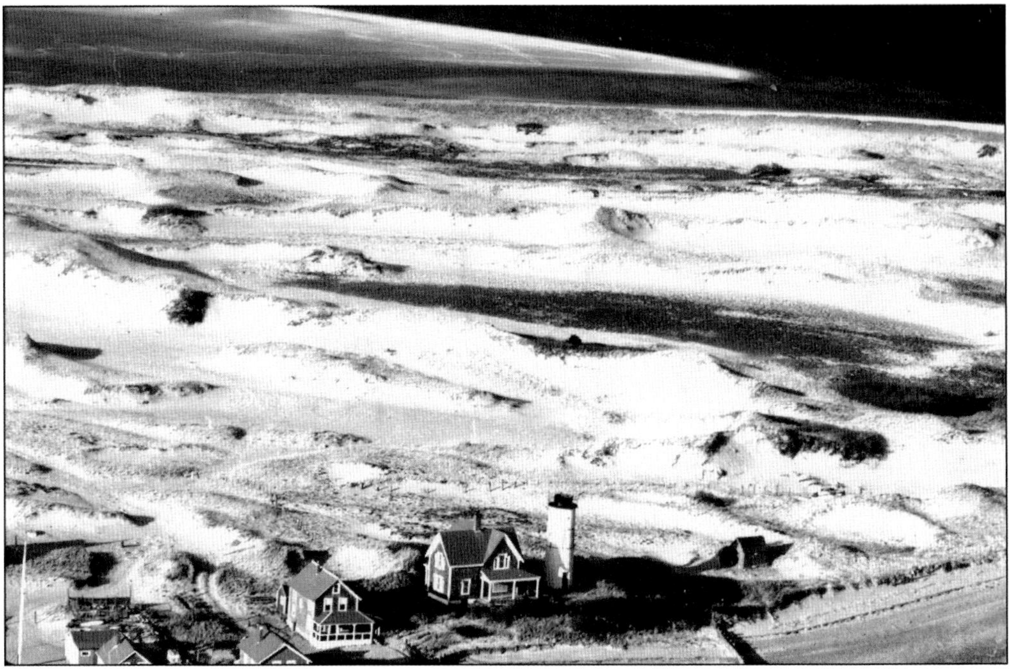

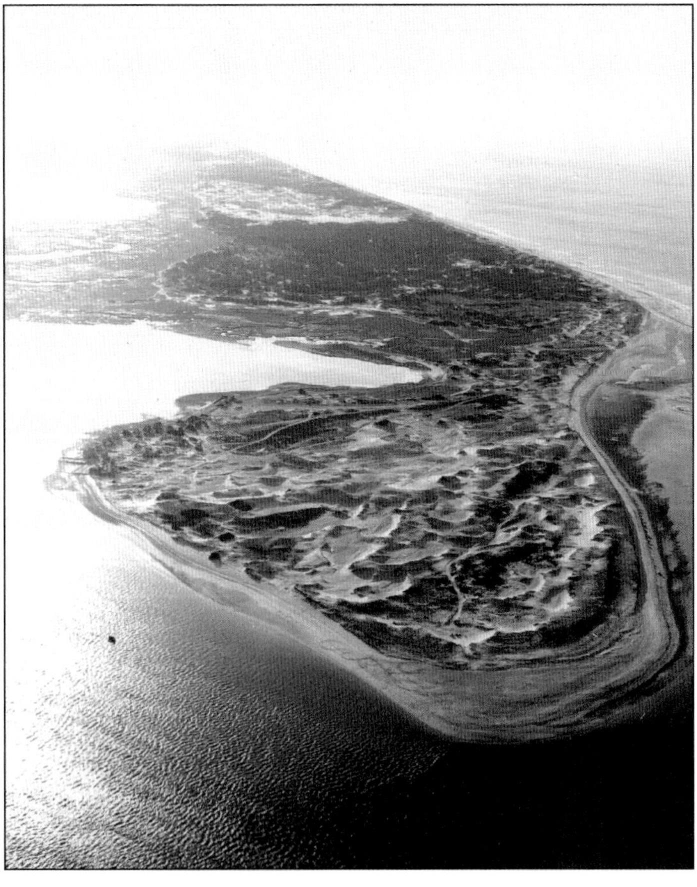

A series over Sandy Neck shows the lighthouse without its lens and the light keeper's house. Also shown is an aerial of the full shoreline of Sandy Neck with its dunes and extension into Cape Cod Bay. Houses on the point and the lighthouse are barely visible on the middle right.

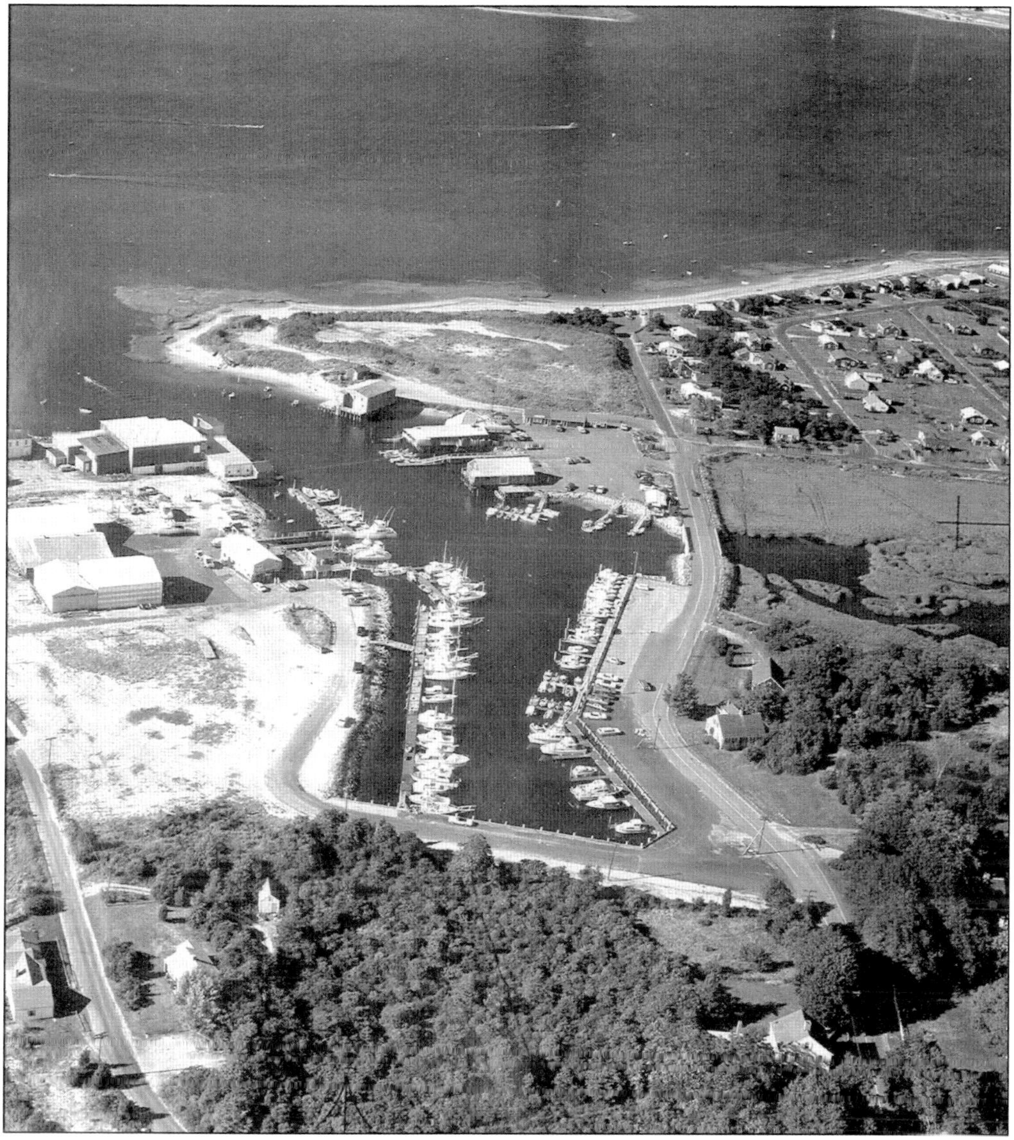

This 1968 photograph shows a detail of Barnstable Harbor in Barnstable Village with the freezer plant, marinas, and boat sheds. Known as the Inner Harbor and somewhat quieter than Hyannis Harbor, it still remains an important boatyard and harbor.

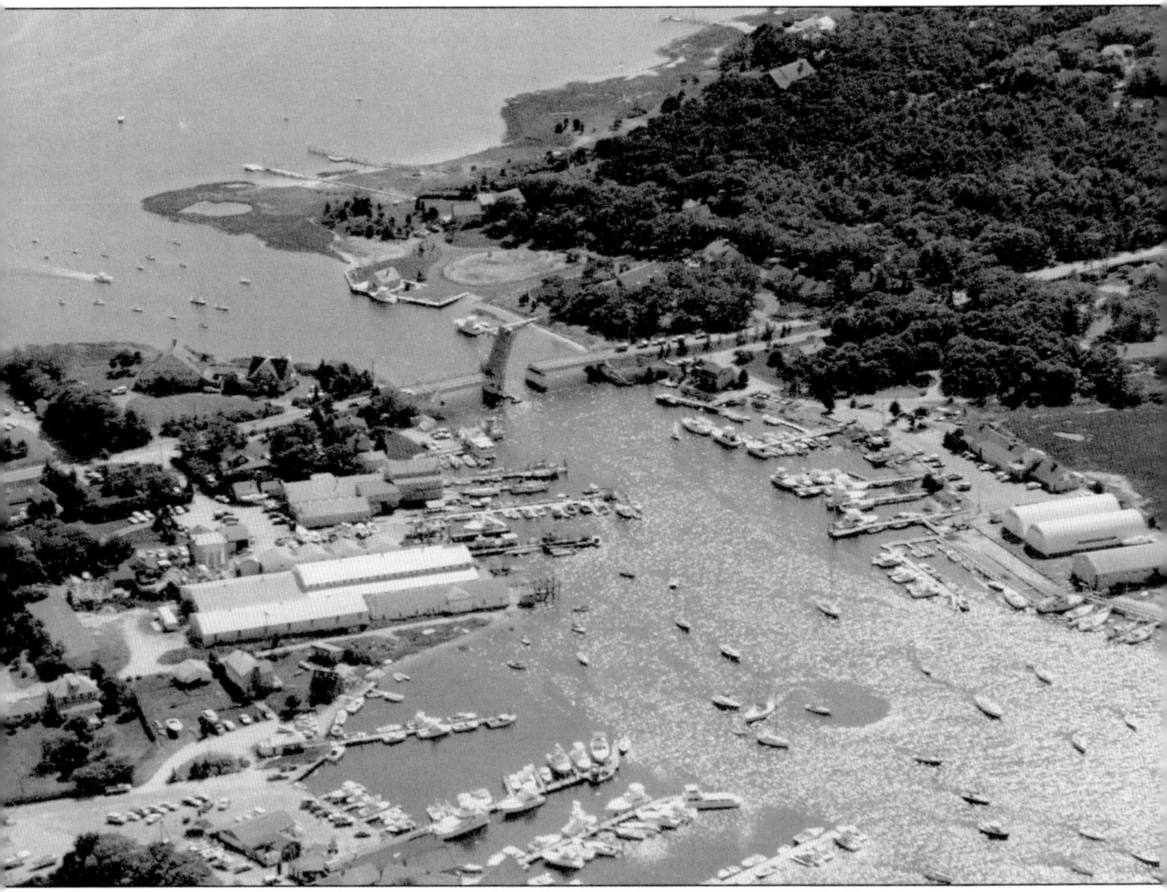

Here is an overview of the Crosby Boatyard in Osterville showing the drawbridge to Oyster Harbors in open position. The Crosby Catboat and Yacht Building Company brought notoriety to this area because of its sensationally designed "as swift as a cat" catboat.

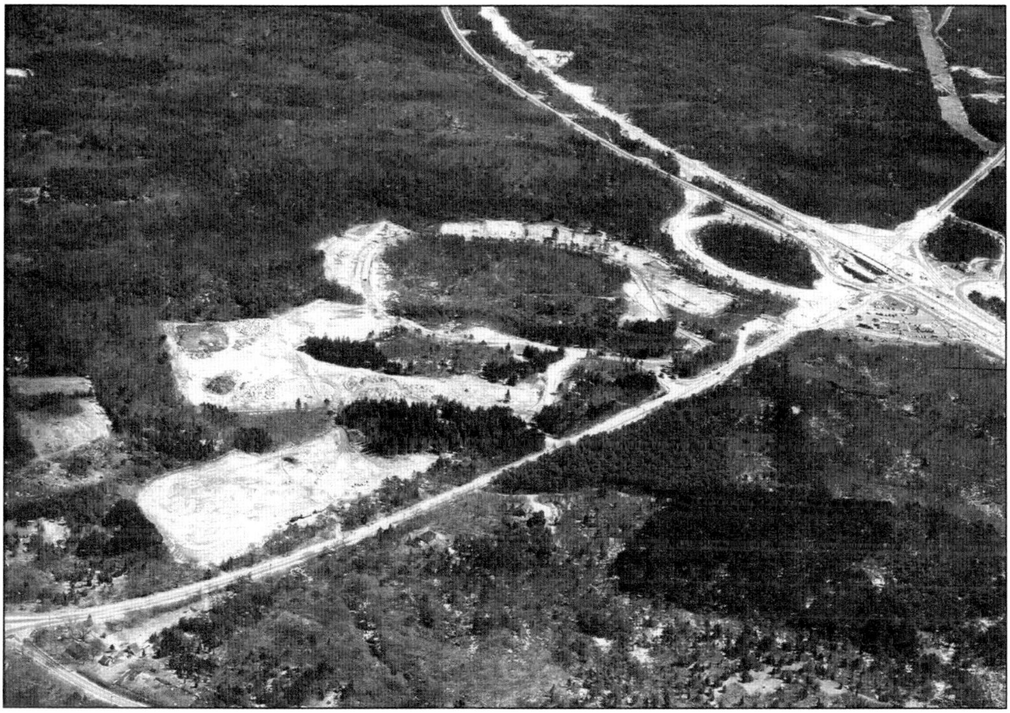

This next sequence shows the development of a new community college campus for Cape Cod. It was built on the sandy knolls of West Barnstable, and Richard Kelsey took key shots on September 13, 1967; July 15, 1969; and later in 1971 to record the birth of the Cape Cod Community College under the direction of second president E. Carleton Nickerson.

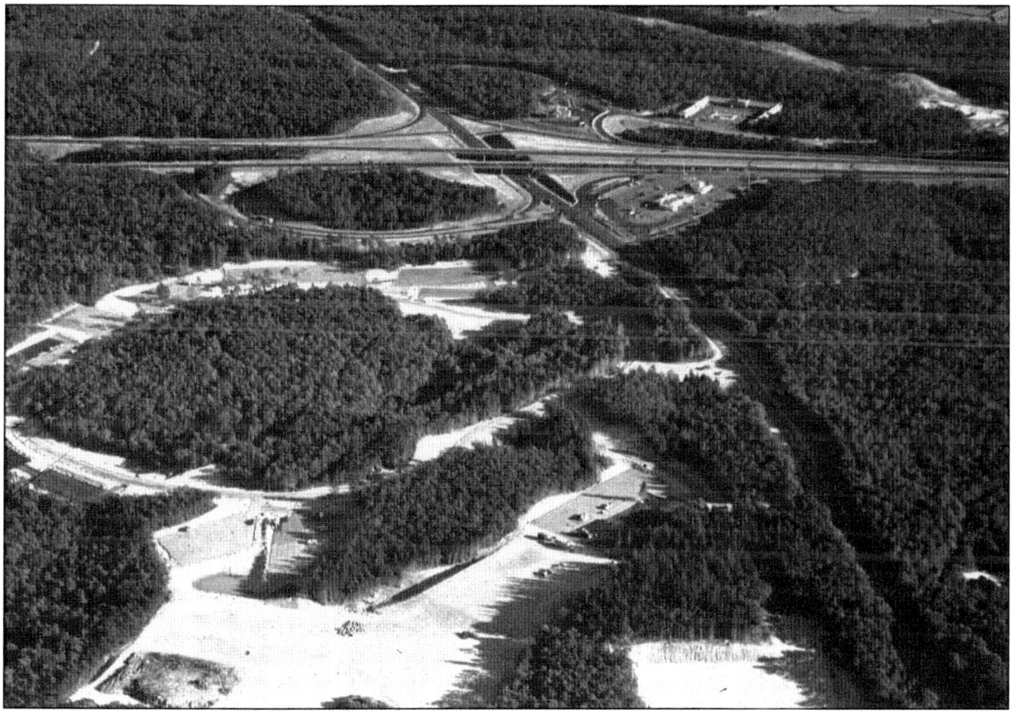

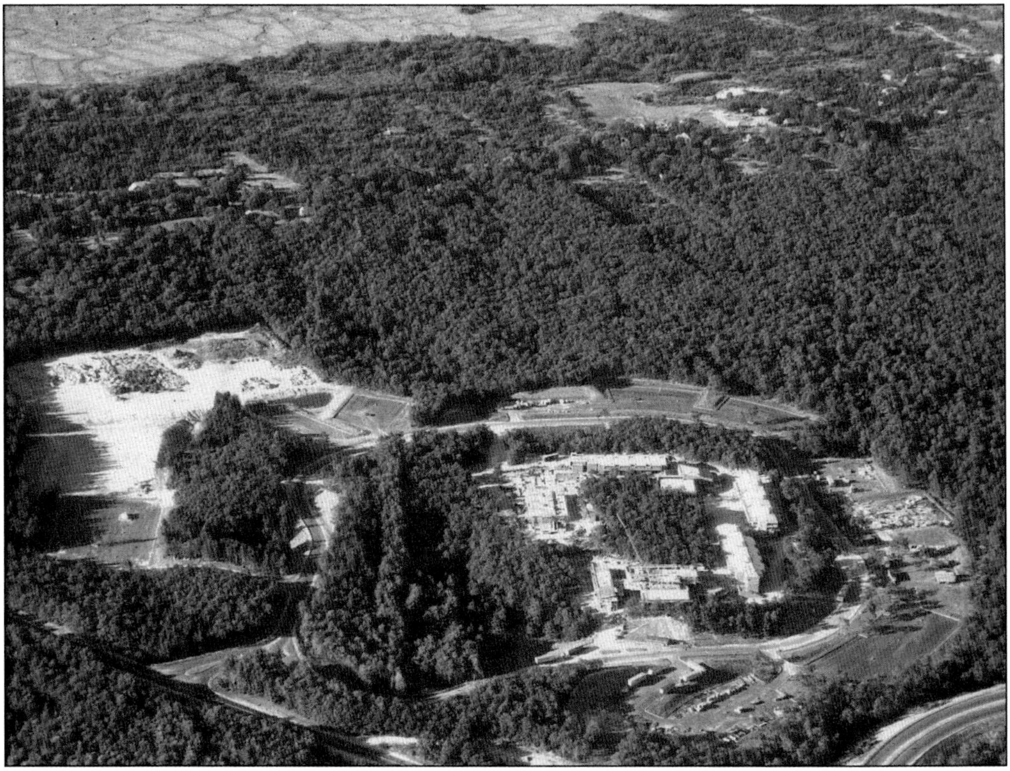

Cape Cod Community College opened its doors of its new campus in 1970 on the 116-acre site with five of the eight buildings designated in its master plan.

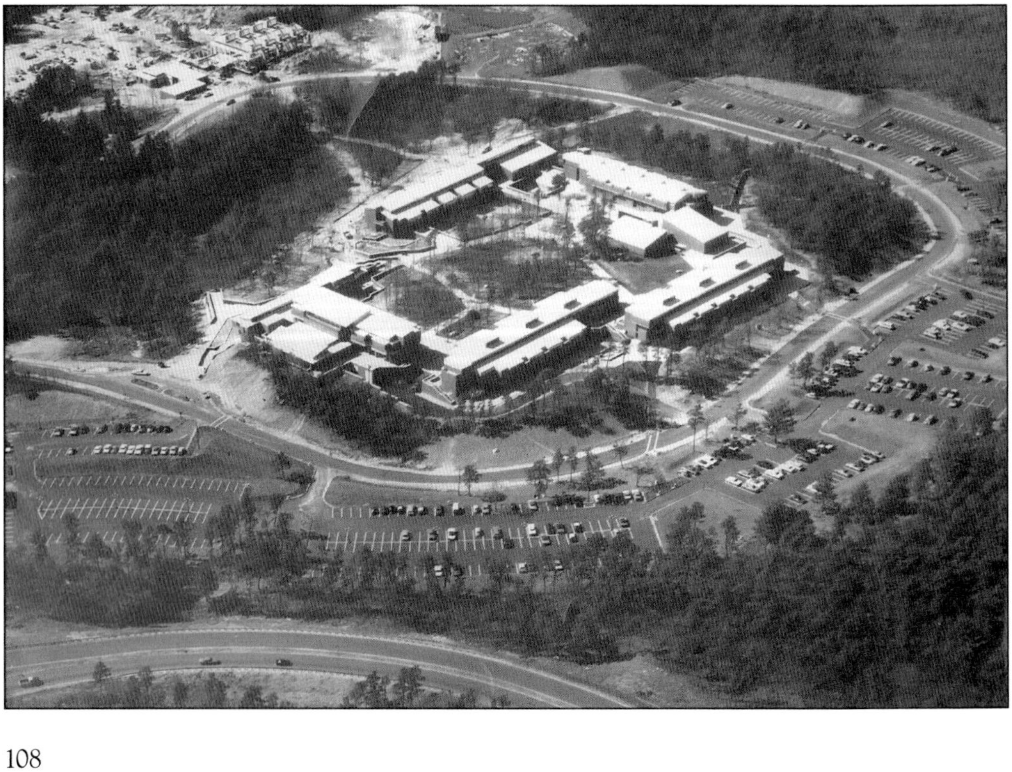

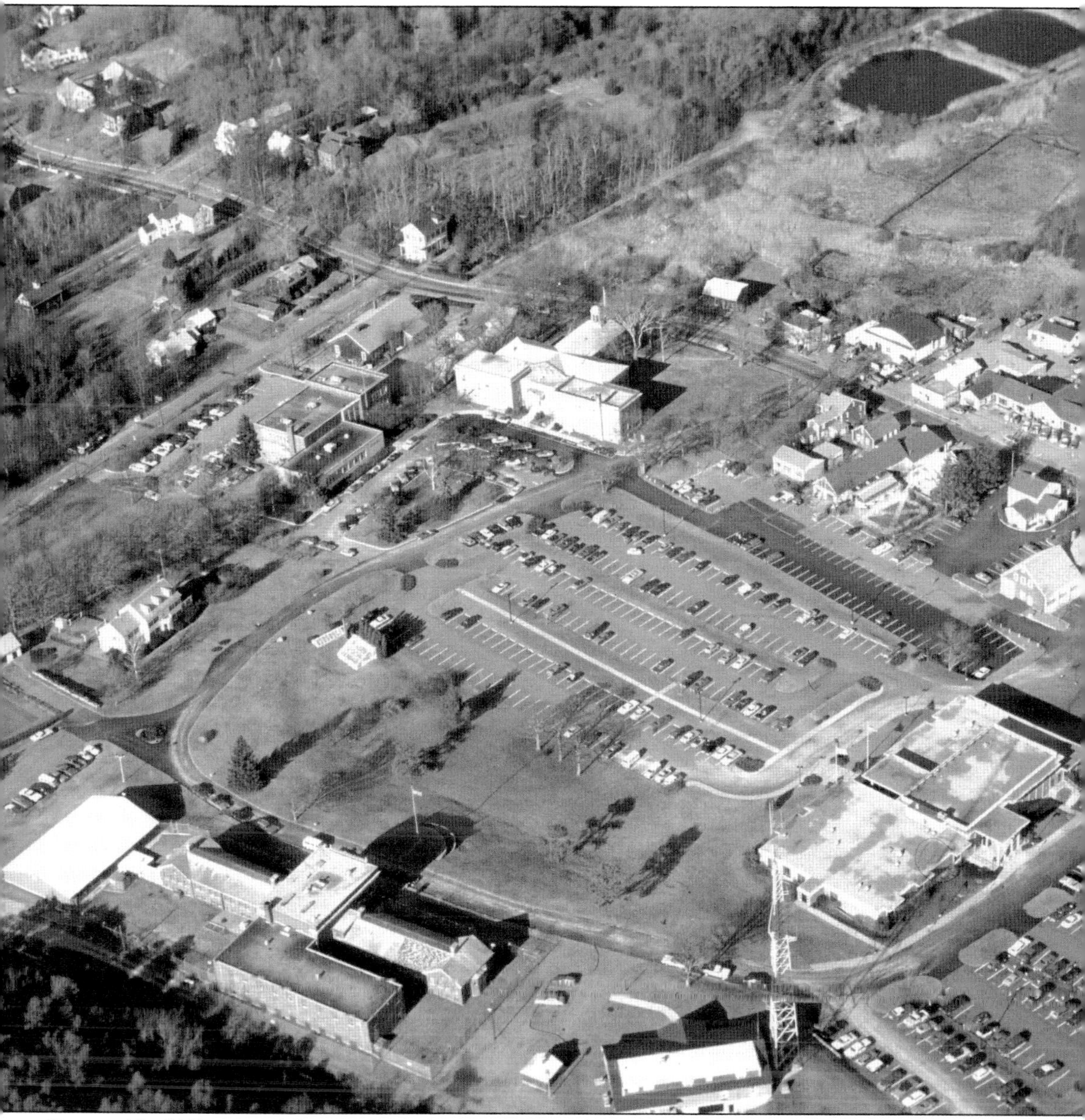

Barnstable Village is delineated in this 1960s-era photograph directly over the Barnstable Courthouse and the Barnstable County Building Complex, the seat of Cape Cod's county government. This granite courthouse, built 1831–1832, was the third courthouse for the county and has been enlarged four times.

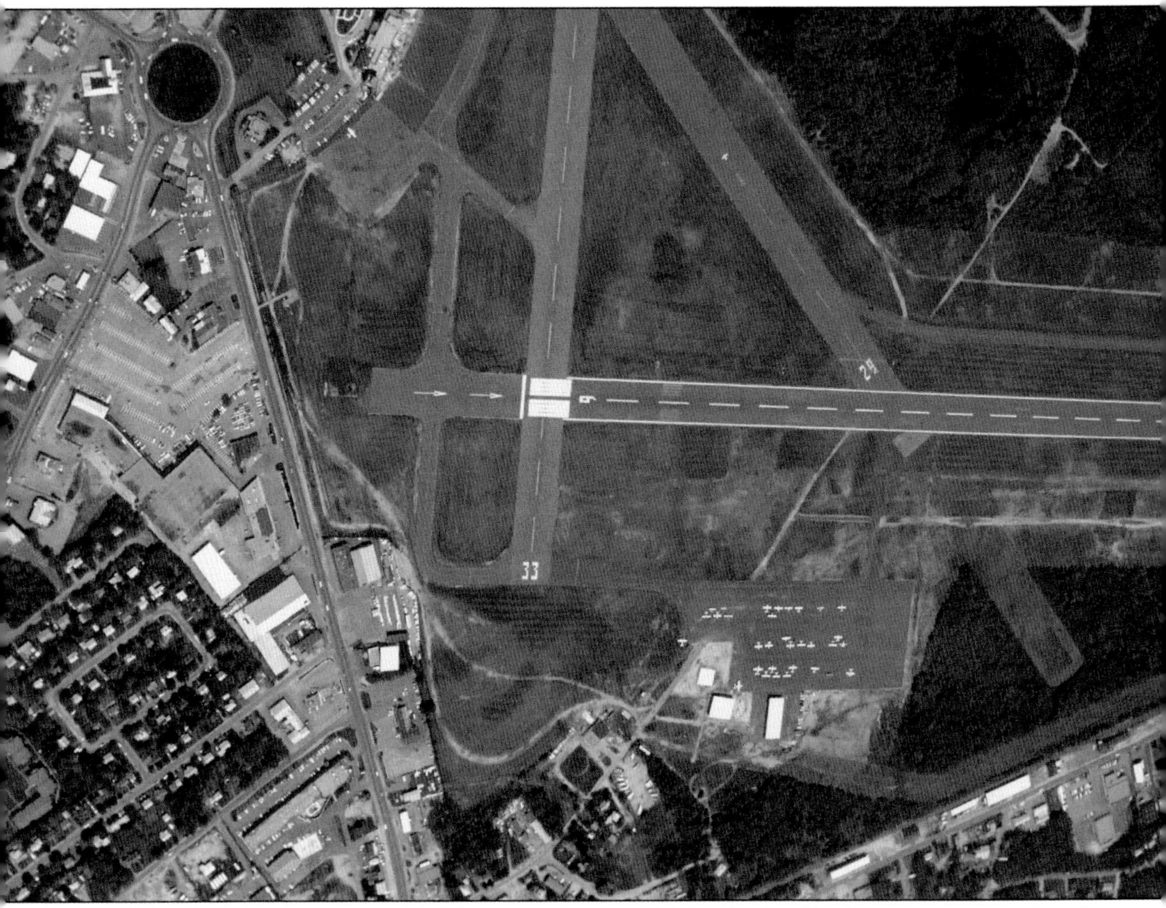

The familiar sight of the Barnstable rotary, just outside the Barnstable Airport, is pictured in the late 1970s. Those with sharp eyes might recognize the roof of the old Red Coach Grill.

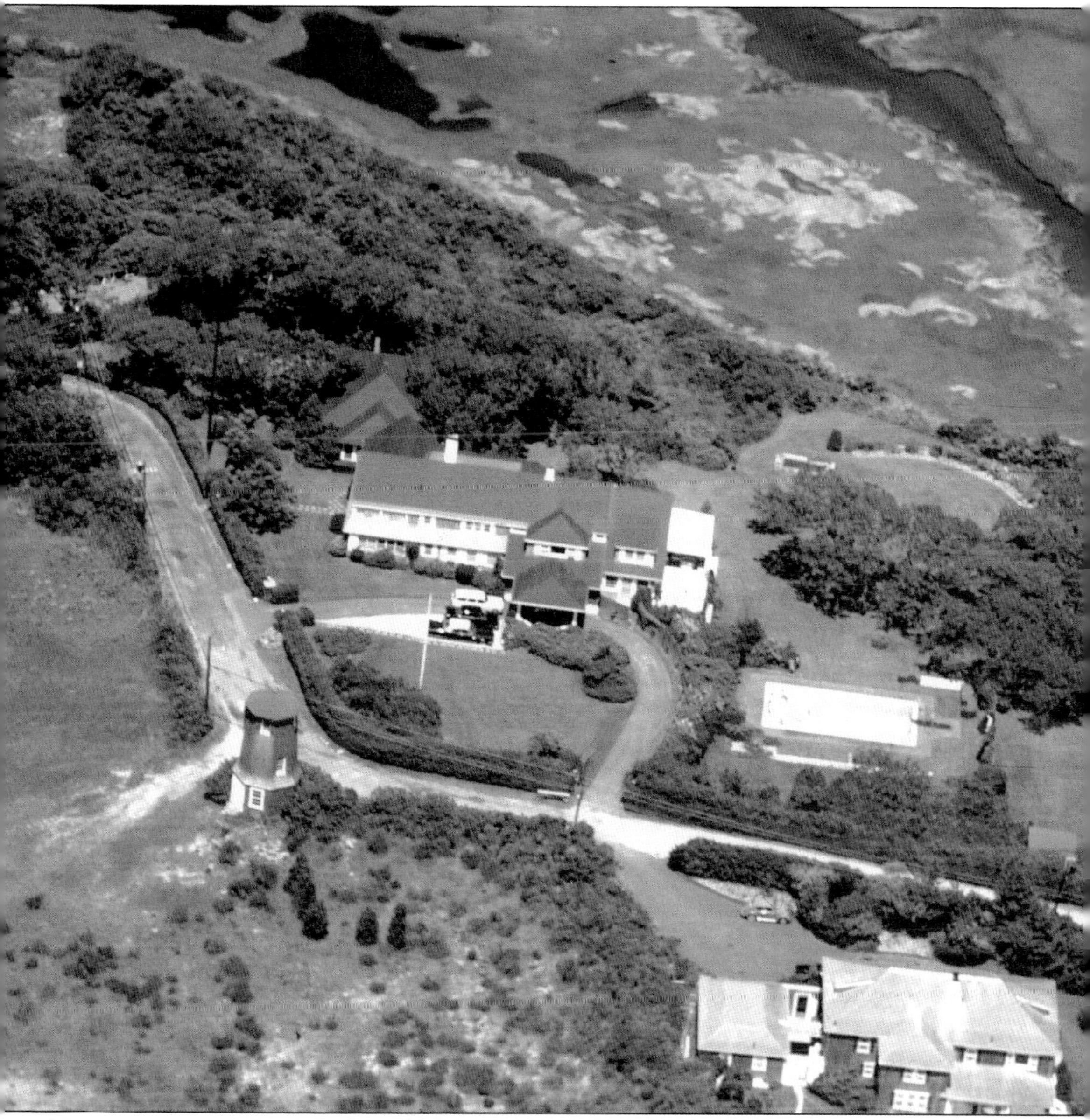

No accounting of Cape Cod would be complete without some reference to the Kennedy Compound, the summer Whitehouse of Pres. John F. Kennedy and family. Squaw Island, shown here, is the home of Joan Bennett Kennedy, the former wife of Edward Kennedy, and is a more isolated property.

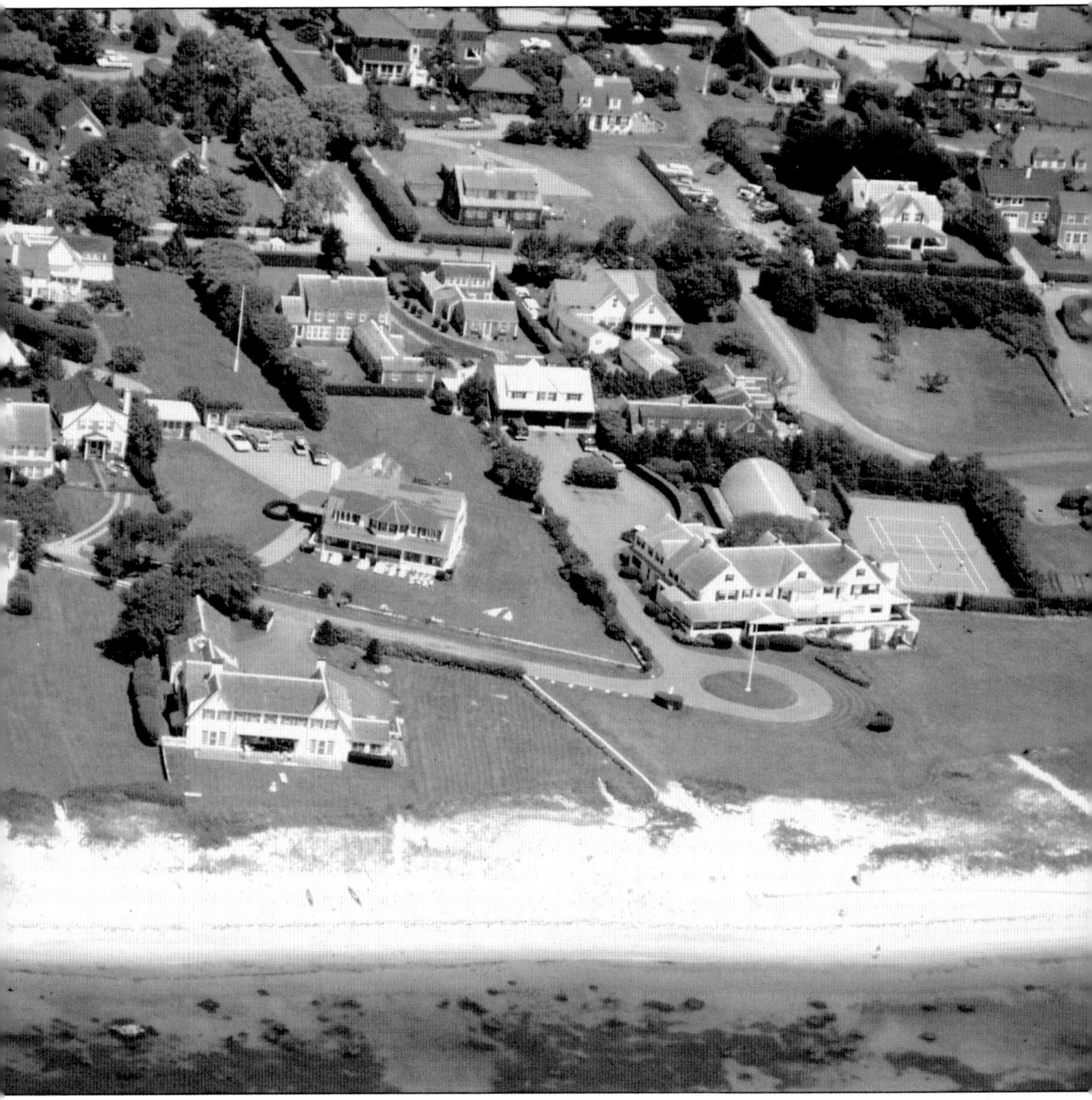

These aerials from the 1970s show the waterfront property as part of a rather congested area of Hyannisport. The influence of the Kennedys on Cape Cod, its growth, development, and popularity is legendary.

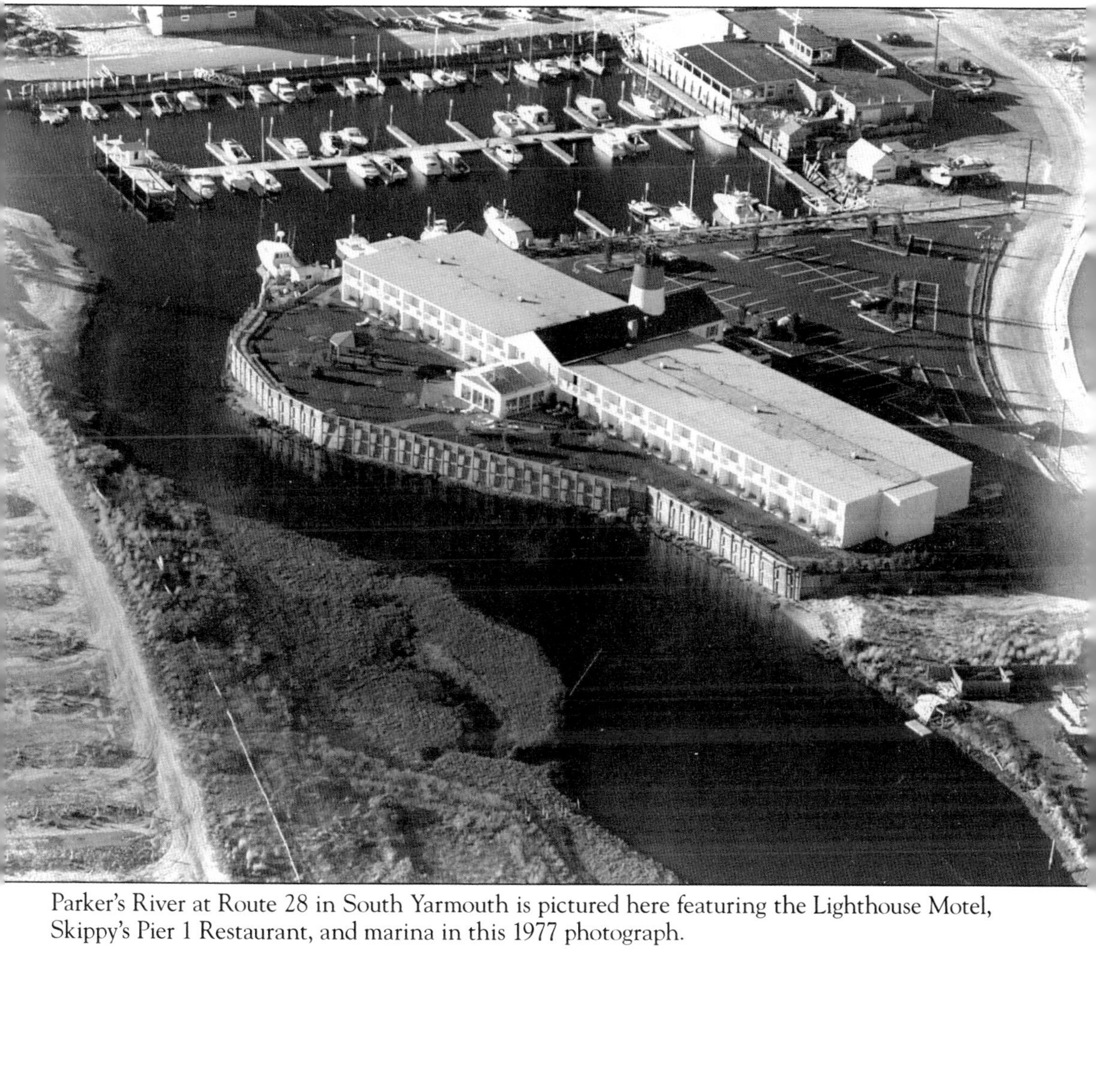

Parker's River at Route 28 in South Yarmouth is pictured here featuring the Lighthouse Motel, Skippy's Pier 1 Restaurant, and marina in this 1977 photograph.

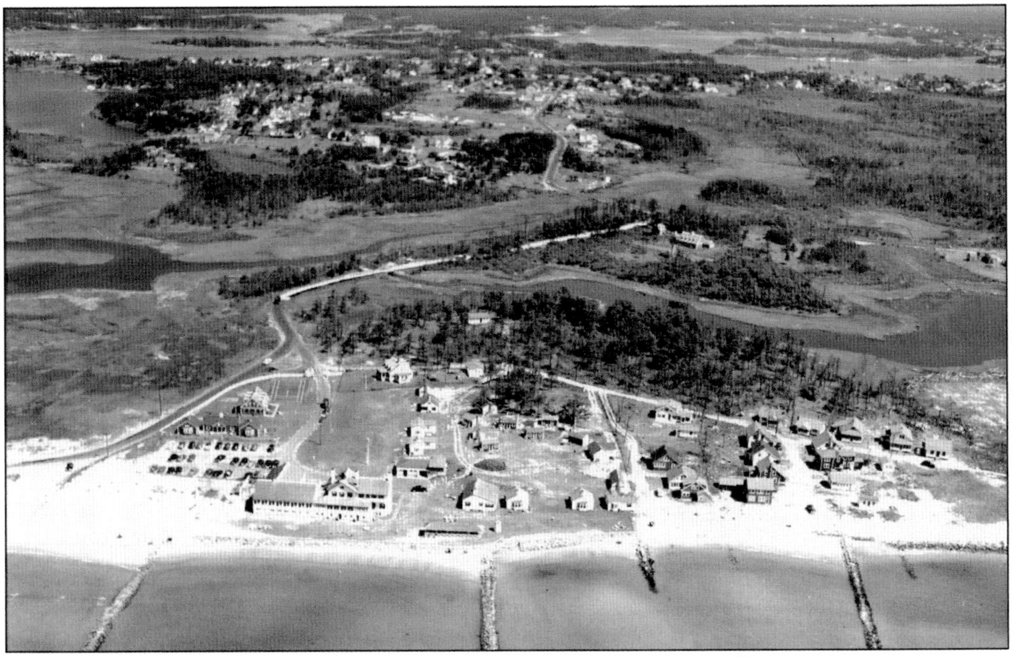

Sesuet Harbor in East Dennis is shown here in 1967. The small village with its community church steeple can be seen in the background. Sesuet Harbor on Sesuet Creek, once the site of the clipper ship–building Shiverick Shipyard, now holds claim to being a major harbor of Cape Cod Bay.

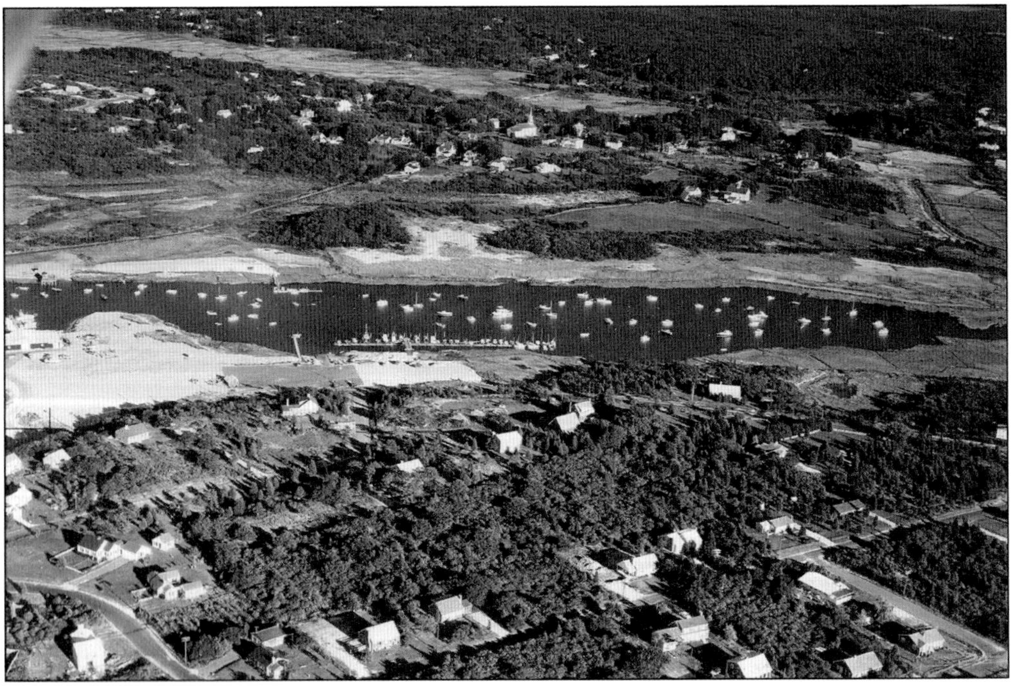

This West Dennis Lighthouse Inn Hotel described itself as an "inn with cottages directly on ocean, around old Bass River lighthouse, where the charm of the old is blended with comfort of the modern."

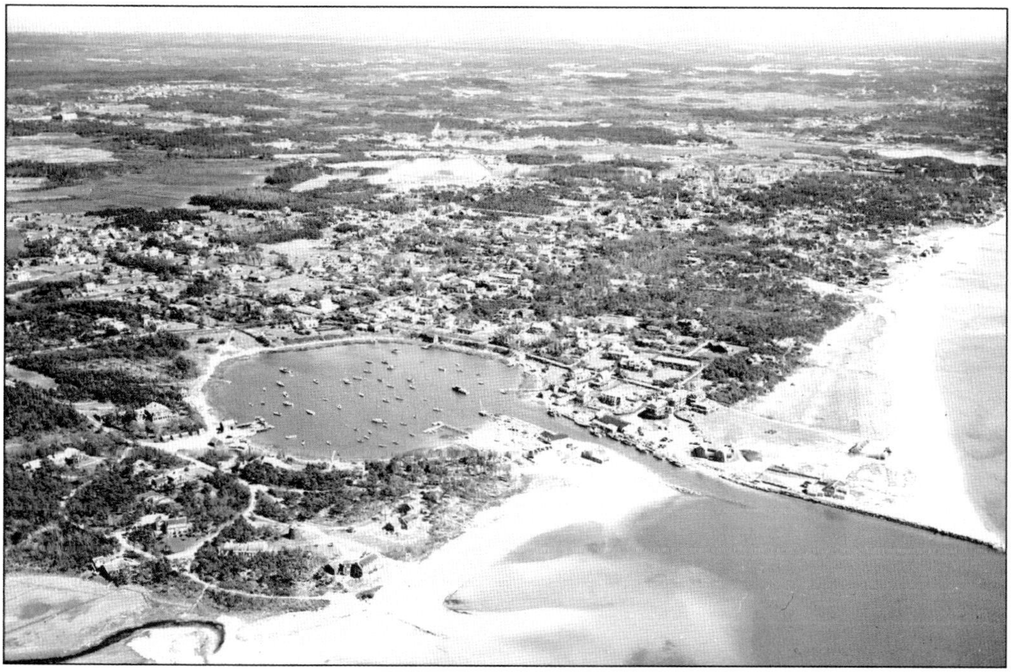

Wychmere Harbor, from overhead, shows the Wychmere Harbor Club and the small protected keyhole inlet looking northeast. Another view of Harwich features Marceline Salvage on Route 24 in Harwich. It is said that Richard Kelsey aerial photographs were business inventory records for the junkyard.

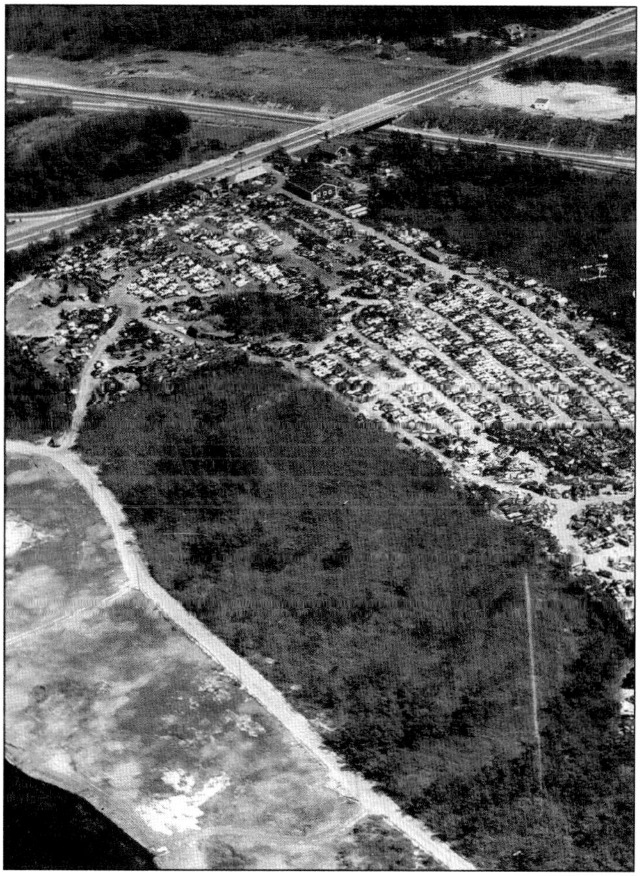

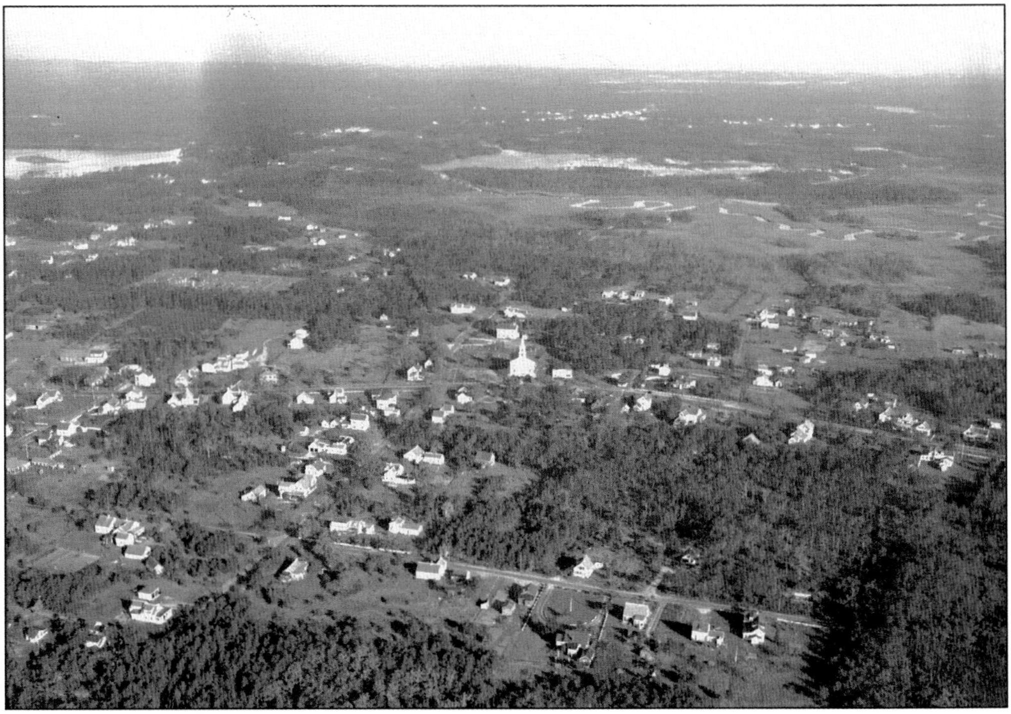

West Harwich is depicted looking north with Bells Neck Reservoir in the background. West Harwich Baptist Church is prominently centered.

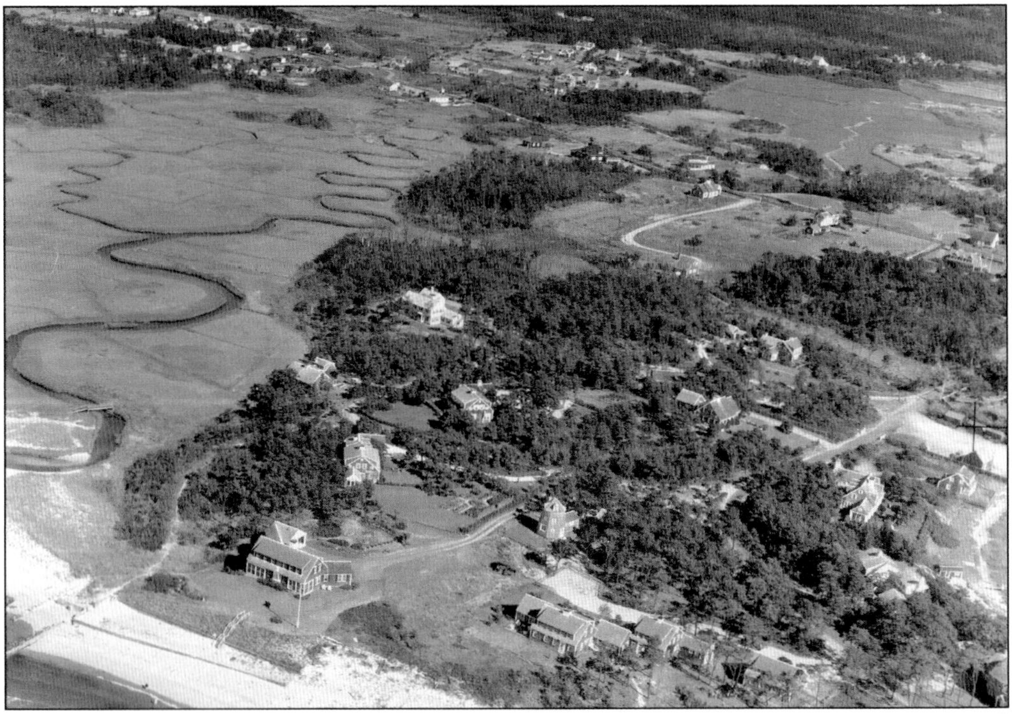

Shown here is Harwichport as seen from overhead with the Herring River and Windmill Point shown.

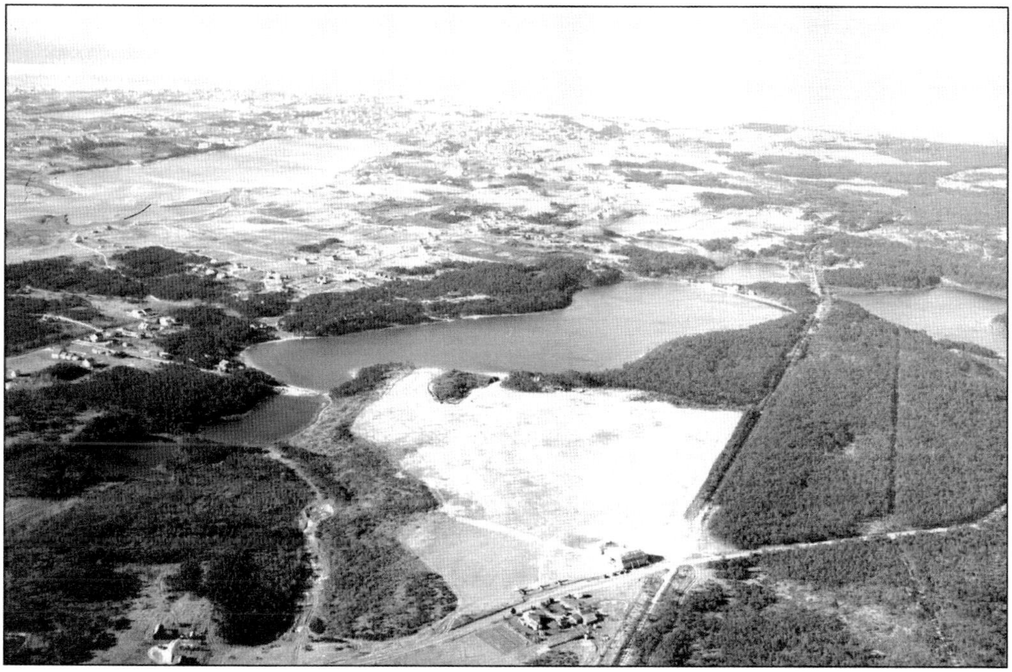

Chatham Municipal Airport in this 1960s photograph (above) shows the wide grassy airfield with the domed hangar. Just beyond the airport is White Pond. In the picture at right, either the downed biplane did not make the approach or it is a seaplane docked on the pond.

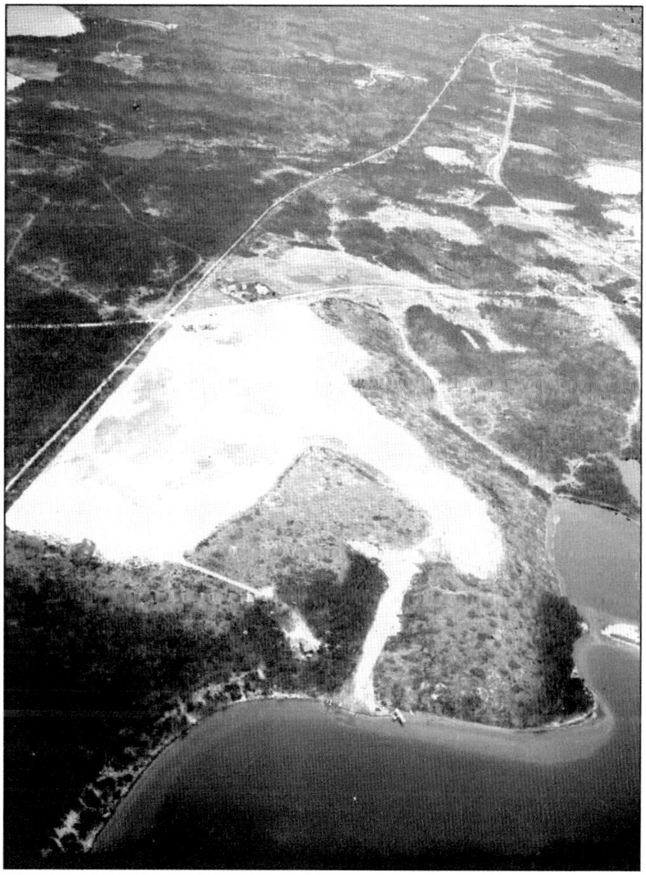

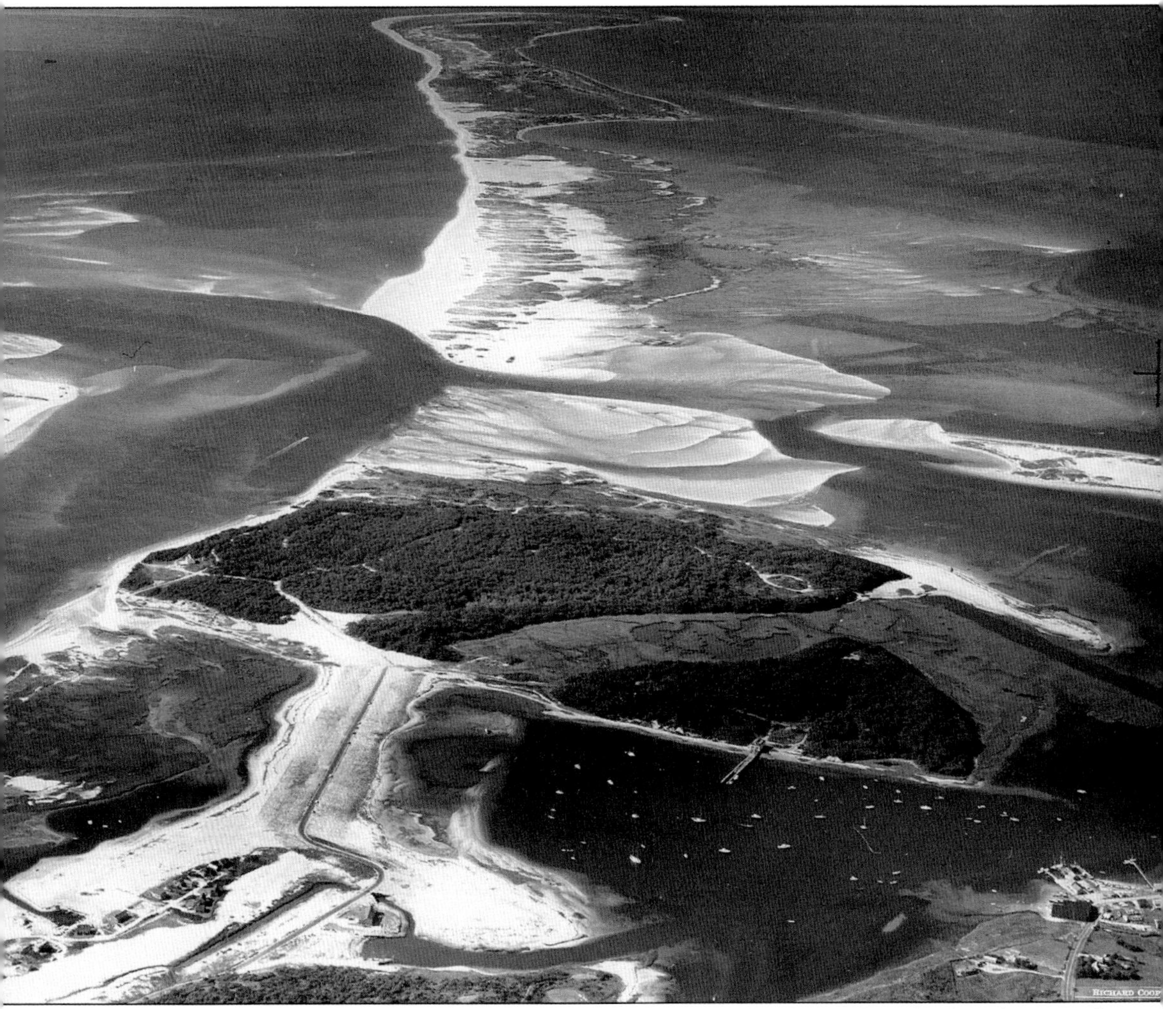

Richard Kelsey's series of photographs on Monomoy clearly shows that he loved to teach geography. Here the length of Stage Harbor Road out to Morris Island with Monomoy beyond was one of his repeated, favorite shots.

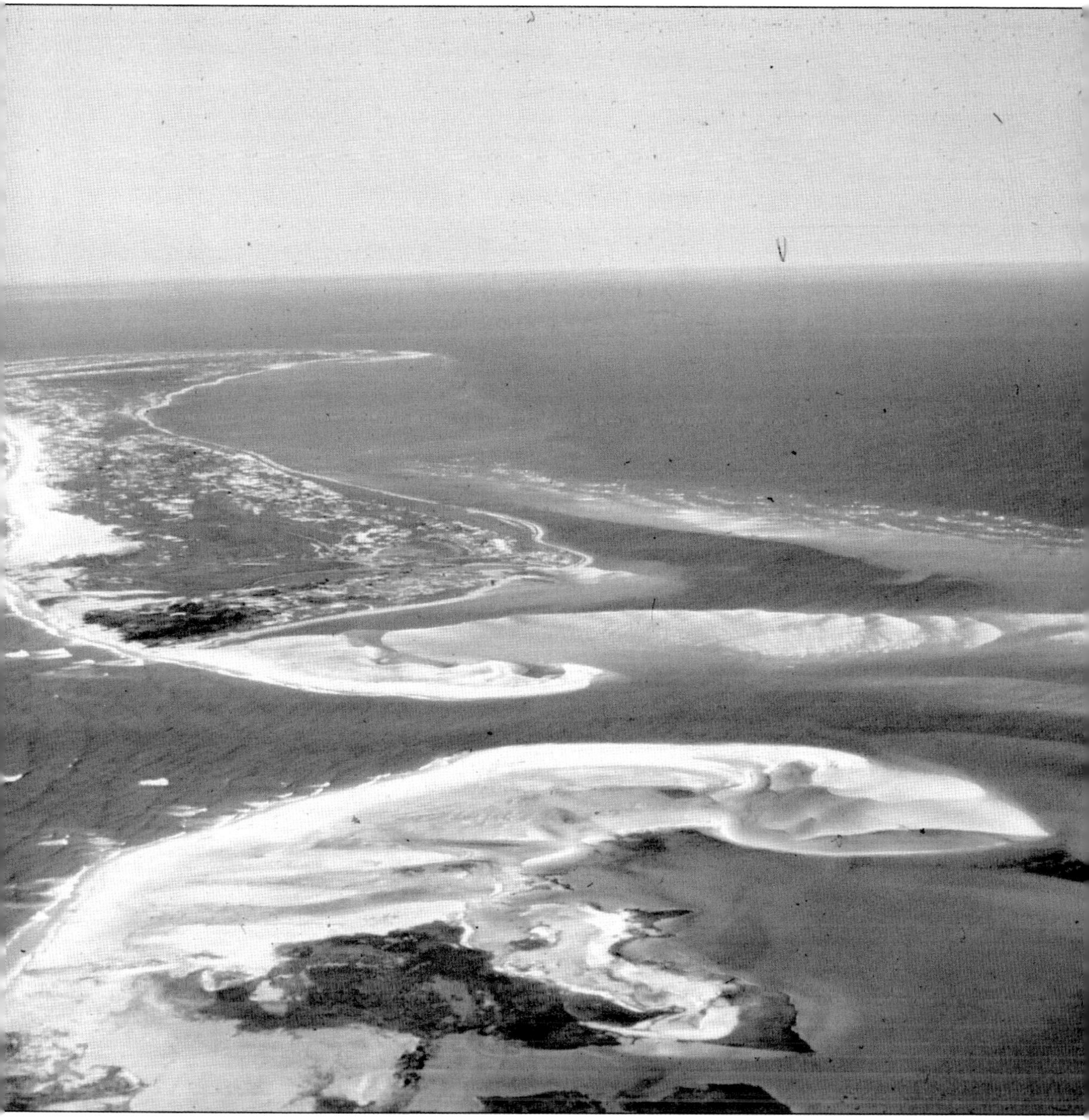

In the nor'easter of 1978, Kelsey was the first person to record the break at Monomoy. This shot and many others became front page news on Cape Cod and beyond. The lessons of erosion on the outer Cape predicted by scientist Graham Giese were recorded and made proof positive by this photograph.

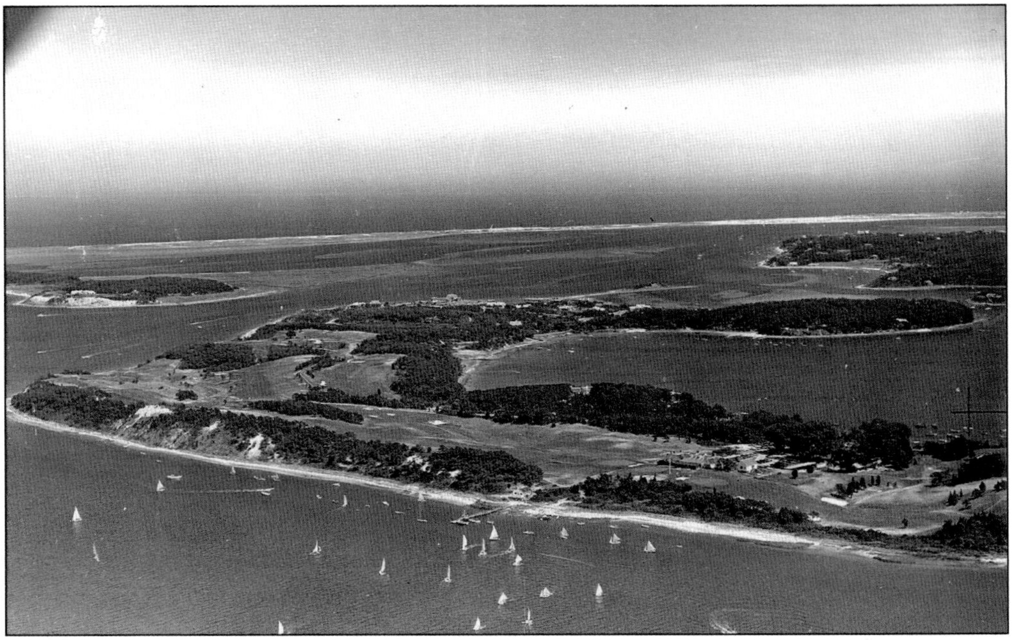

Views of Nickerson Neck with its private Eastward Ho Championship Gold Links are reproduced here. As described in a publicity brochure, "the first nine holes stretch away to the east toward the Atlantic Ocean, which may be seen from every fairway and green, and the last nine lie to the west along the shores of the magnificent Pleasant Bay."

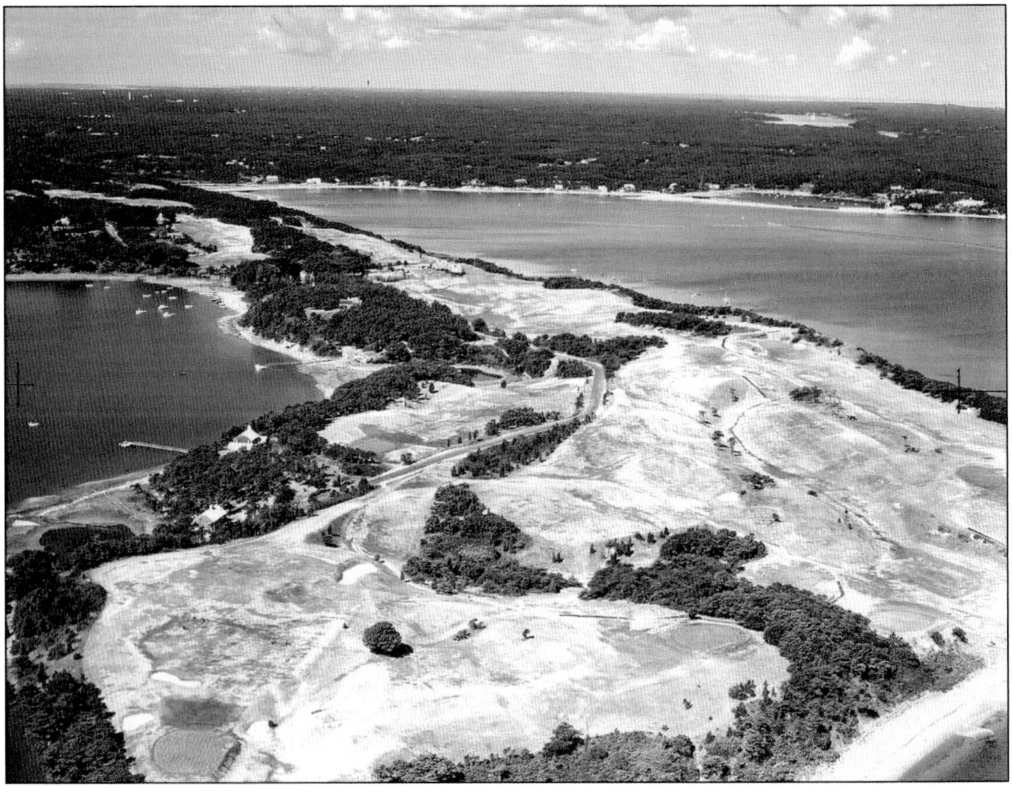

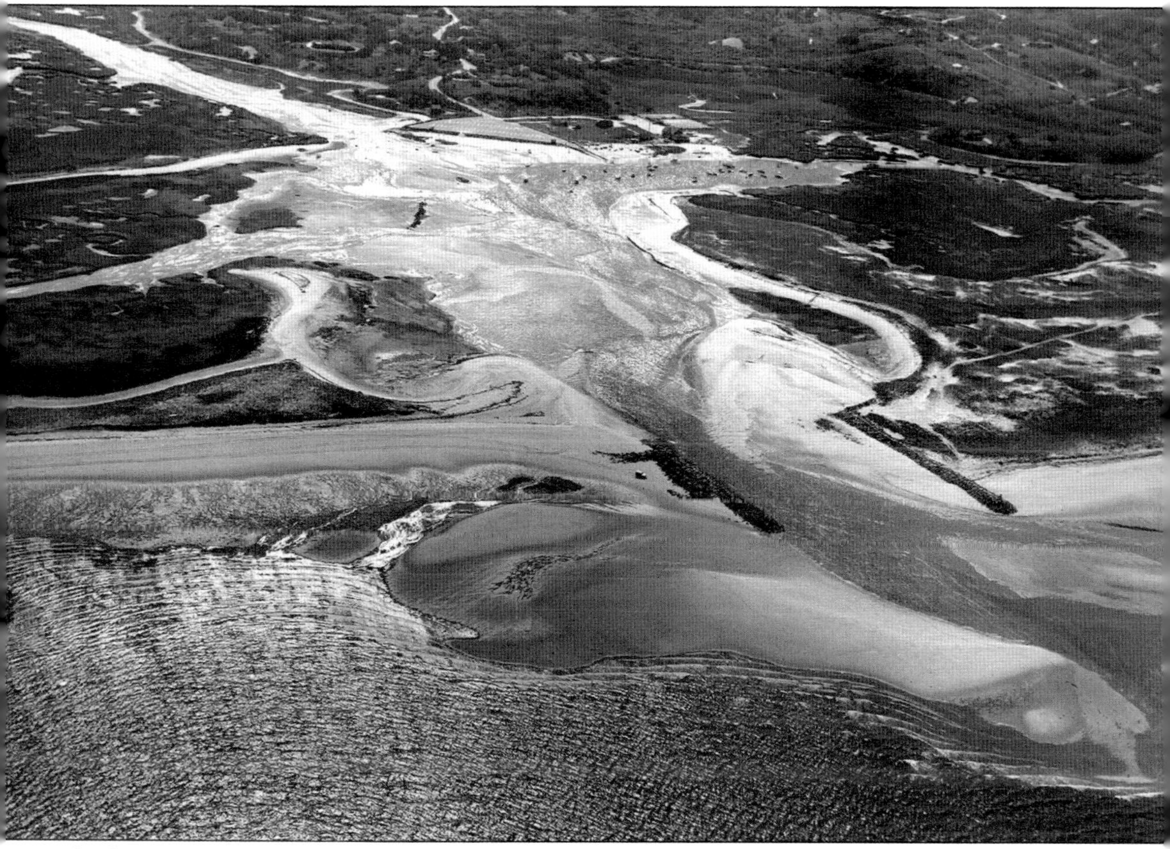

The flats of Truro and the Pamet River stand out in this high-altitude shot over the lower Cape. As Shebnah Rich explained in his 1884 history of Truro, "the hollows of Truro are perhaps more regular than any other part of the Cape. They are delightfully sheltered from the bleak winds and storms."

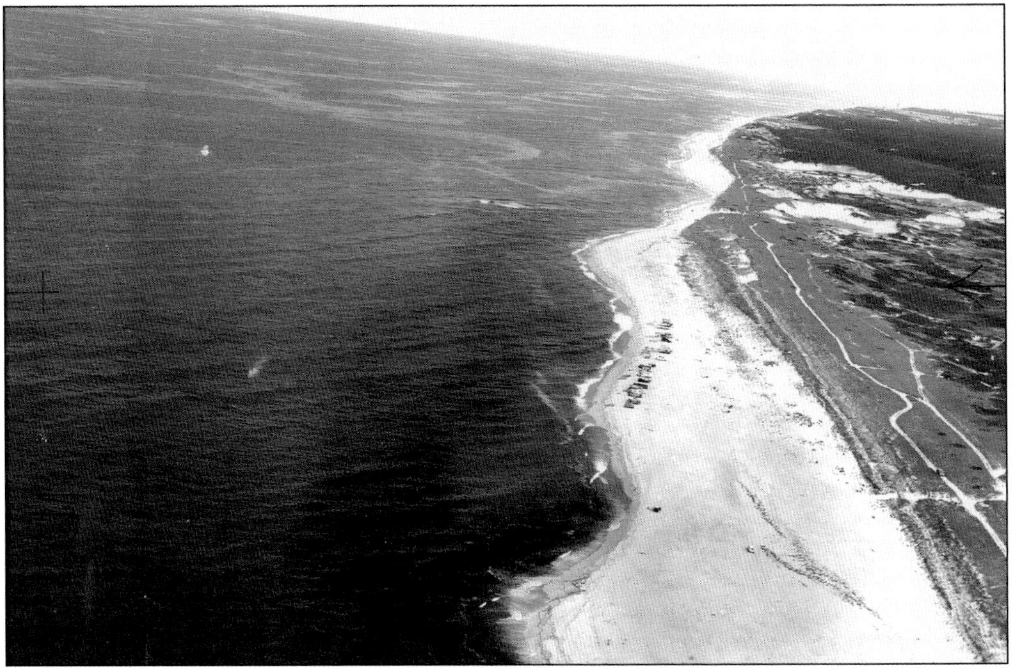

Aerials of beach buggies or off-road vehicles along outer Cape Cod beaches have had a long history on Cape Cod. The Massachusetts Beach Buggy Association was first formed on September 3, 1940, at Nauset Beach in Orleans and adopted its code of ethics. Its debate with environmentalists restricting the use of dune access is ongoing, but the freedom and enjoyment of these caravans seem complete.

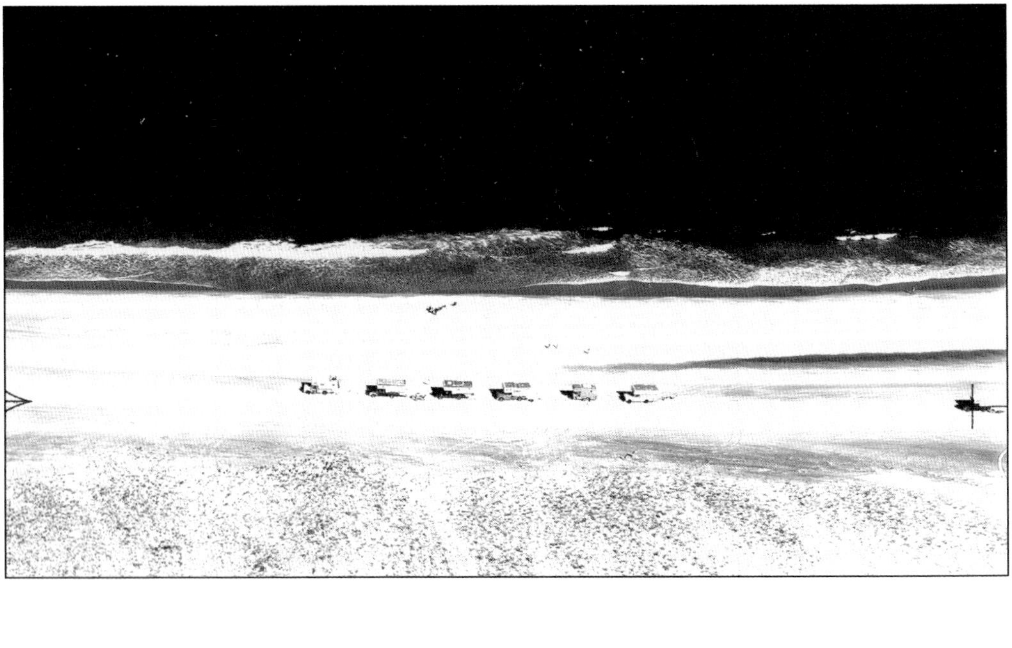

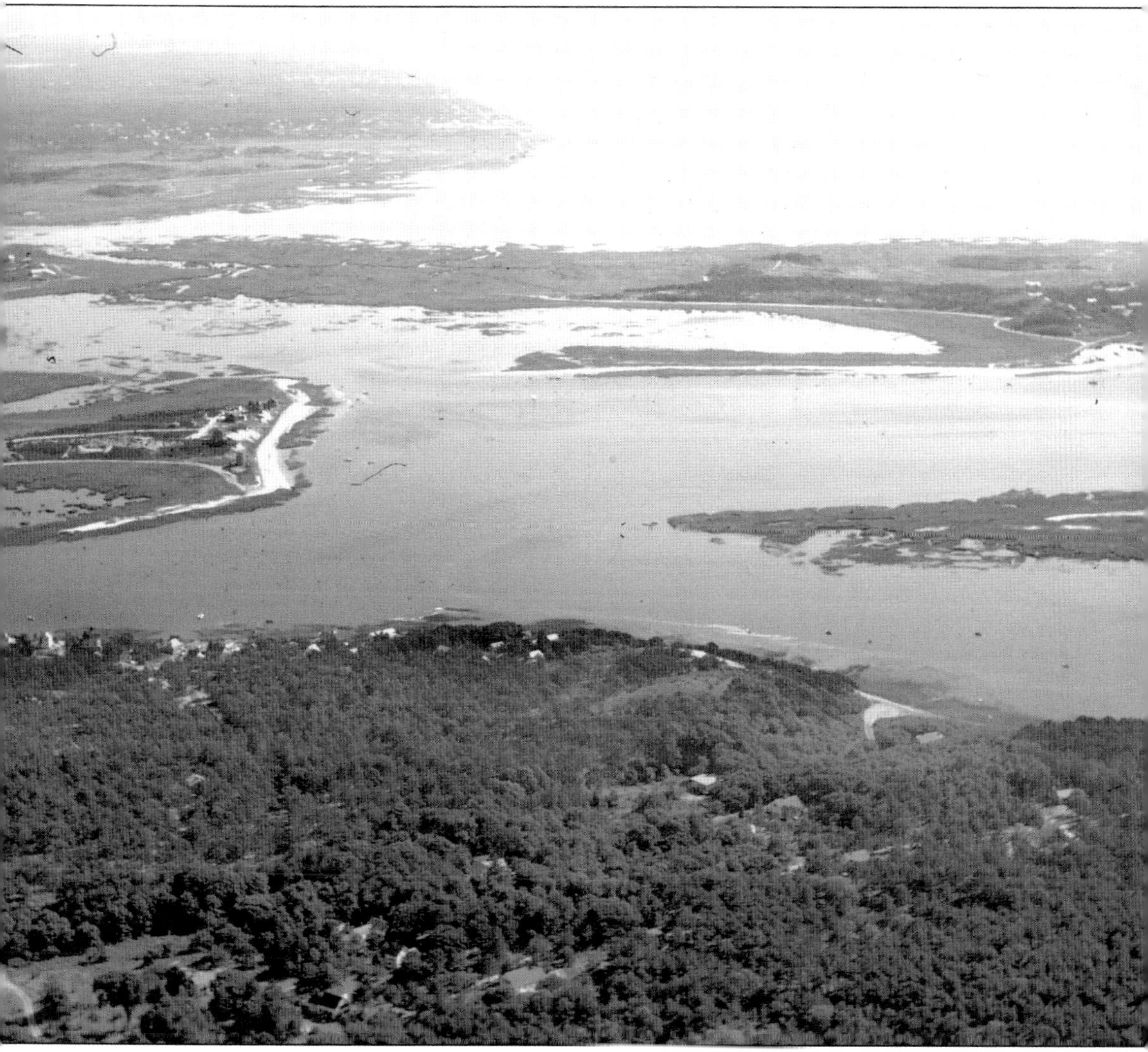

Wellfleet with its series of ponds, Long Pond, Great Pond, and Gull Pond, looks out into the waters of Cape Cod Bay. A Wellfleet Chamber of Commerce publication described the area: "Wellfleet has the great good fortune to lie between the open Atlantic and sheltered Cape Cod Bay. From 'coast to coast' the countryside is a study in variety, tranquility, and great natural beauty."

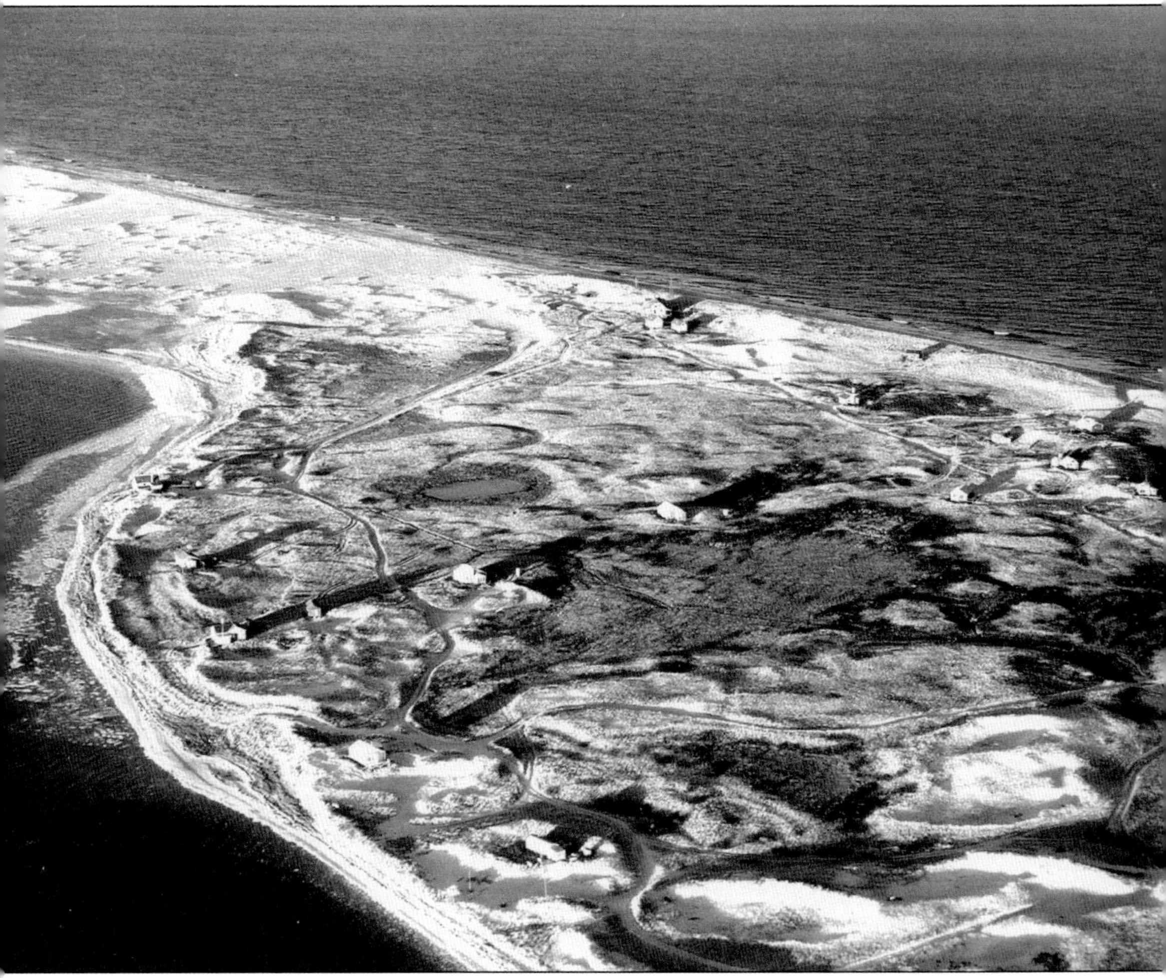

North Beach in Chatham and the dune shack community of about nine properties represent living as close to nature as legally possible in current times. Living on the edge of a spit of sand close to the edge of this country is a rare experience.

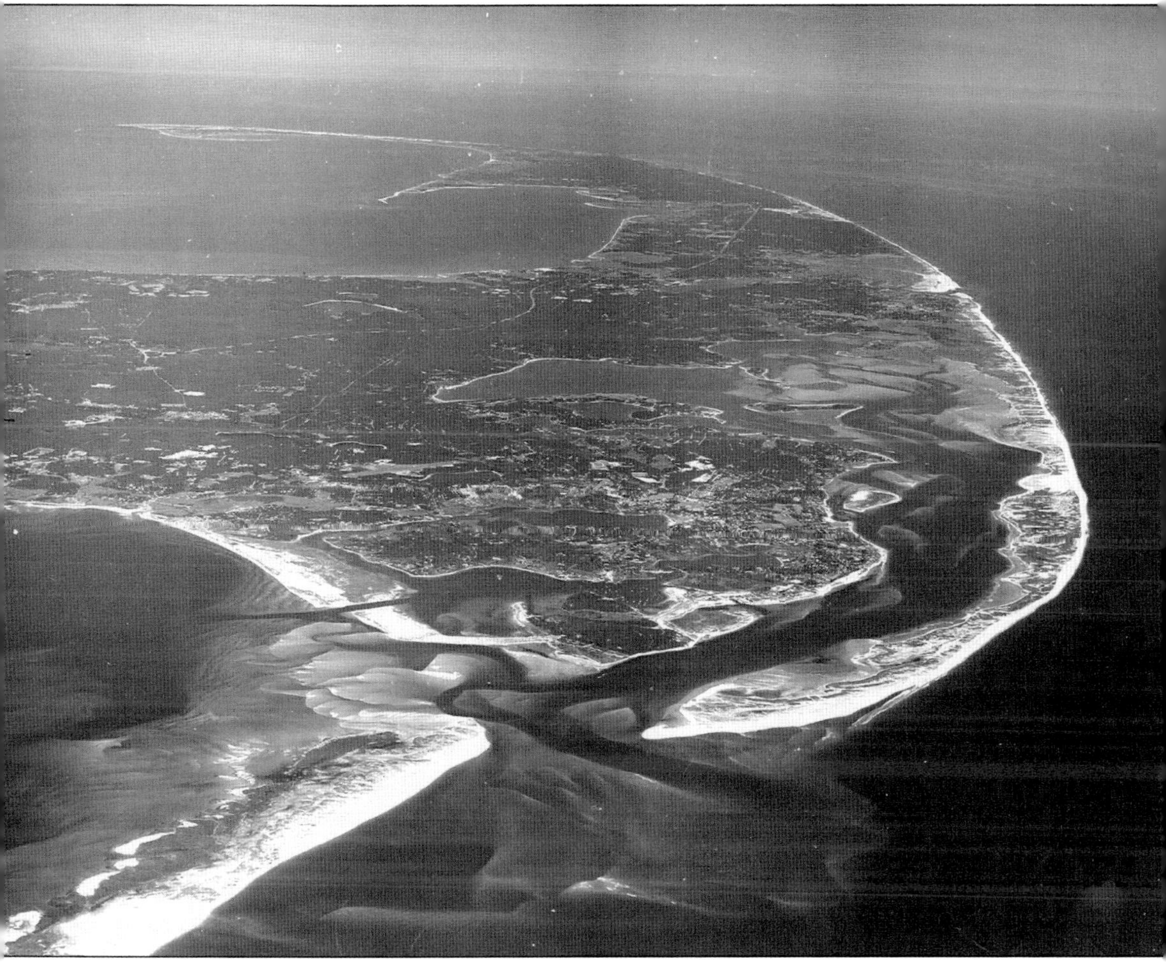

The outer Cape is caught in this classic Richard Kelsey view all in one long, high-powered photograph. It is described in the 1953 Cape Cod Handbook as, "one of the most beautiful stretches of beach in America runs from Race Point to Highland Light. Between this stretch of Lonely beach and Spain there is nothing but the broad expanse of the Atlantic Ocean."

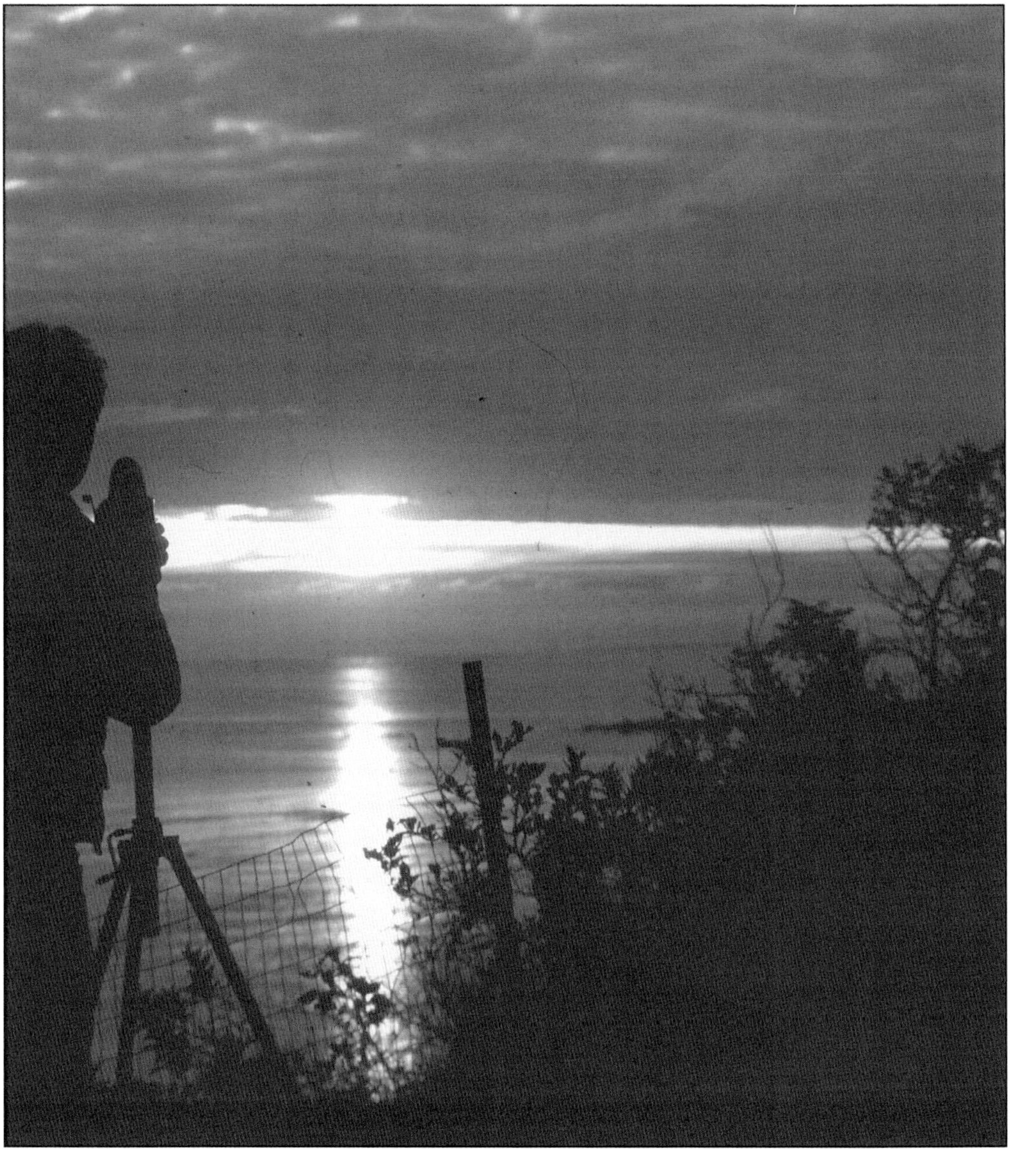

Richard Kelsey was forever chasing sunsets and depicted them in full color photography. This Brewster sunset with the shadow of a photographer in 1978 seems an appropriate conclusion to this brief tribute to his work.

Bibliography

Brewster Board of Trade. *Brewster: the Heart of Cape Cod.* West Yarmouth, MA: Leyden Press, 1968.

Cape Cod Chamber of Commerce. *Cape Cod Vacationer: Directory of Cape Cod activities and attractions.* Hyannis, MA: Cape Cod Chamber of Commerce, 1960.

Cape Cod Chamber of Commerce. *Cape Cod.* Boston: Spaulding-Moss Company, 1950.

Cape Cod Chamber of Commerce. *Cape Cod: the alluring vacationland.* Hyannis, MA: Cape Cod Chamber of Commerce, 1966.

Cape Cod Chamber of Commerce. *Sportsman's Guide to Cape Cod.* Hyannis, MA: Cape Cod Chamber of Commerce.

Cape Playhouse. *Cape Playhouse: Dennis on Cape Cod, Massachusetts; 50th Anniversary.* Dennis, MA: Dennis Playhouse, 1976.

Eastham Chamber of Commerce. *Eastham "Vacationist's Handbook" Cape Cod, Mass.* Lexington, MA: Hancock Press, 1951.

Eastwood Hi! a Championship Gold Links. Boston: Walton Advertising and Printing Company.

Harwich Board of Trade. *Harwich, Cape Cod, Massachusetts: the Town on the Sound.* Harwich Port, MA: Central Cape Press.

McCue, James W. *Cape Cod Holiday.* Silver Lake: self-published, 1944.

Orleans Bicentennial Committee. *Camps of Orleans 1900–1988: Collection of histories written for the Orleans Bicentennial Committee.* Orleans, MA: Orleans Bicentennial Committee, 1997.

Sandwich Board of Trade. *Sandwich, Cape Cod, Massachusetts: the Oldest Town on the Cape.* West Yarmouth, MA: Leyden Press.

Webber, Bernard. C. *Chatham, "the lifeboatmen."* Orleans, MA: Lower Cape Publishing Company, 1985.

Wellfleet Chamber of Commerce. *Welcome to Historic Wellfleet for Your Cape Cod Vacation!* Wellfleet, MA: Wellfleet Chamber of Commerce, 1960.

Wychmere Trustees. *Wychmere Seashore Cottages, Cape Cod, Harwich, Mass.* Brooklyn: 1909.